IMAGES
of America

SMITHFIELD

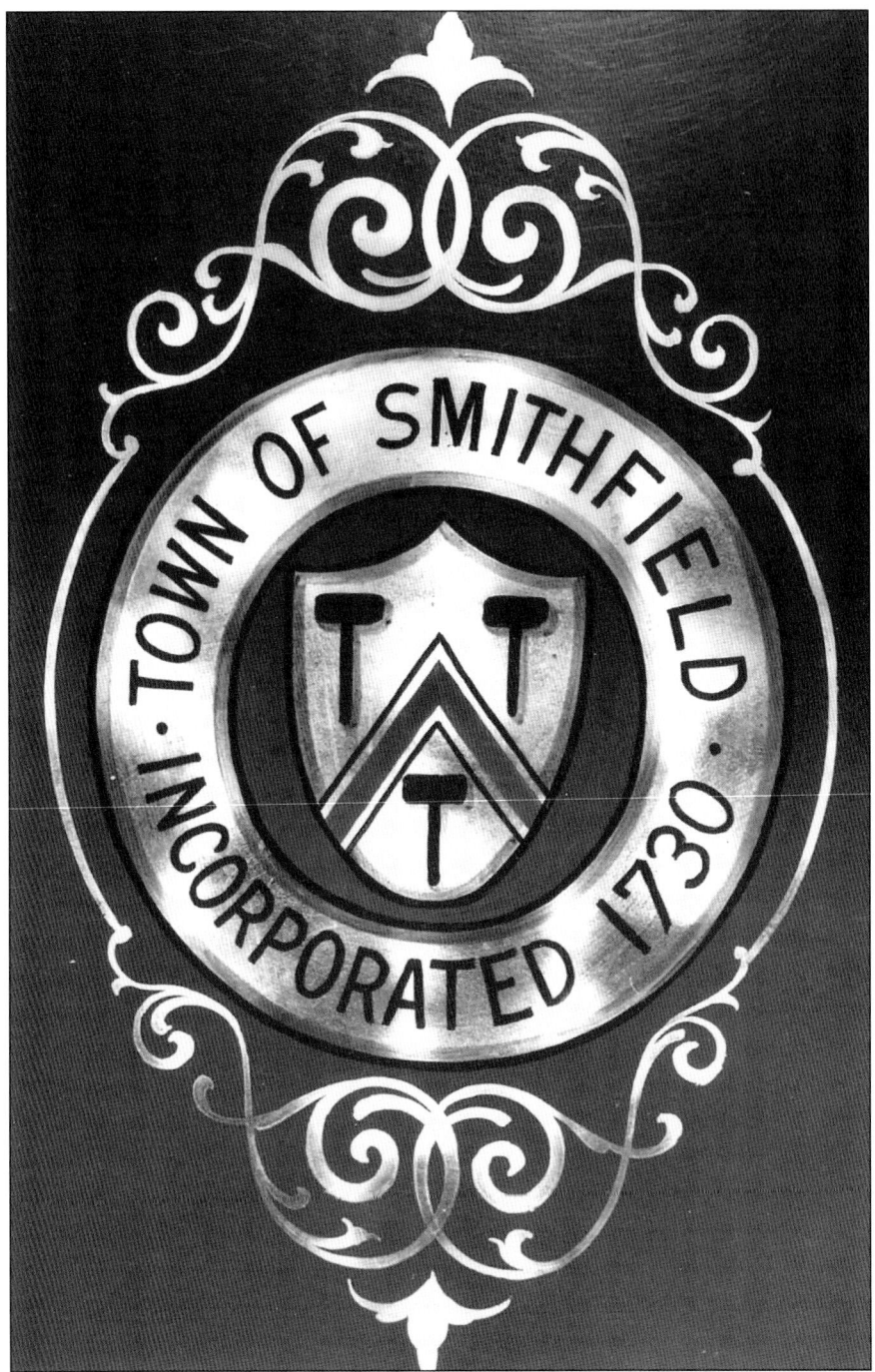

This image shows an early Smithfield town seal. (Ken Brown Sr.)

On the cover: This photograph shows Sidney M. Appleby (1846–1929) and an unidentified man working in the fields that used to surround the Smith-Appleby House on Stillwater Road. Sidney married Sarah Cozzens of Centerdale, and they had one child, Maria C. Appleby, who was the last of the Applebys to live in the Smith-Appleby House. (Historical Society of Smithfield.)

IMAGES of America
SMITHFIELD

Ken Brown Sr., Jim Ignasher,
and Bill Pilkington

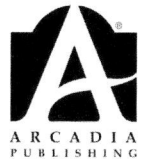

ARCADIA
PUBLISHING

Copyright © 2008 by Ken Brown Sr., Jim Ignasher, and Bill Pilkington
ISBN 978-0-7385-5538-6

Published by Arcadia Publishing
Charleston, South Carolina

Printed in the United States of America

Library of Congress Catalog Card Number: 2007931701

For all general information contact Arcadia Publishing at:
Telephone 843-853-2070
Fax 843-853-0044
E-mail sales@arcadiapublishing.com
For customer service and orders:
Toll-Free 1-888-313-2665

Visit us on the Internet at www.arcadiapublishing.com

This book is dedicated to the citizens of Smithfield.

Contents

Acknowledgments 6

Introduction 7

1. Houses of Worship 9
2. Honoring Veterans 17
3. Smithfield Police Department 25
4. Smithfield Fire Department 37
5. Mills and Mill Villages 51
6. Early Smithfield Schools 61
7. Stagecoaches, Taverns, Trains, and Planes 69
8. A Smithfield Photo Album 85

ACKNOWLEDGMENTS

Thank you to all who contributed. This book would not have been possible without you. The photograph credit legend for this book is as follows: Tim Arup (TA), Diane (Dorgan) Bennett (DDB), Don Brown (DB), Ken Brown (KB), Ken Brown Jr. (KB Jr.), John Joseph Carlton (JC), Kerrie L. Doyle (KD), John Emin Jr. (JE), Frank Floor (FF), Alfred Gobeille (AG), Allison Jaswell Molis (AJM), Charles and Louise Lachapelle (CLL), Greenville Public Library (GPL), Historical Society of Smithfield (HSS), Priscilla W. Holt (PH), Jim Ignasher (JI), William Kelley (WK), Leo Kennedy Jr. (LK), Todd Manni (TM), Joseph P. Mollo III (JPM), Bill Pilkington (BP), Anthony Poliseno (AP), Alfred E. Schenck (AS), Chester Sleboda (CS), Smithfield Fire Department (SFD), and Smithfield Police Department (SPD).

All royalties from this book go to the Historical Society of Smithfield.

Introduction

The state of Rhode Island and Providence Plantations was founded in 1636 when Roger Williams and four other men fled Massachusetts to escape religious persecution. They traveled by boat up what is now known as the Providence River and came ashore at a site known as Slate Rock where they saw it would be a good place to begin a settlement. Believing they had reached safe haven through God's divine intervention, they named the settlement Providence.

In the 1600s, what is today the town of Smithfield was considered "the outlands" of Providence—a wild and untamed region where only the most self-reliant people dared to venture and settle. But settle they did, and within 80 years talk of incorporation as a town began. There were many advantages to incorporation, among them local self-government and no longer having to travel to Providence or Newport to attend to local business.

Smithfield incorporated on February 20, 1730 or 1731, depending on which town records one looks at. (Even today, the town seal has two dates.) At the time of incorporation Smithfield was much larger than it is today for it originally included the present-day towns of Lincoln and North Smithfield, as well as the city of Central Falls and a portion of Woonsocket. In all, an area of about 73 square miles.

On March 8, 1871, 140 years after municipal incorporation, Smithfield was divided into three separate municipalities and the town of Smithfield became what it is today. This division was not without controversy, as there were some who favored it and some who did not. At the time of the division, the towns of Lincoln and North Smithfield were established with Central Falls remaining part of Lincoln until 1895.

Prior to the division, Central Falls had been the industrial and business center for Smithfield. It is for this reason that anyone wishing to examine Smithfield town records predating 1871 must go to the Central Falls City Hall to see them.

In its earliest days, Smithfield was primarily an agricultural community, but by the early 1800s mills and factories began to appear, bringing industry to the town. The villages of Stillwater, Georgiaville, Esmond, and Greenville became manufacturing centers that by the 1870s warranted construction of a railroad through town. The mills continued to thrive well into the 20th century until forced to close due to economic recession and cheaper labor in other states. By the late 1900s, the mills and the railroad were gone, and today Smithfield can be called a suburban "bedroom community" because many people who live here work someplace else.

A major agricultural industry of Smithfield was, and to a small degree still is, apple growing. In fact, the town itself has been referred to as "Apple Valley" due to the many orchards and farms that once dotted the region. Many of these orchards have been lost to development and suburban sprawl. Longtime Smithfield residents can still remember the farms that once occupied land now paved over by condominiums and shopping malls. Many say it is a shame that what made Smithfield a pleasant town to live in is quickly disappearing. That is the reason for this book. To try and give a glimpse of Smithfield in the "old days."

People love to look at old pictures. The moment after a photograph is taken it becomes historical. It is a visual record of how a particular person, place, or thing looked at that exact moment in time. Some early photographers knew this and captured what they saw on film so that images of what they saw 100-plus years ago are available today. It is not until things change that people realize how glad they are to have preserved these images of the past. It is then they say, "Look at the funny clothes," "I remember that building," and "My father had a car just like that one."

But it is not just the way things were that residents remember, they also recall how things were done compared to today, before the days of electricity, automobiles, iPods, and cell phones.

This book contains images of days gone by in Smithfield, but it also gives a brief account of the way things were done in the old days. It is not that those days were necessarily better, although some might argue they were, they were just different; and the present day will one day too become the old days.

In 1881, Thomas Steere published the first historical book about Smithfield called *History of the Town of Smithfield from Its Organization, in 1730–1, to Its Division, in 1871*. Very little has been published since.

There is much more that could be said about the history of Smithfield here than space will permit. This book is not intended to be an in-depth report containing every detail of town history, but instead designed to give a brief overview of the many aspects of the town.

The images in this book are considered vintage today, but at one time they were not. It is hard to imagine the photographs taken today will one day be looked at by future generations as vintage, quaint, or even historical. But they will be. So take a picture of something so future generations can see what life was like in Smithfield in 2008.

One
HOUSES OF WORSHIP

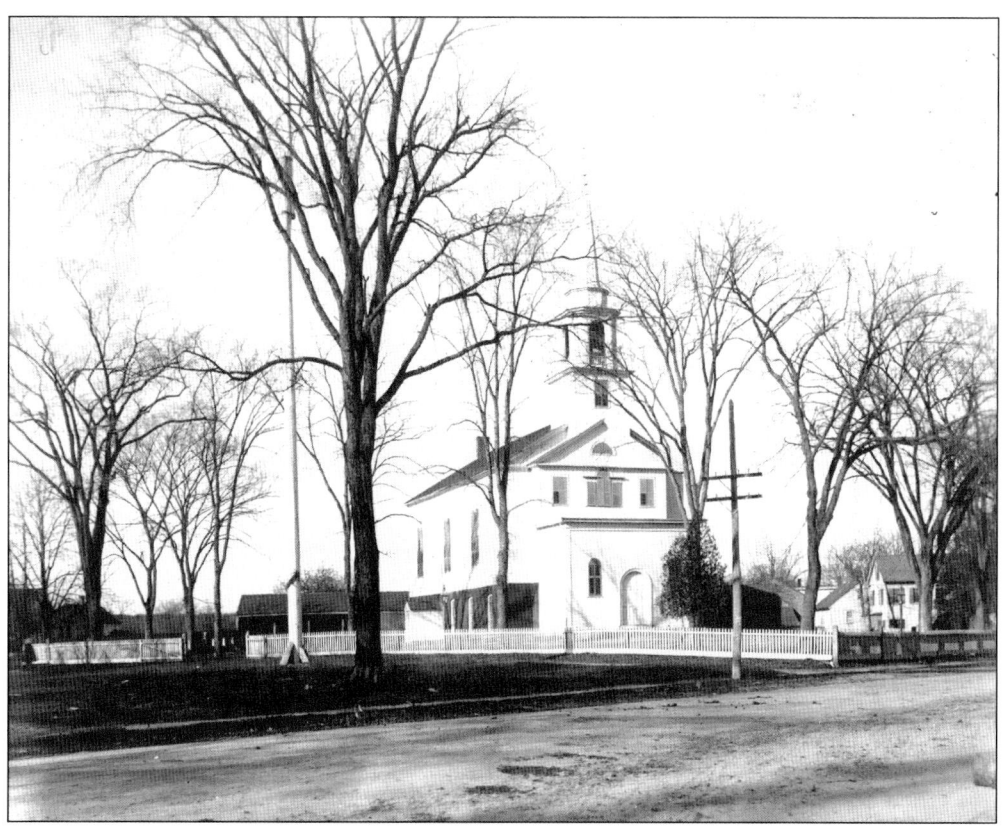

The Greenville Baptist Church is seen as it looked about 1900. This is perhaps the oldest church in Smithfield, dating from 1822. (PH.)

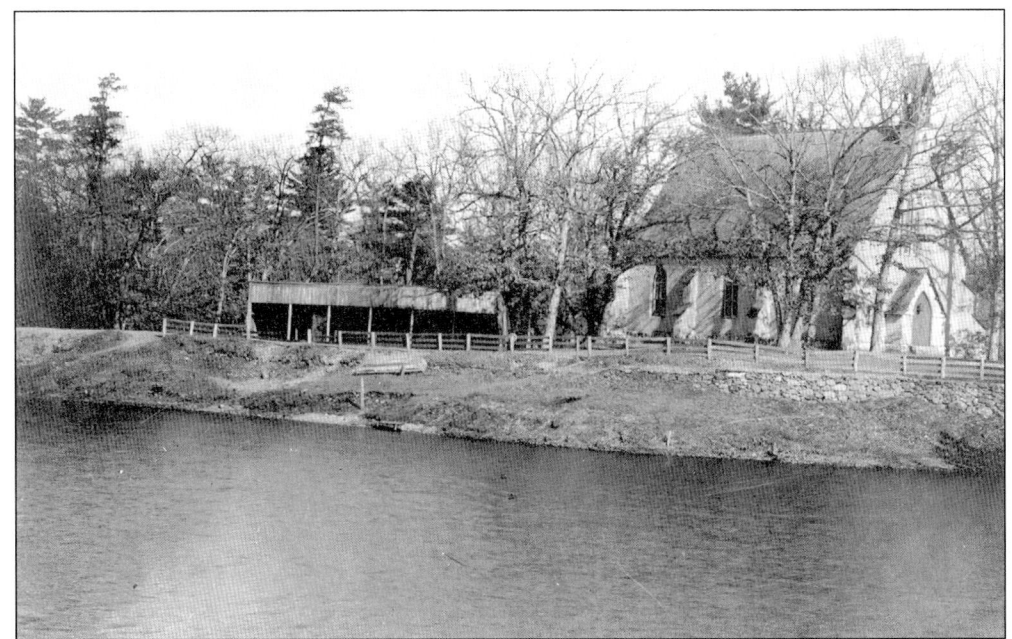
The old Georgiaville Baptist Church stood from 1857 to 1906 where the Georgiaville Beach parking lot is today. It is said that baptisms took place in Georgiaville Pond. (TA.)

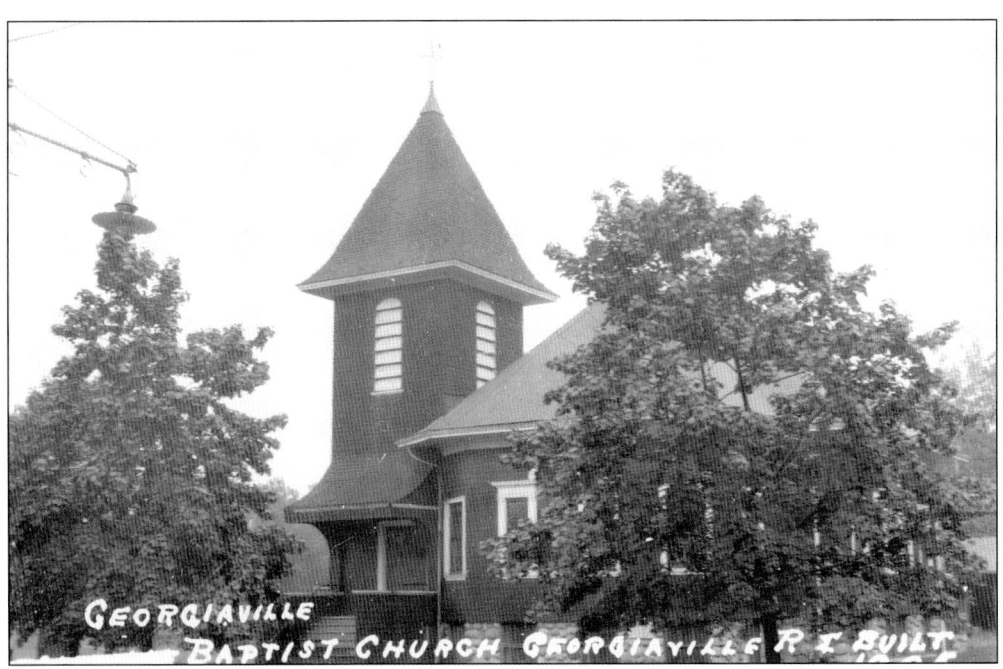
The present-day Georgiaville Baptist Church was built in 1906. (HSS.)

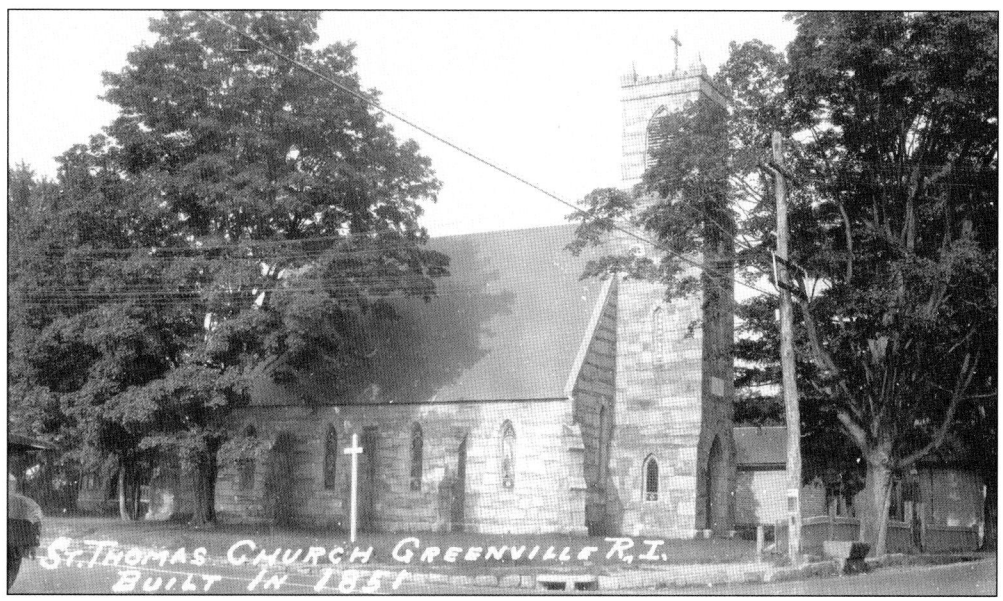
This 1931 view is of St. Thomas Church in Greenville. Note the space for the water trough for horses, and later cars, in front. (HSS.)

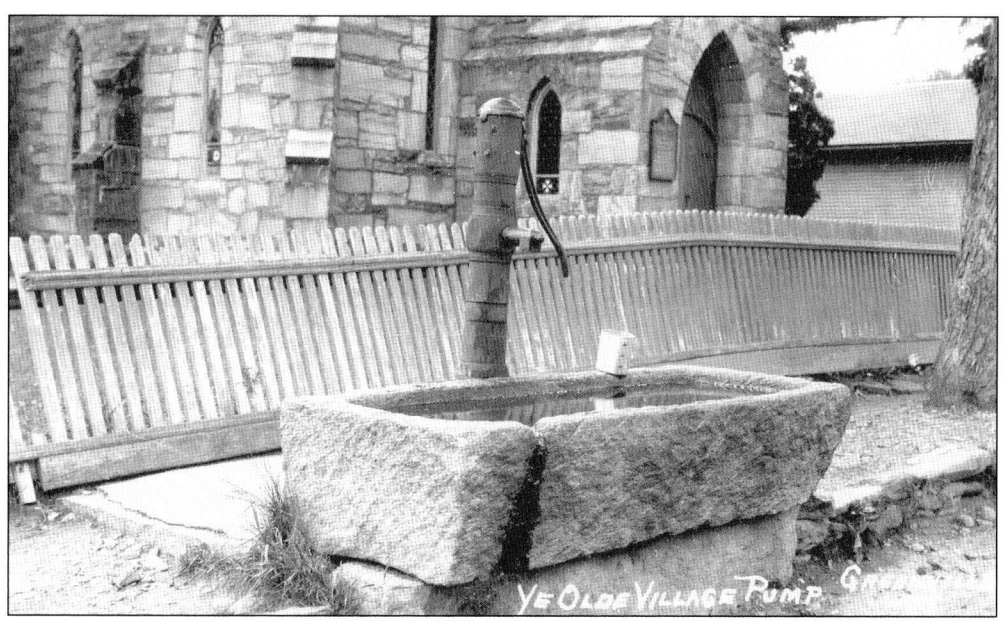
This hand-cut, stone water trough now sits on the Greenville Common. (HSS.)

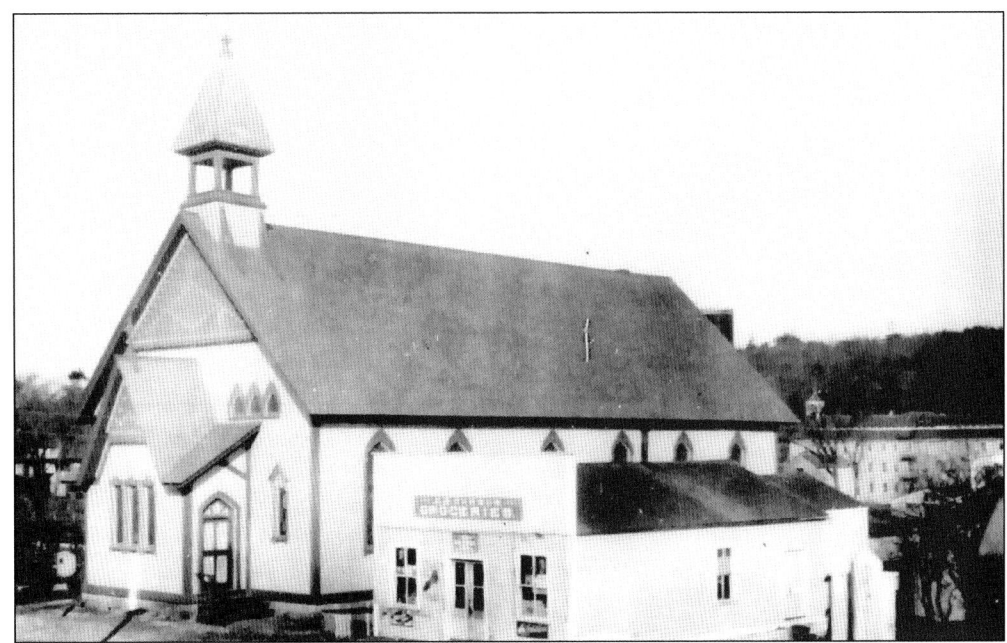
The old St. Michael's Church stood on Homestead Avenue in Georgiaville. Built in 1875, it served until the current St. Michael's opened on Farnum Pike in 1967. (FF.)

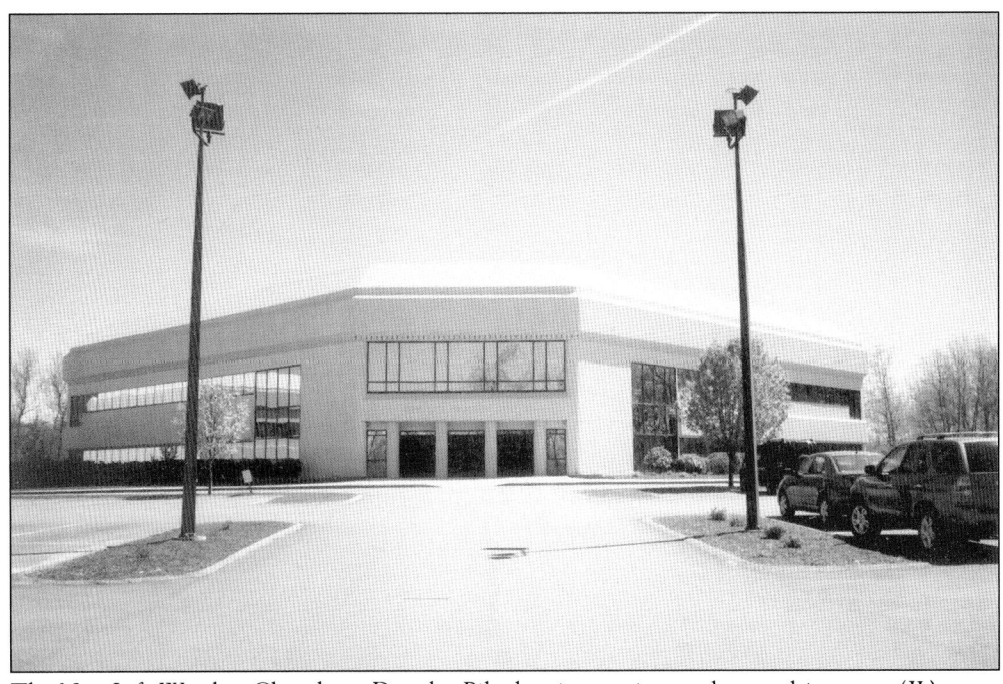
The New Life Worship Church on Douglas Pike has impressive modern architecture. (JI.)

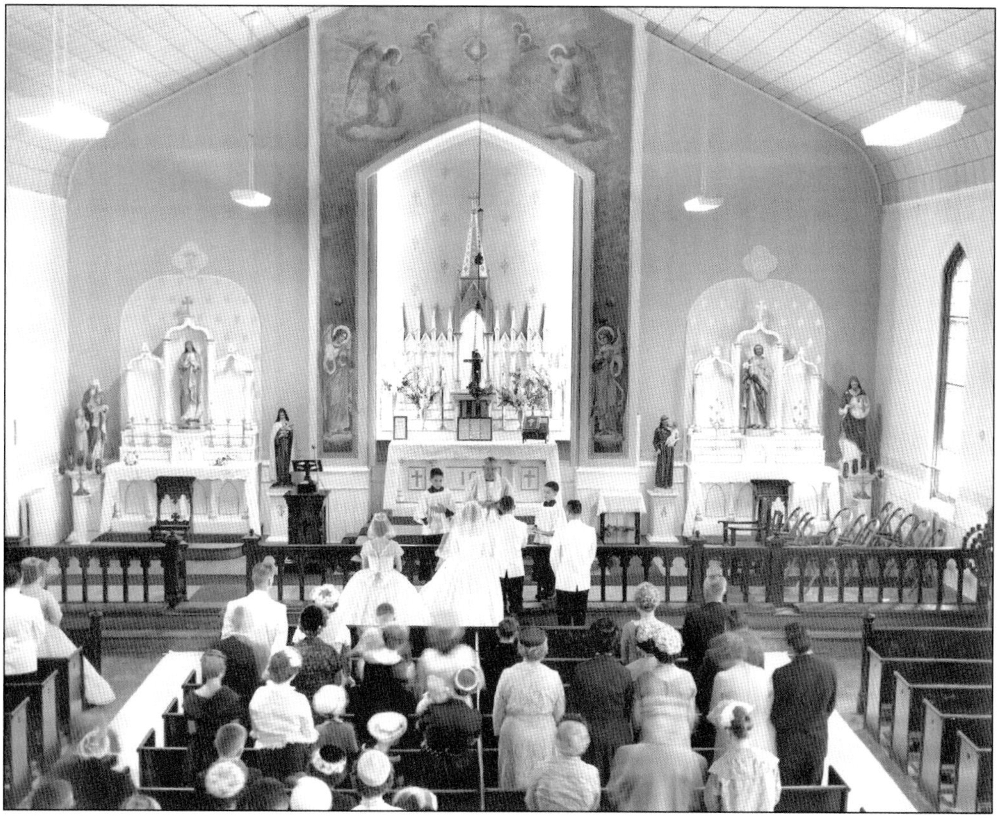

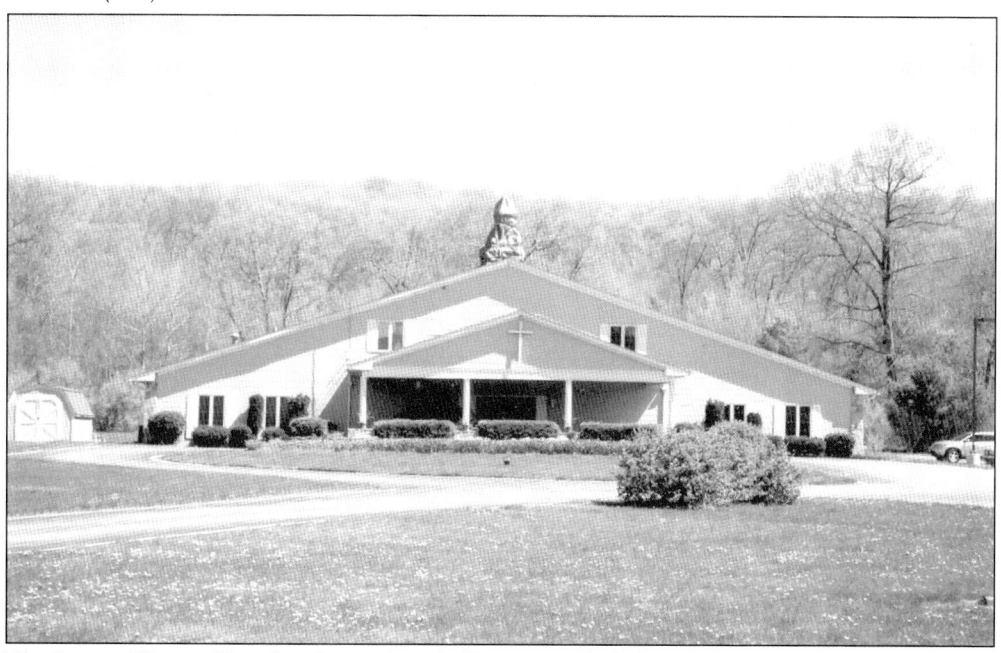

This wedding photograph taken in 1962 shows an interior view of the old St. Michael's Church. (KB.)

The Living Waters Church is located on Stillwater Road. (JI.)

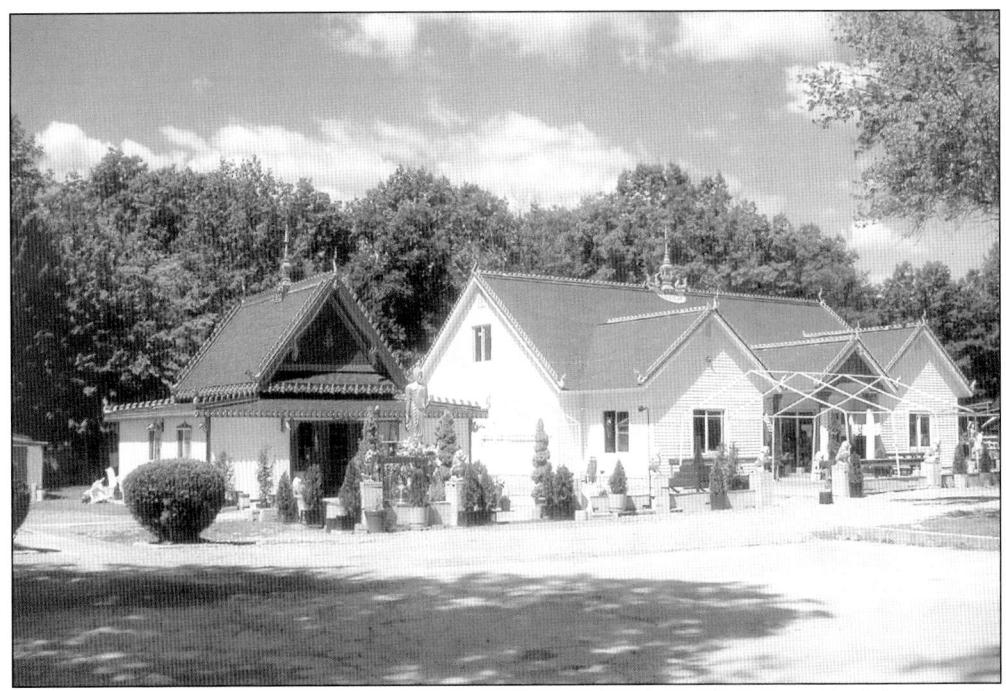

The beautifully ornamented Wat Lao Buddhovath Temple is located on Lime Rock Road. (JI.)

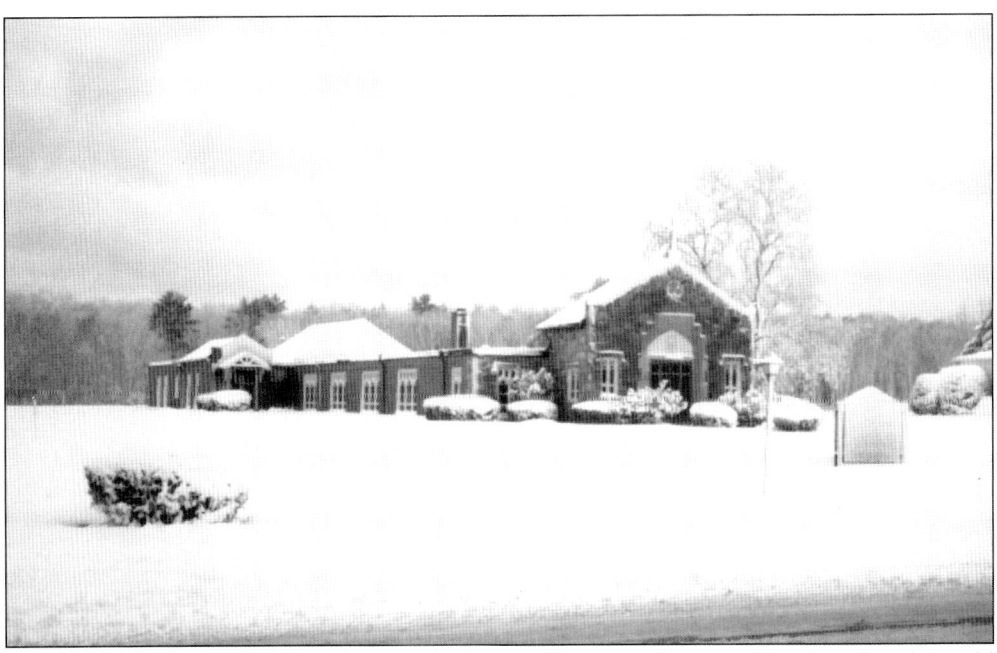

This 1987 photograph shows the second St. Philip's Church on Putnam Pike. It replaced the old wooden St. Philip's Church on Smith Avenue that is still standing today. The second church was torn down in 1989 so the present St. Philip's Church could be constructed. (JI.)

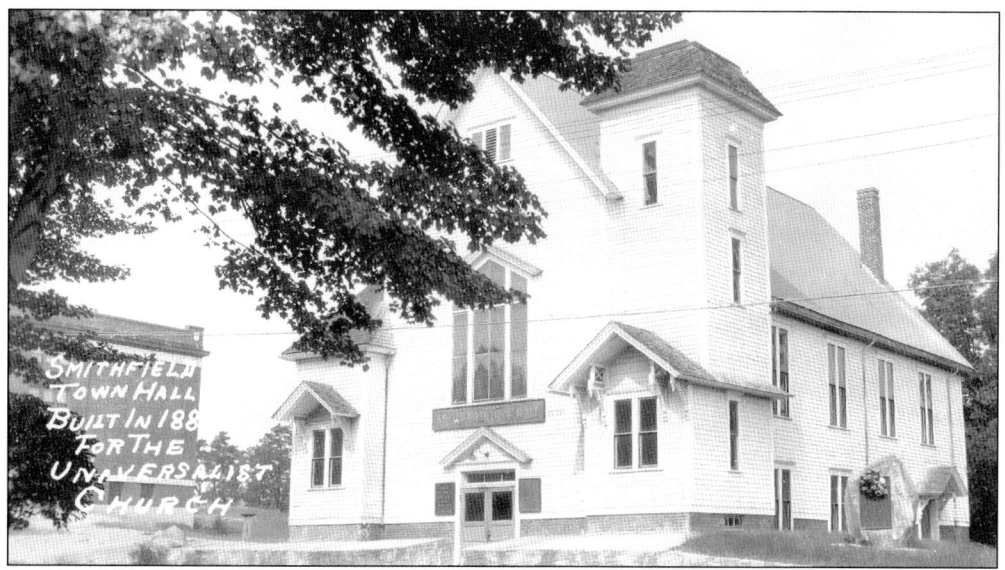

This building in Georgiaville was constructed in 1888 as a Universalist church and later served as the Smithfield Town Hall. Today it is a Veterans of Foreign Wars (VFW) post and has been totally remodeled since this photograph. (HSS.)

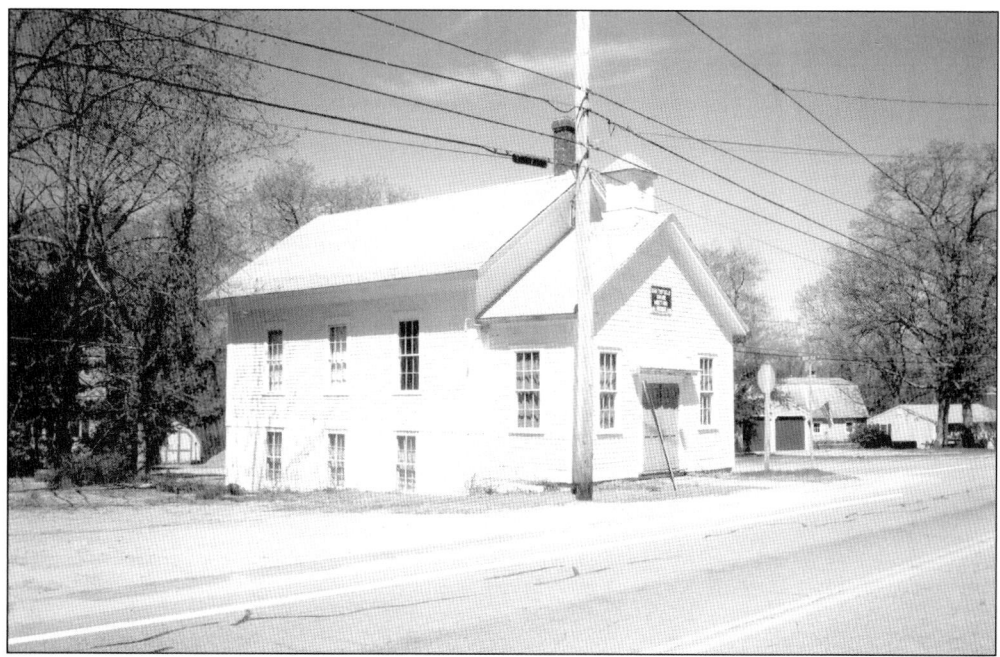

The Smithfield Union Meeting House, also known as the Union Chapel, on Branch Pike at Brayton Road, was built in 1860. (JI.)

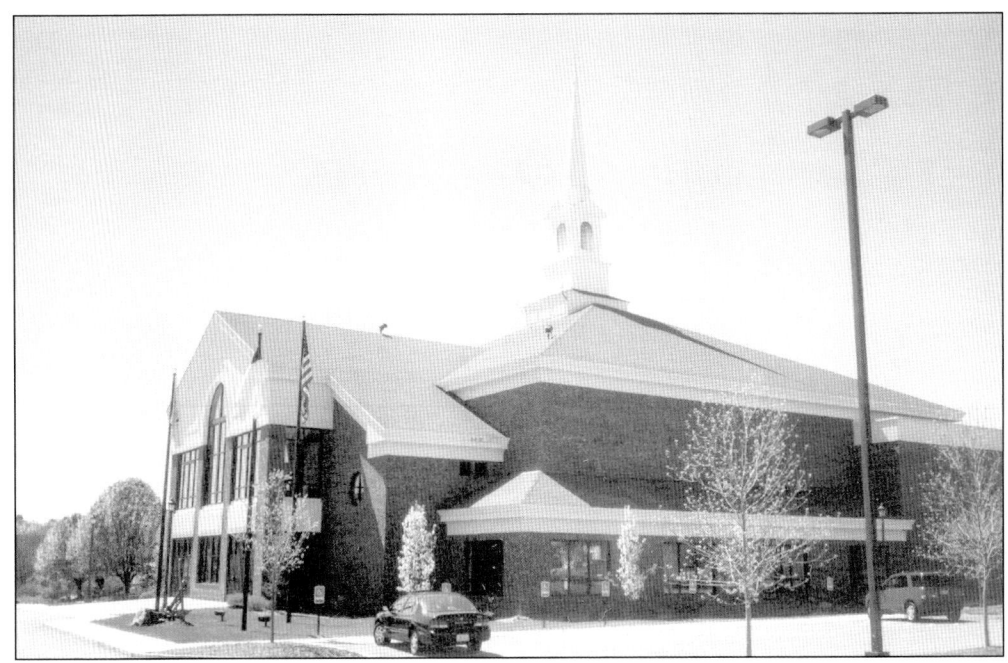

The above photograph shows the Rhode Island Baptist Church on Douglas Pike. (JI.)

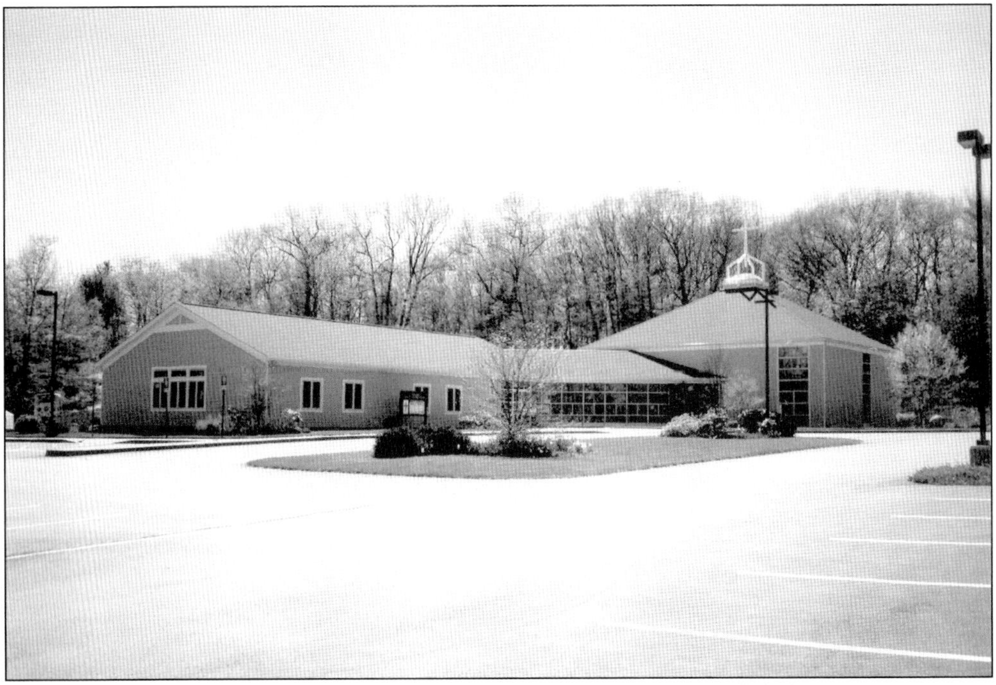

The Our Redeemer Lutheran Church is located on Cedar Swamp Road. (JI.)

Two
HONORING VETERANS

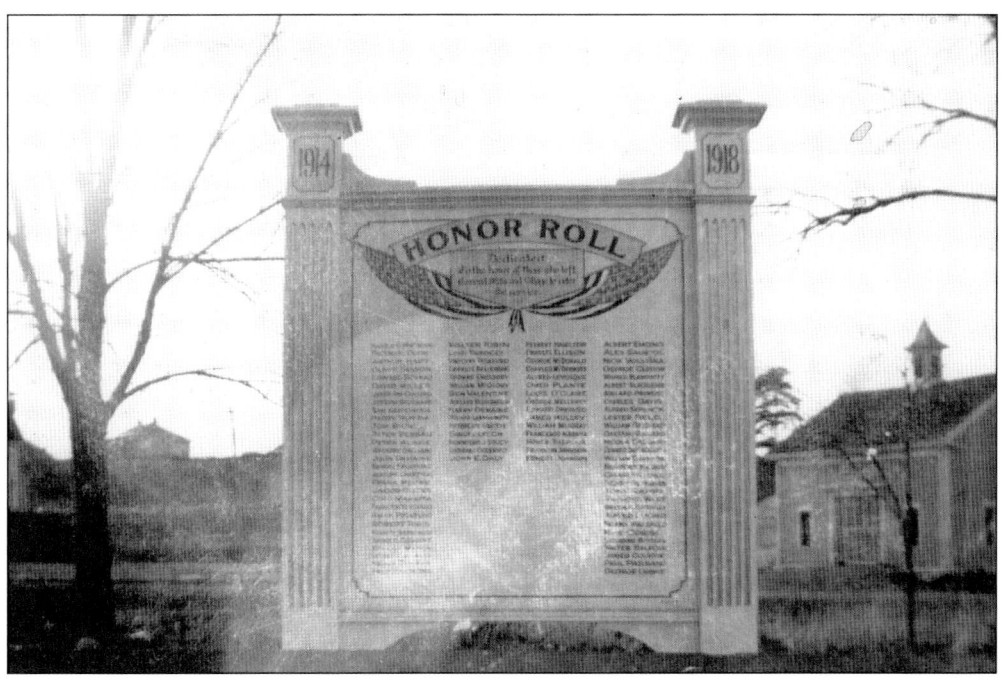

Smithfield's oldest veteran memorials date from World War I. Before that, only the graves of the individual veterans had been marked. The honor roll sign pictured above no longer exists. It was dedicated to those of the village of Esmond and those who worked at the Esmond Mills who served in World War I. (AS.)

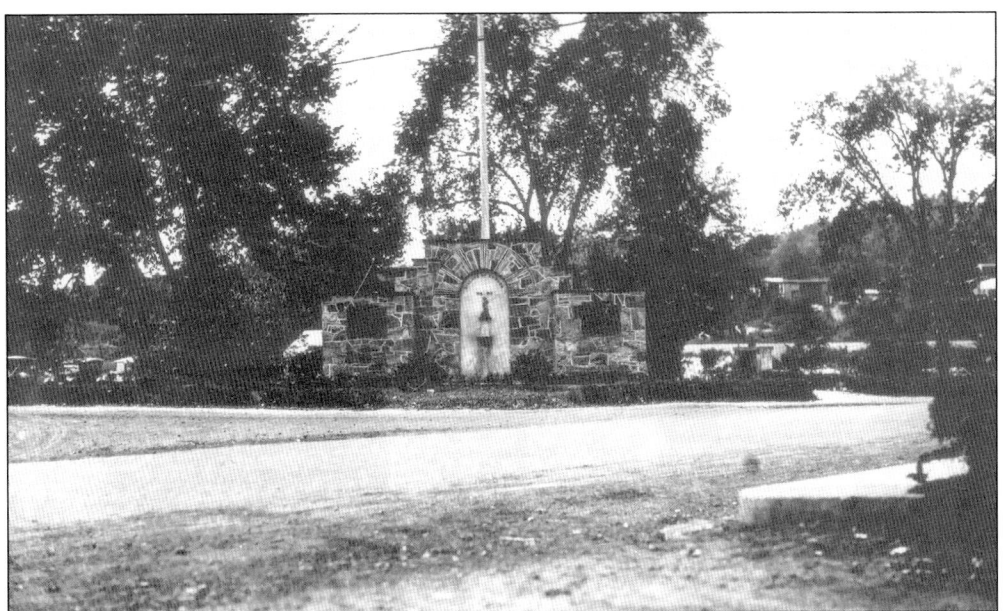

A permanent World War I monument was constructed by the owners of the Esmond Mills after the war. It stood at the corner of Esmond Street and Waterman Avenue where Esmond Park is today. This site is also known as Alexander M. Balfour Square. (AS.)

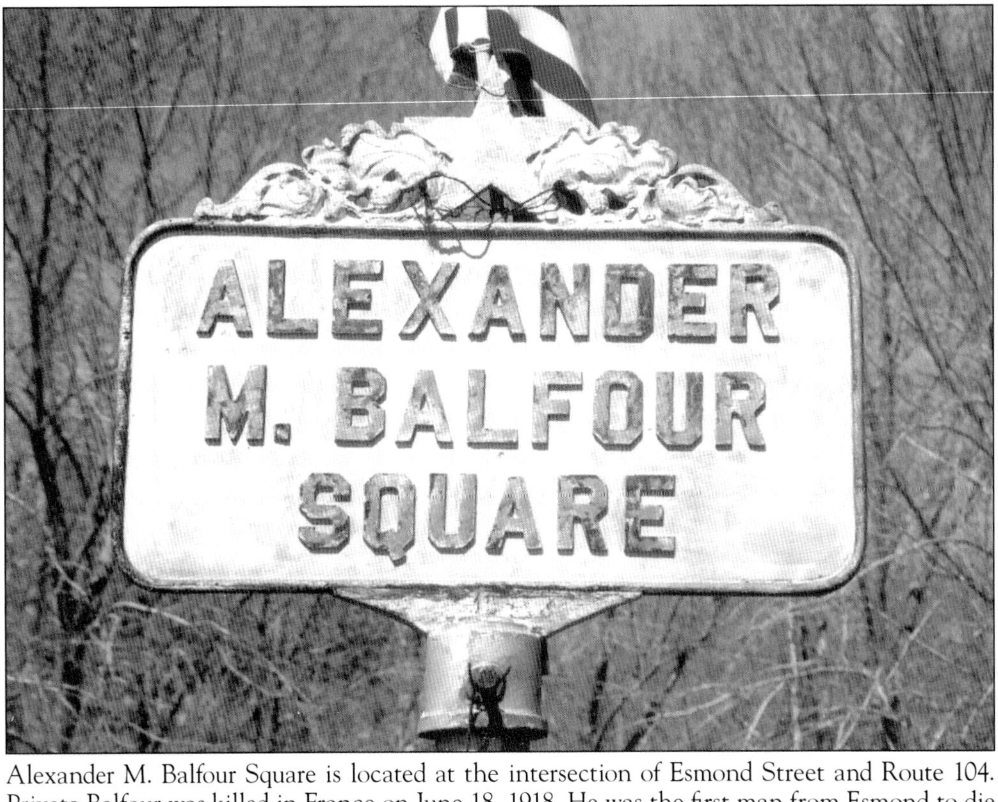

Alexander M. Balfour Square is located at the intersection of Esmond Street and Route 104. Private Balfour was killed in France on June 18, 1918. He was the first man from Esmond to die in World War I. (JI.)

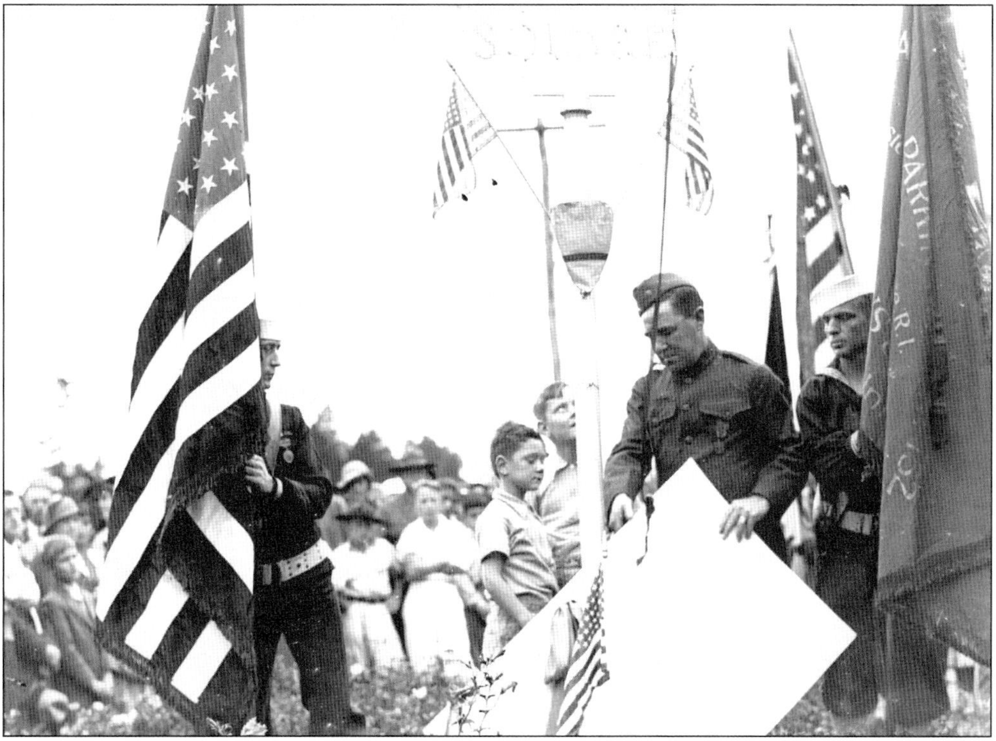

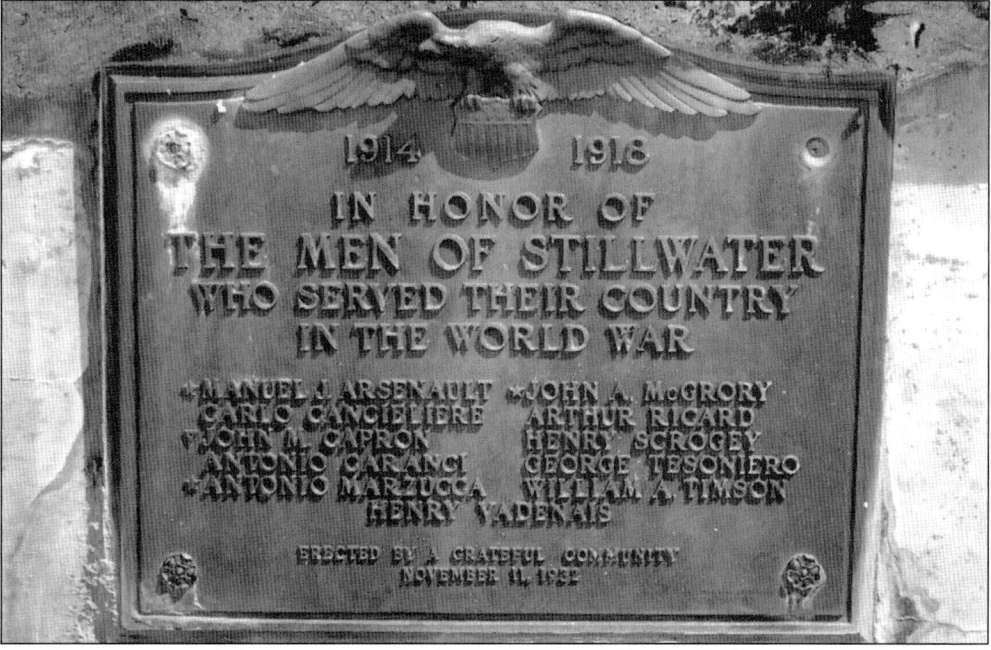

The dedication of Prescott J. Williams Square at the corner of Route 44 and Route 116 took place in 1934. Alfred Schenck is holding the American flag, Prescott J. Williams II and his brother Andrew stand next to the monument pole. (AS.)

This plaque on the Capron Road Bridge honors the men of Stillwater who served during World War I. (JI.)

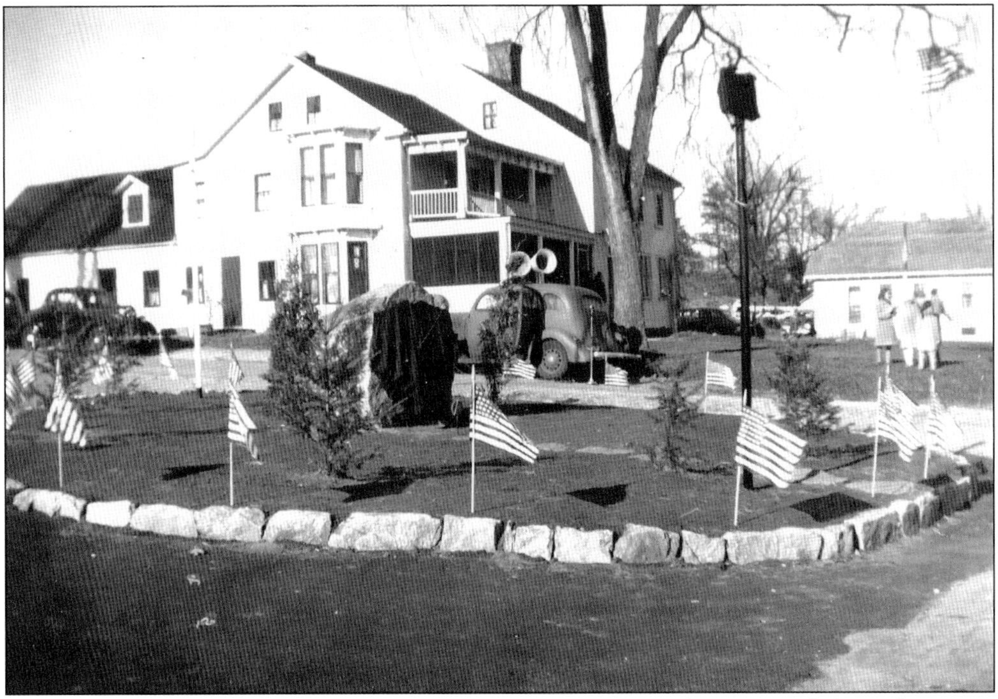

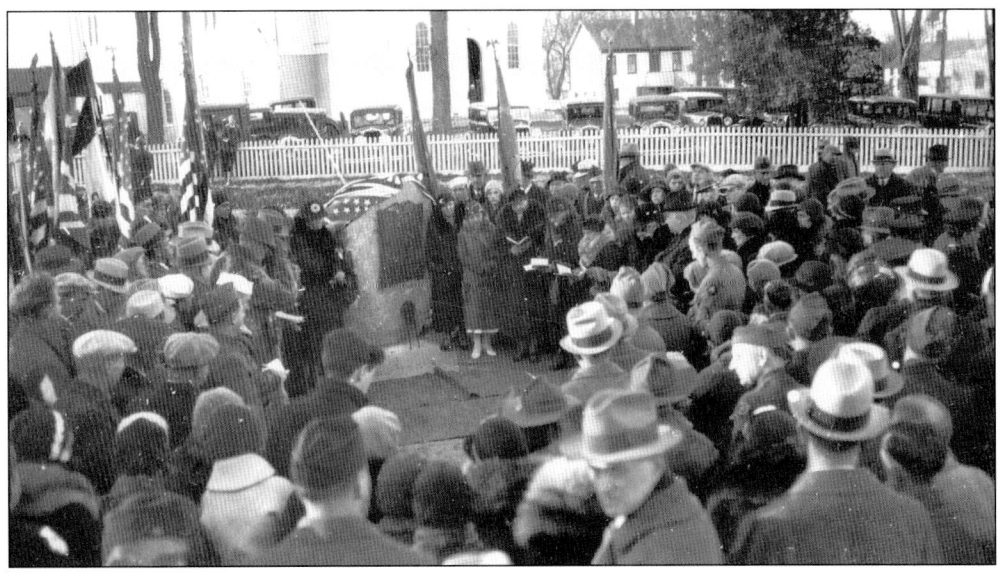

The World War II memorial in Spragueville was very different when it was dedicated at Swan Road and Pleasant View Avenue. This intersection has been redesigned since this photograph was taken, and it is today known as Payette Square. (AS.)

This photograph shows the dedication ceremony of the World War I monument on the Greenville Common in 1932. (HSS.)

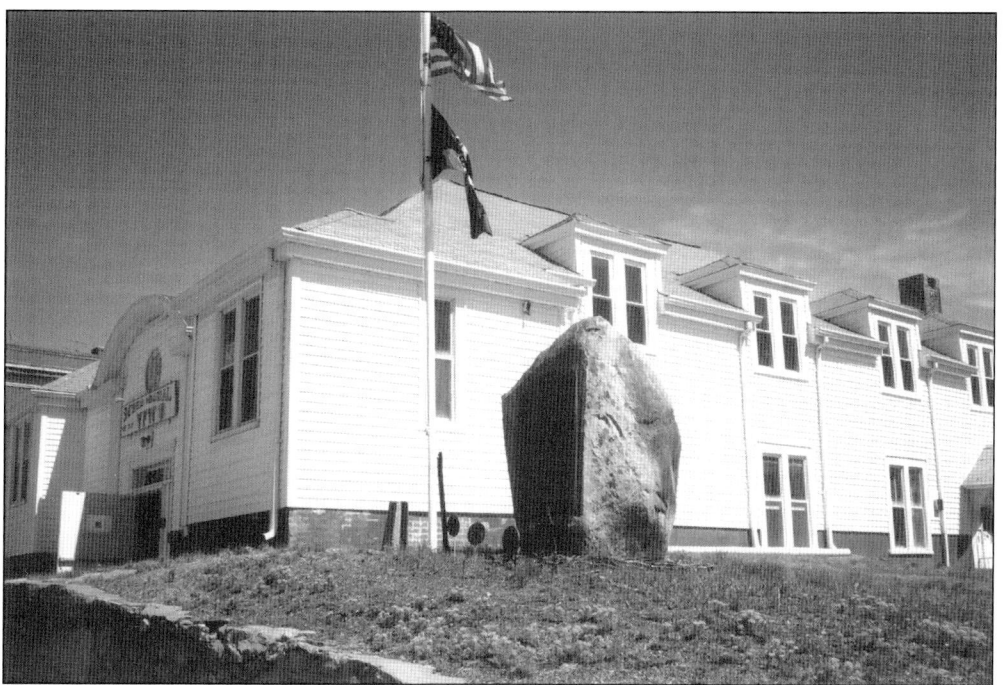

The World War I monument honoring the men of Georgiaville sits next to the VFW post on Farnum Pike. (JI.)

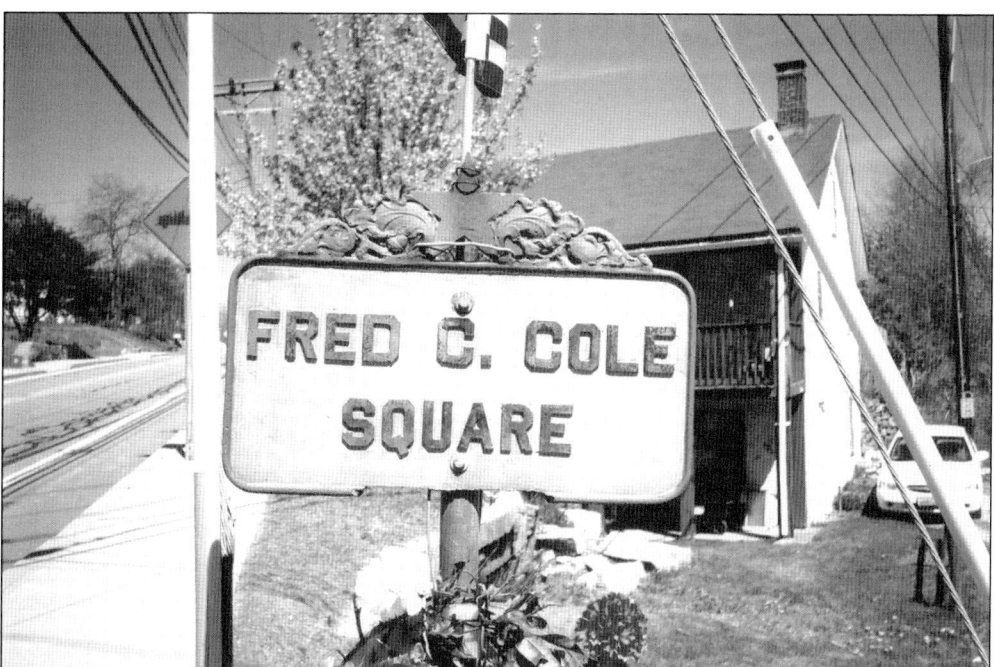

Fred C. Cole Square is located at Farnum Pike and Homestead Avenue in Georgiaville just south of the VFW post. Cole was killed in action during World War I. (JI.)

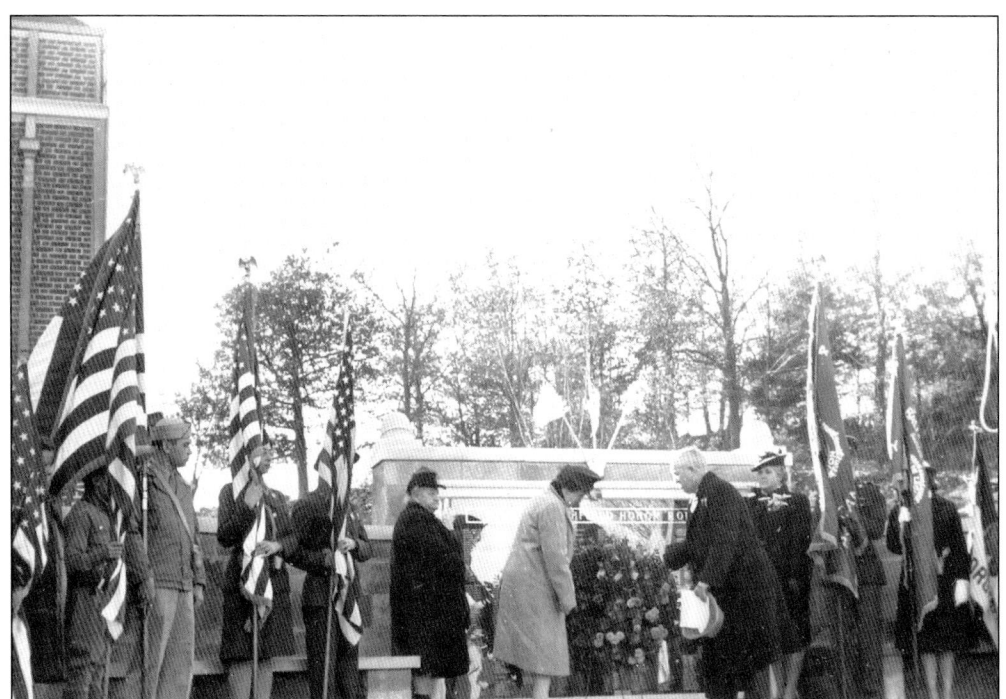

This photograph depicts the dedication of the veterans' memorial outside town hall just after World War II. The memorial originally had a glass front that protected the names of Smithfield veterans underneath; however, it was later replaced by a marble slab, as seen below. (AS.)

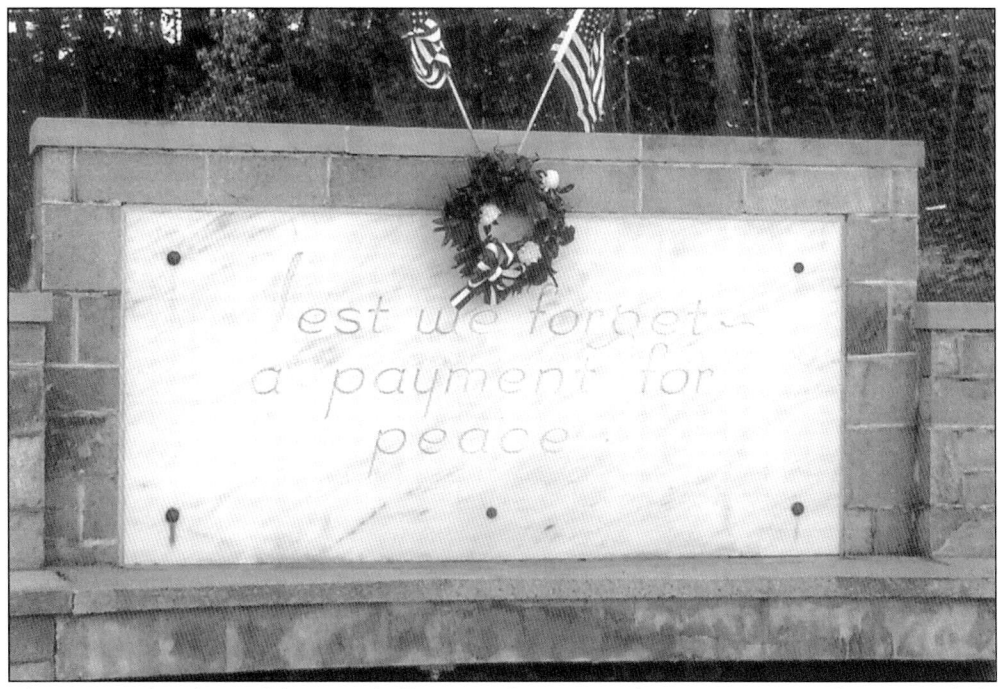

The memorial in front of the town hall now reads, "Lest we forget—a payment for peace." (JI.)

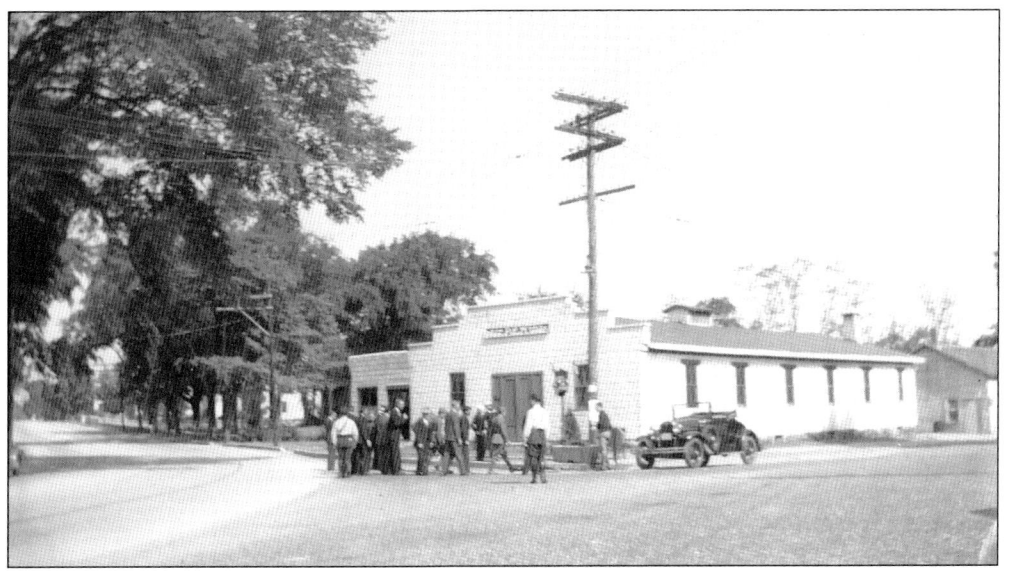

This photograph shows the intersection of Route 44 (in a view looking west) and Austin Avenue in 1937. The officials in the photograph are in the process of dedicating the intersection as Pvt. Ernest E. Austin Square. Austin was killed in France on October 10, 1918. (AS.)

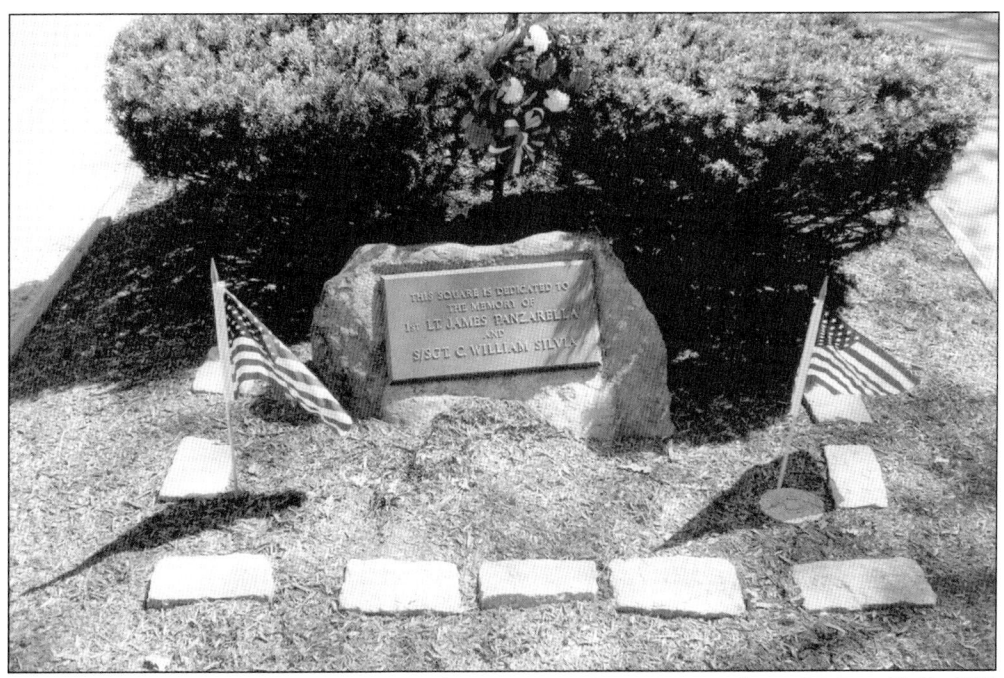

A memorial on Whipple Road at Route 7 honors 1st Lt. James Panzarella and S.Sgt. Clifford W. Silvia, two Smithfield men killed in action during the Vietnam War. (JI.)

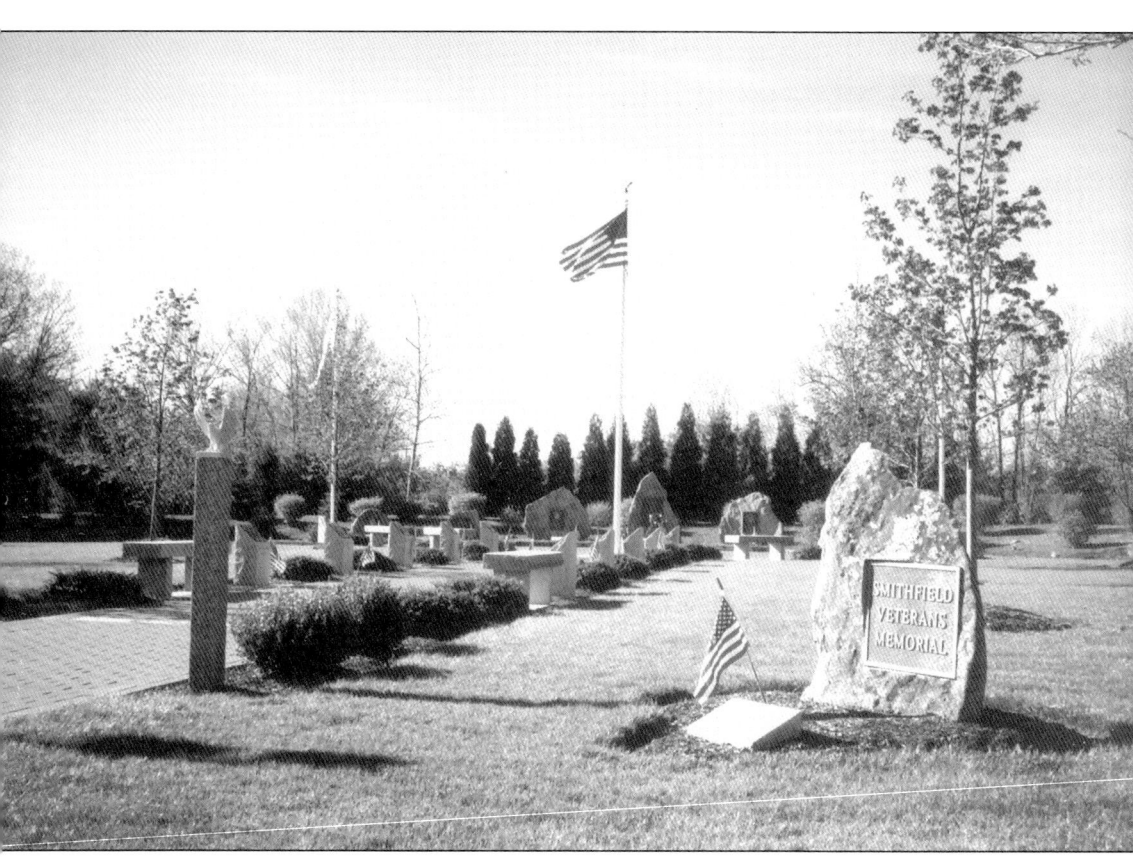

The Smithfield Veteran's Memorial in Deerfield Park was dedicated on November 11, 2001, the 83rd anniversary of the end of World War I—the war that was supposed to be "the war to end all wars." It was designed to honor all veterans from every branch of the armed services who have served in every U.S. armed conflict from the Revolutionary War to the present day. Behind every name is a story. Most of the stories have been lost to history, but they are the citizens of Smithfield who answered the call to duty. Some of them never came back. They all deserve sincere gratitude. (JI.)

Three
SMITHFIELD POLICE DEPARTMENT

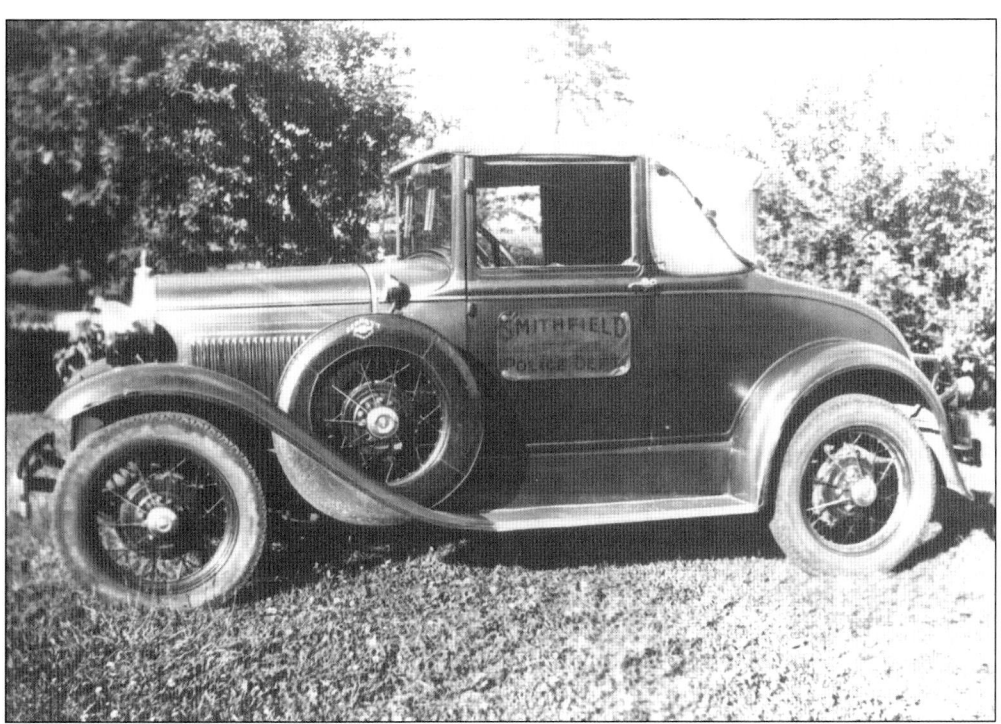

Before the days of automobiles, police constables patrolled on horseback, bicycle, or foot. This photograph depicts what is perhaps Smithfield's first police car, an early Ford Model A. It was capable of achieving speeds up to 60–65 miles per hour, which was considered very fast for its day. It lacked all the equipment found on a modern cruiser, but it was a vast improvement over horses. (SPD.)

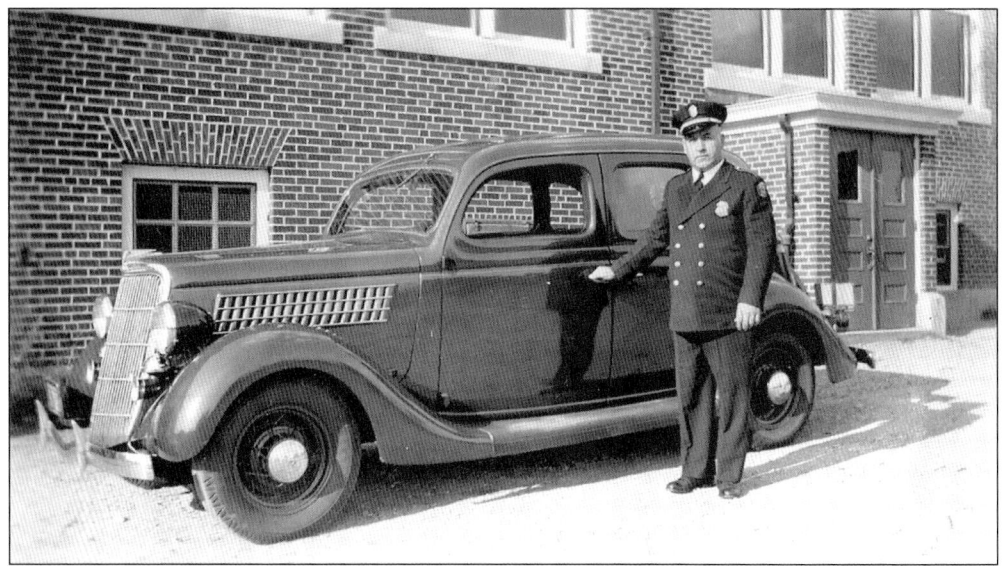

This photograph, taken in 1935, shows chief of police William Kelley next to a 1935 Ford. In the 1930s, Smithfield had a part-time chief of police who was appointed by the town council. The chief was assisted by several special officers who received little if any pay. (WK.)

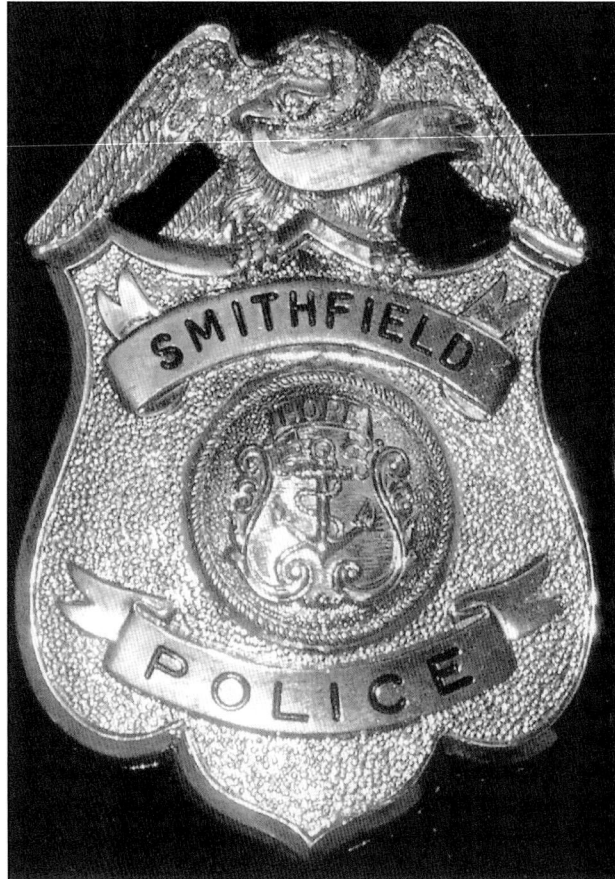

To the left is an example of an early Smithfield patrolman's badge worn by both permanent and reserve officers until about 1973. When the badge style was changed for permanent officers, the reserve officers continued to wear this style. (JI.)

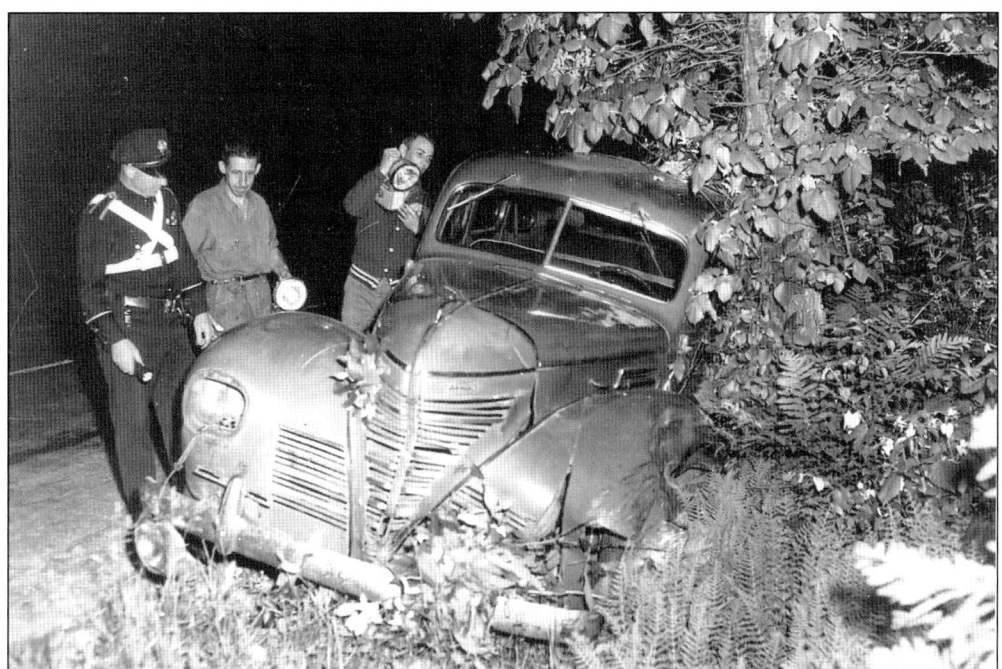

Officer Adolph Schenck investigates an accident on Douglas Pike in 1951, while Alfred Angel and Milton Corey look on. In 1951, a Smithfield patrolman worked 54 hours a week and earned about $2,100 a year. That works out to about 77¢ per hour! (AS.)

To the right is a second-issue Smithfield police uniform patch worn from about 1950 to 1973. It replaced an earlier version first worn in the 1930s that had the same basic design but was round. (See the photograph of Chief Kelley on page 26.) (JI.)

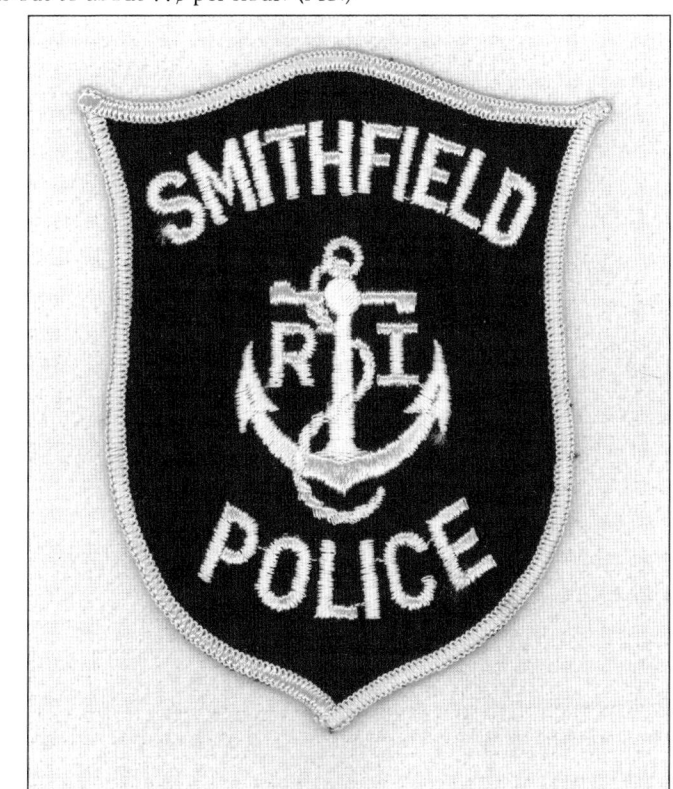

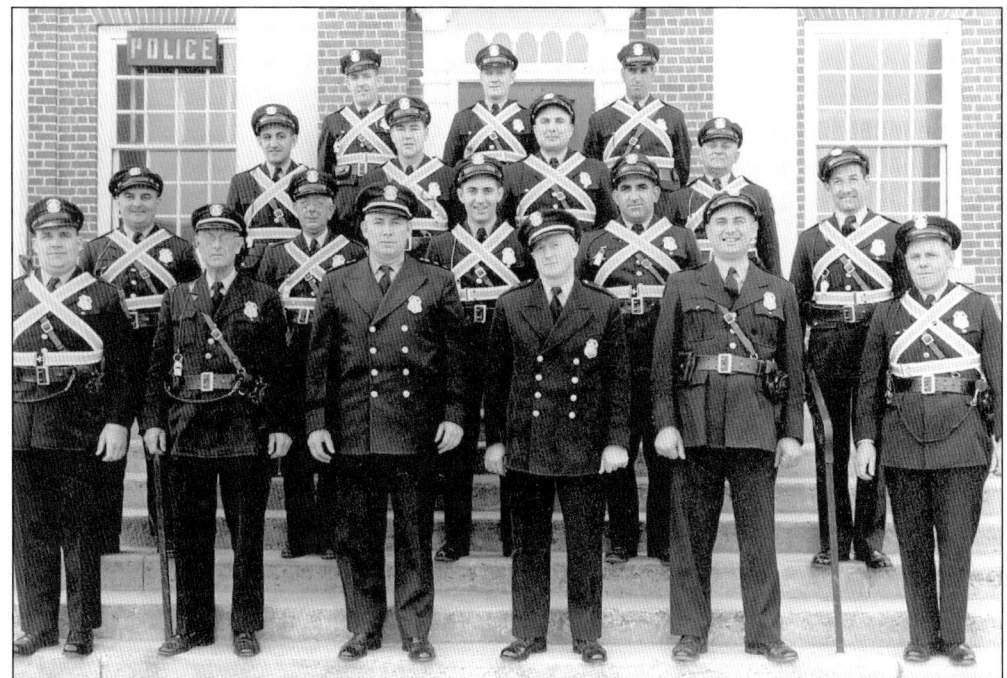

Smithfield established its first permanent police department in 1950 under an act of the Rhode Island General Assembly. This photograph was taken in 1955 in front of the town hall, which at the time housed the police station in the basement. (SPD.)

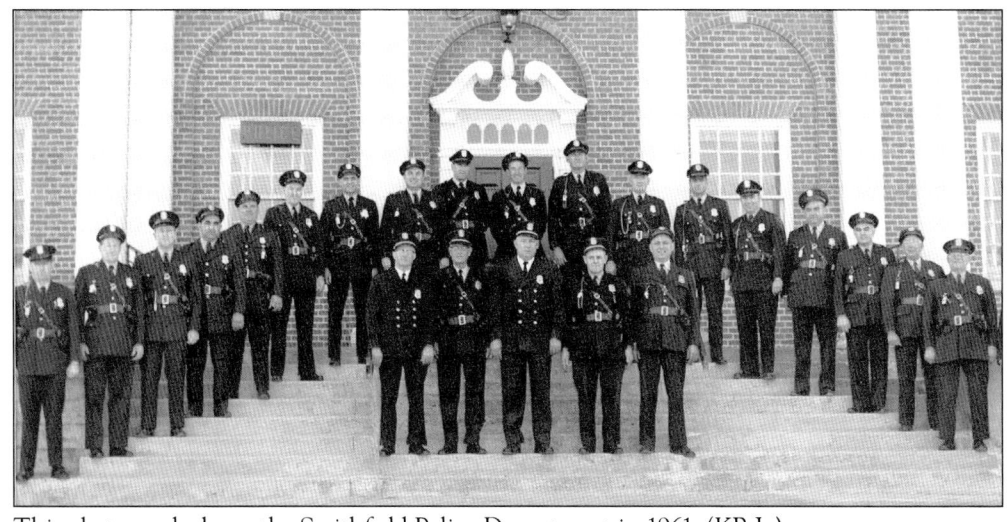

This photograph shows the Smithfield Police Department in 1961. (KB Jr.)

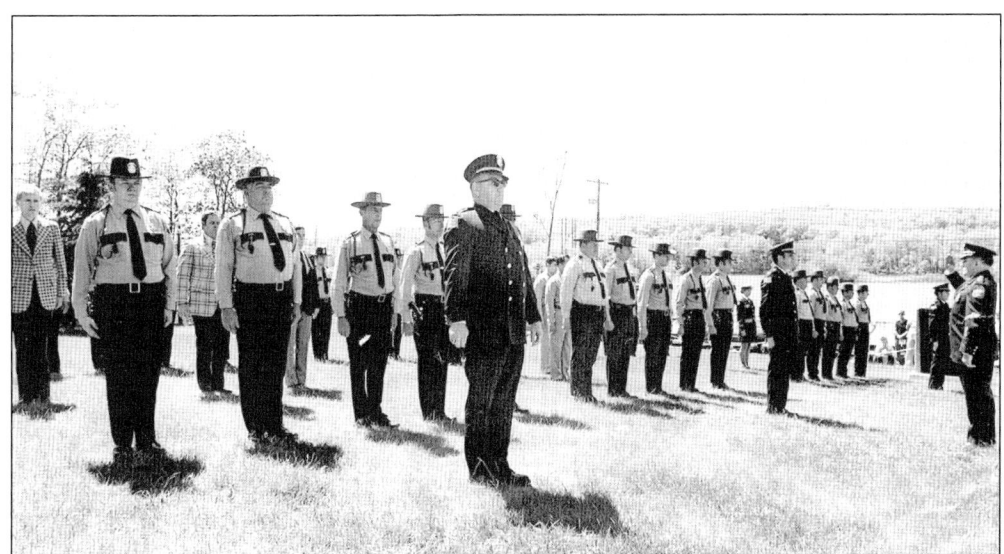

A police Memorial Day ceremony in front of the police station on Pleasant View Avenue is shown in 1976. Members of the department once wore blue uniforms. (KB Jr.)

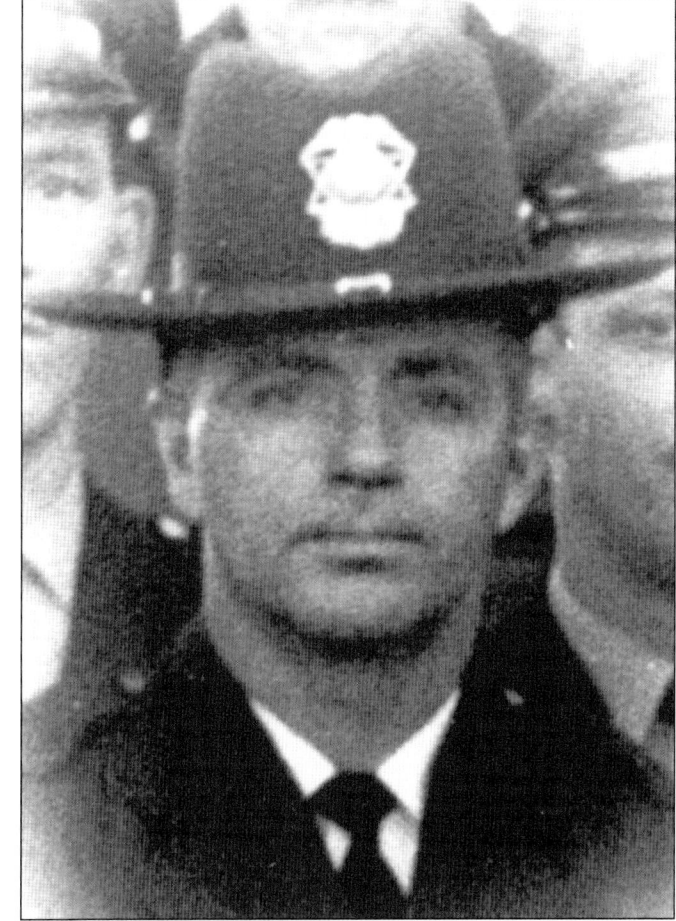

On December 10, 1968, patrolman Norman G. Vezina died in the line of duty while attempting to rescue a small child who had fallen through the ice on a local pond. He joined the department as a reserve officer in November 1966 and was sworn in as a permanent officer on May 1, 1968. He was promoted to sergeant posthumously. Today memorials to him are located in the police station and at Deerfield Park. (SPD.)

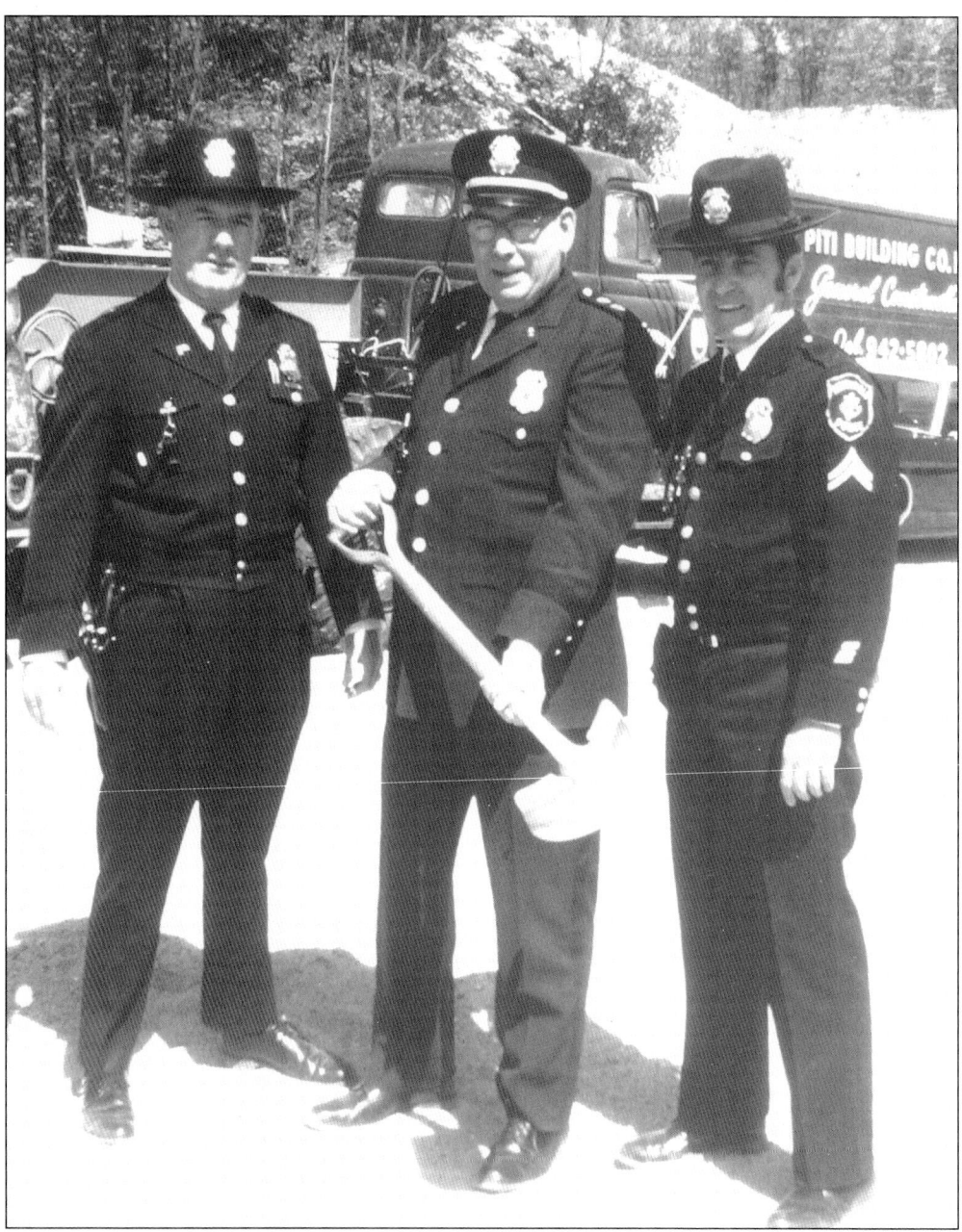

By 1970, the department had outgrown its quarters at the town hall, and it was decided that a new station should be built. A parcel of land on Pleasant View Avenue was donated to the town by Burton and Mary Mowry, and a groundbreaking ceremony was held on May 27, 1972. From left to right are Deputy Chief Jim McVey, Chief Arthur Gould, and Cpl. Saverio Serapiglia. (TM.)

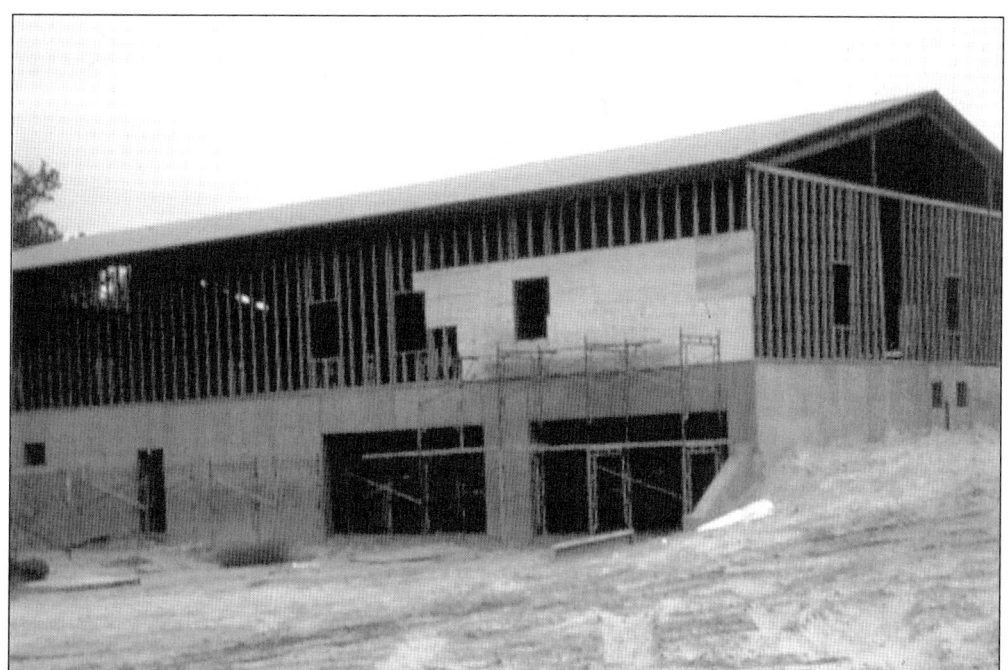

This photograph shows the rear of the present police station under construction in 1972. Many of the officers helped to keep construction costs down by voluntarily working on the project on their days off. On November 18, 1972, the department officially moved into the new station. The final cost of the project was $387,600. (KB Jr.)

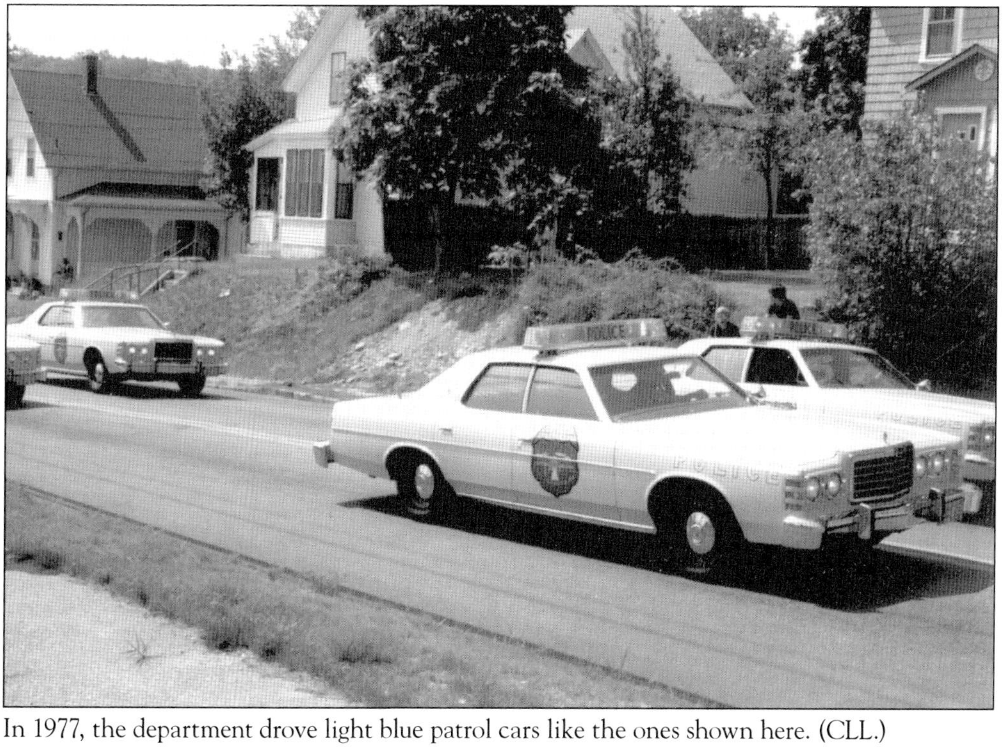

In 1977, the department drove light blue patrol cars like the ones shown here. (CLL.)

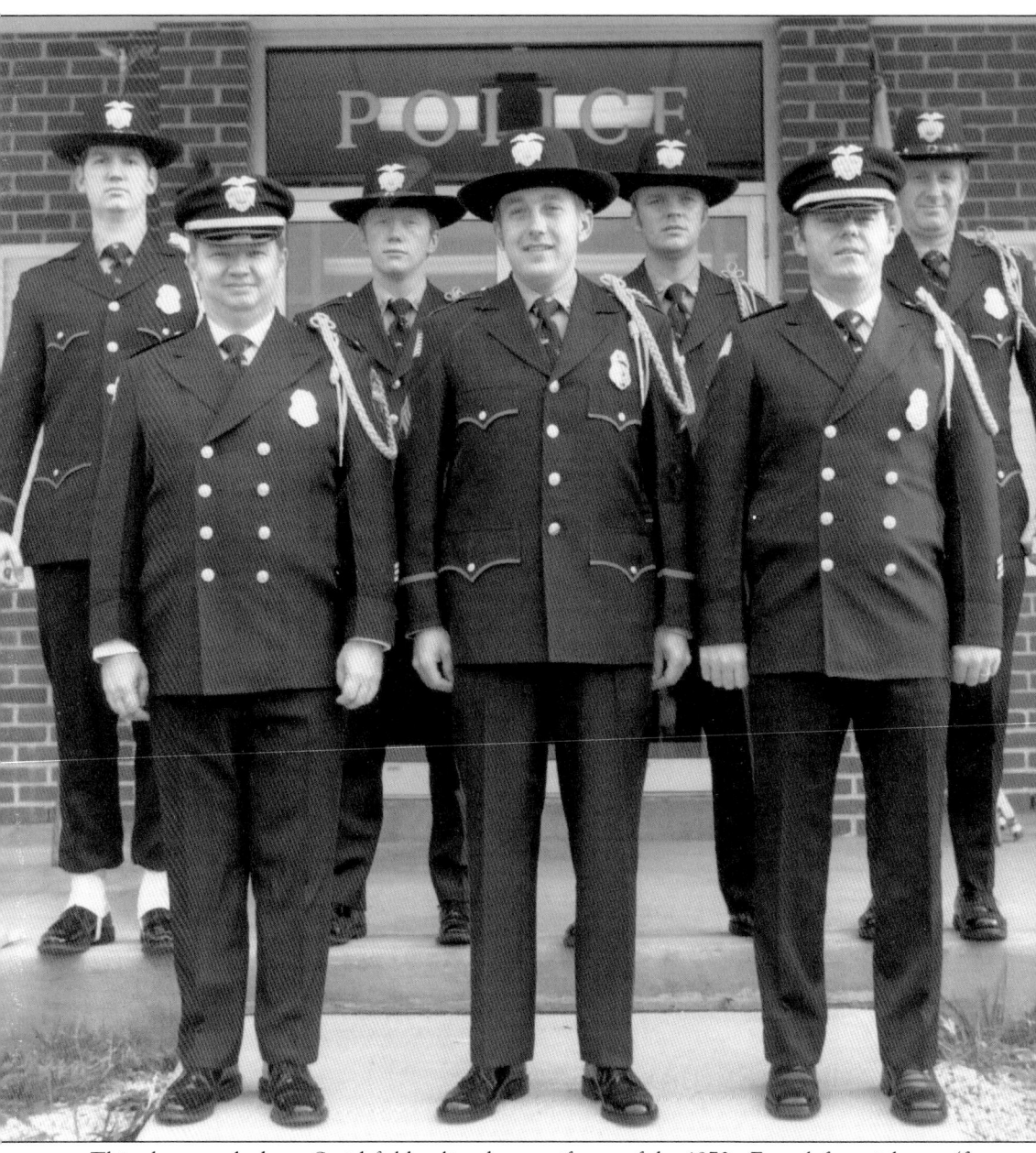

This photograph shows Smithfield police dress uniforms of the 1970s. From left to right are (first row) Raymond Trombley, Curtis Pollard, and Robert Kerwin; (second row) Prescott J. Williams III, Thomas Hickey, John Whitecross, and Jack Hart. (KB Jr.)

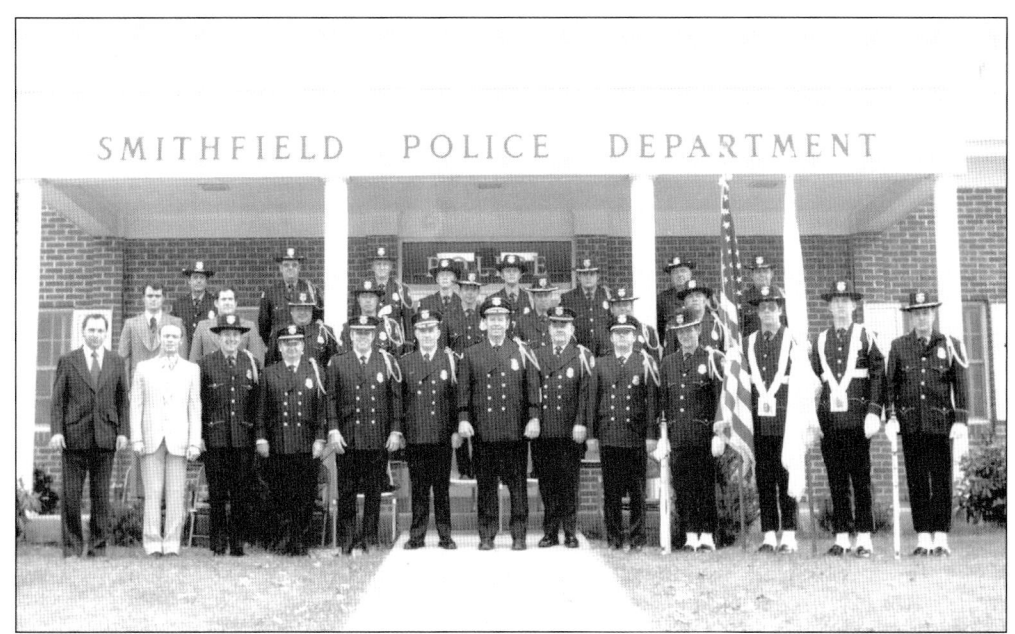
Permanent police officers are seen around 1976. (KB Jr.)

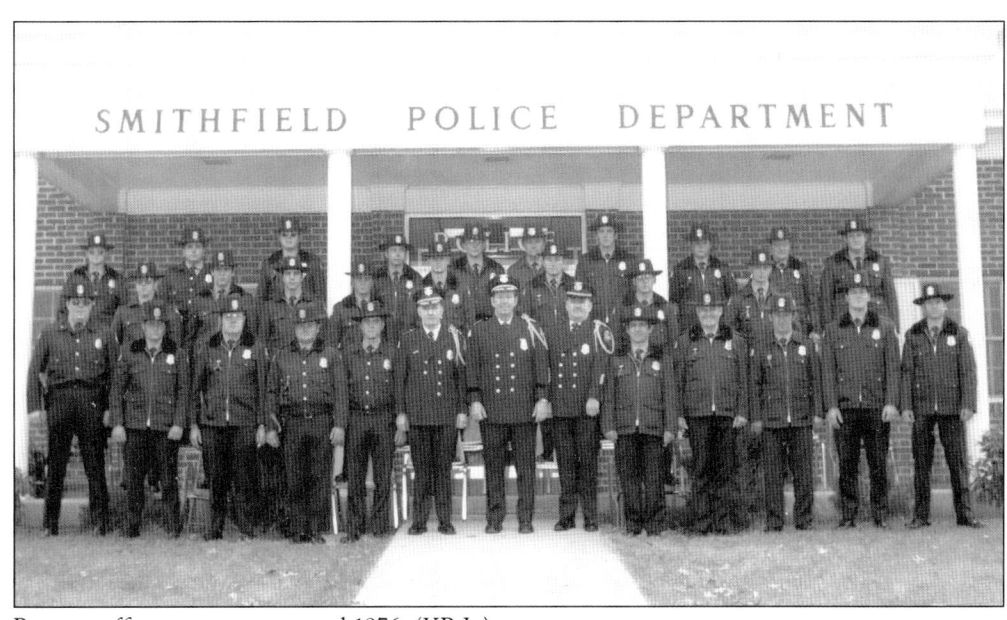
Reserve officers are seen around 1976. (KB Jr.)

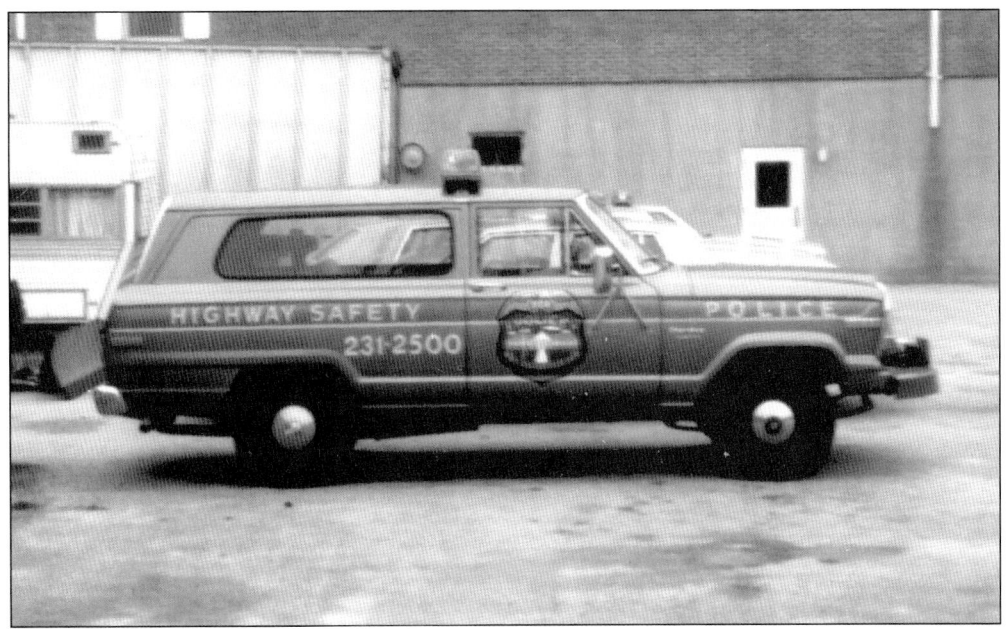

This highway safety Jeep was used by the department in the early 1980s. (JI.)

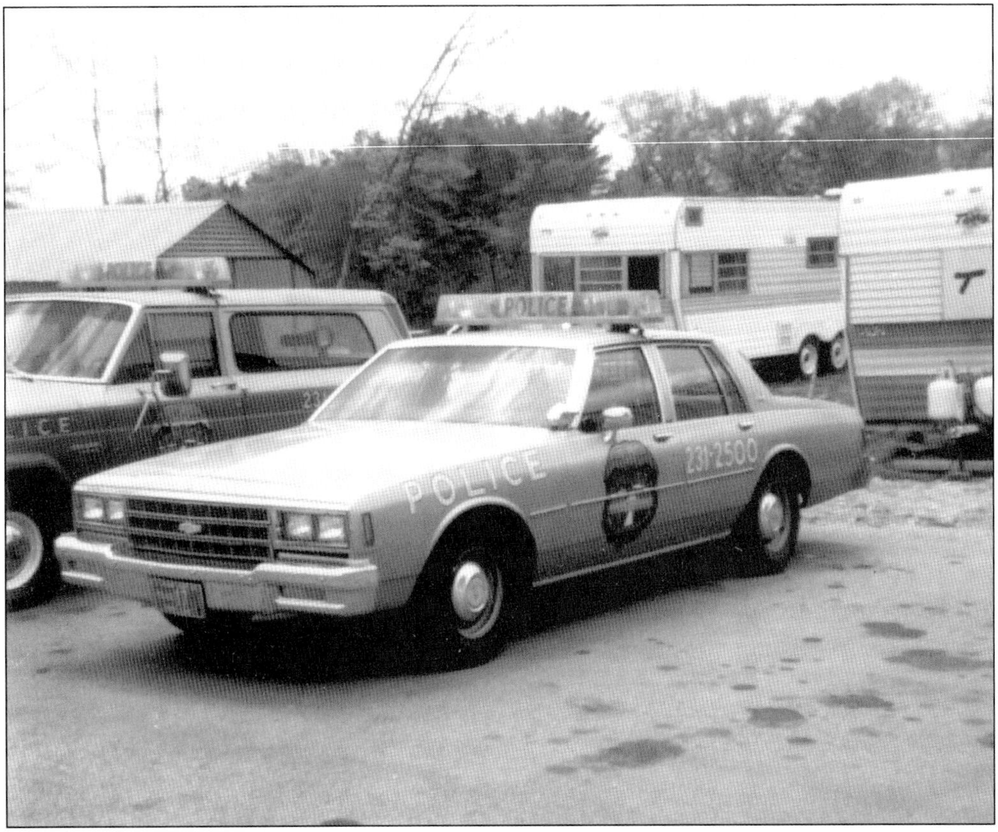

This photograph, taken in 1983, shows a Chevrolet police car. In the late 1970s, the department changed its uniforms and cruisers from blue to gray. (JI.)

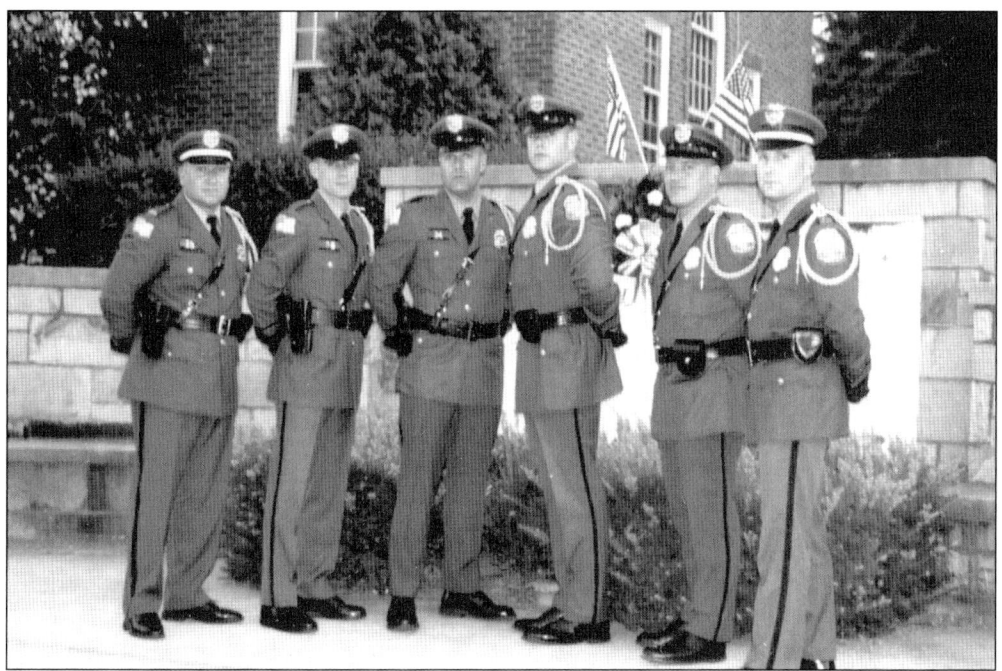

The officers in this 2002 photograph are wearing the old-style honor guard uniforms. From left to right are Kenneth Brown Jr., Michael Smith, Christopher Taylor, Joseph Marcello, Dennis Paul, and Michael Mousseau. (KB Jr.)

The current-issue uniform shoulder patch has been worn since 1973. The patch was designed by three members of the department: Deputy Chief James H. McVey, Capt. Prescott J. Williams II, and Lt. Saverio E. Serapiglia. The finished artwork was done by Frank Iafrate. (JI.)

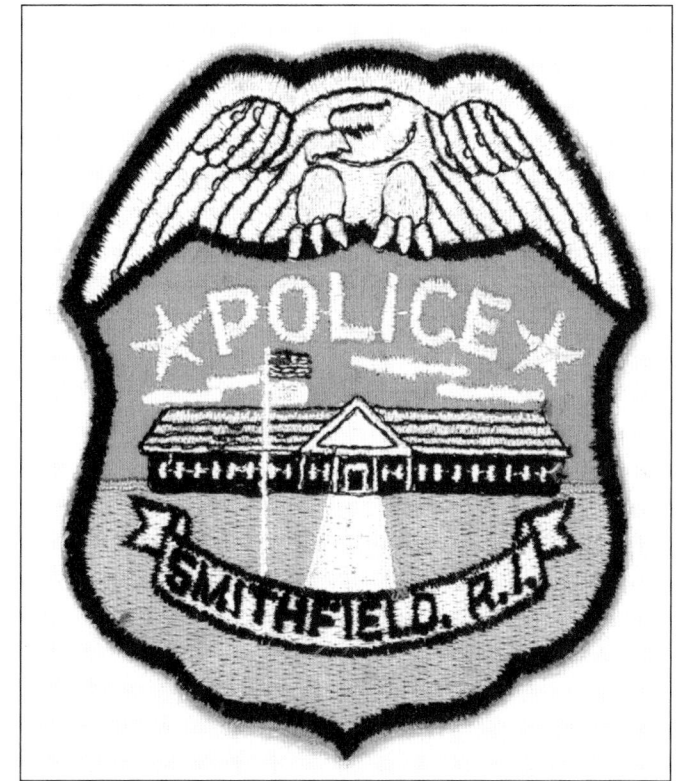

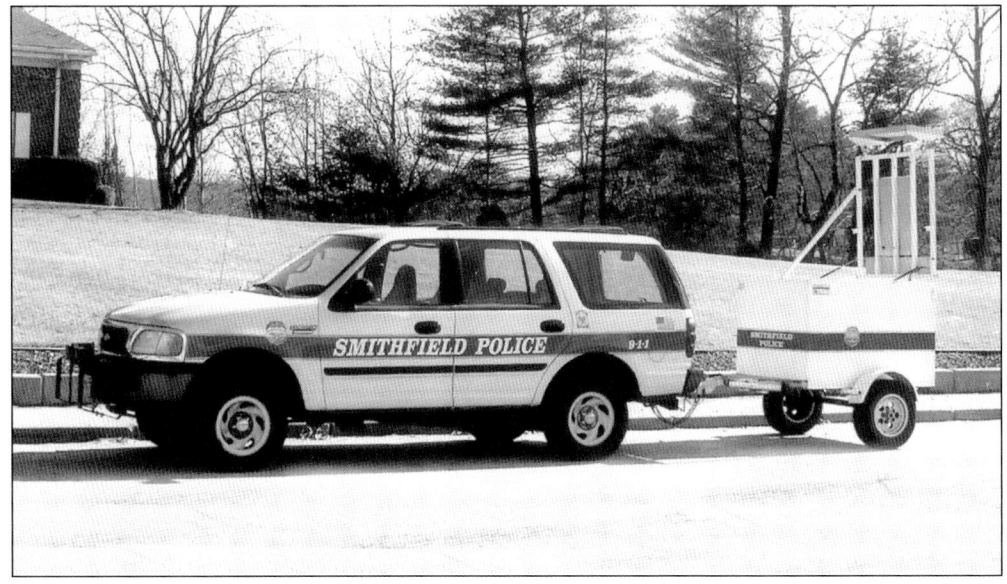

This photograph, taken in 2007, shows a vehicle assigned to the department's traffic division. It can tow a trailer used to regulate traffic flow. (JI.)

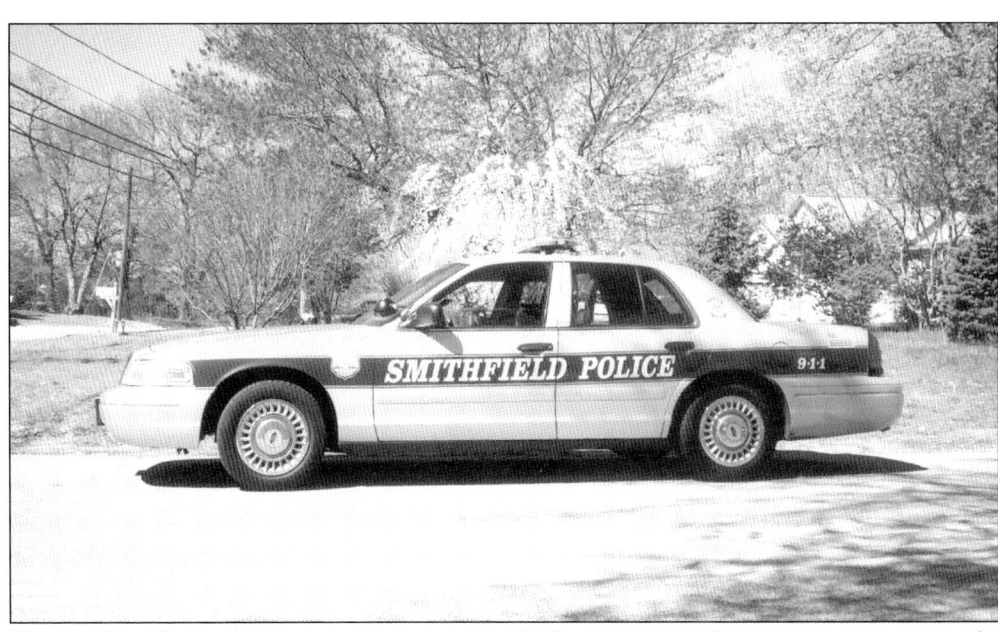

This modern Ford police cruiser is equipped with the most up-to-date resources necessary for today's police officer. It will one day look as obsolete as the department's first 1930 patrol car. (JI.)

Four
SMITHFIELD FIRE DEPARTMENT

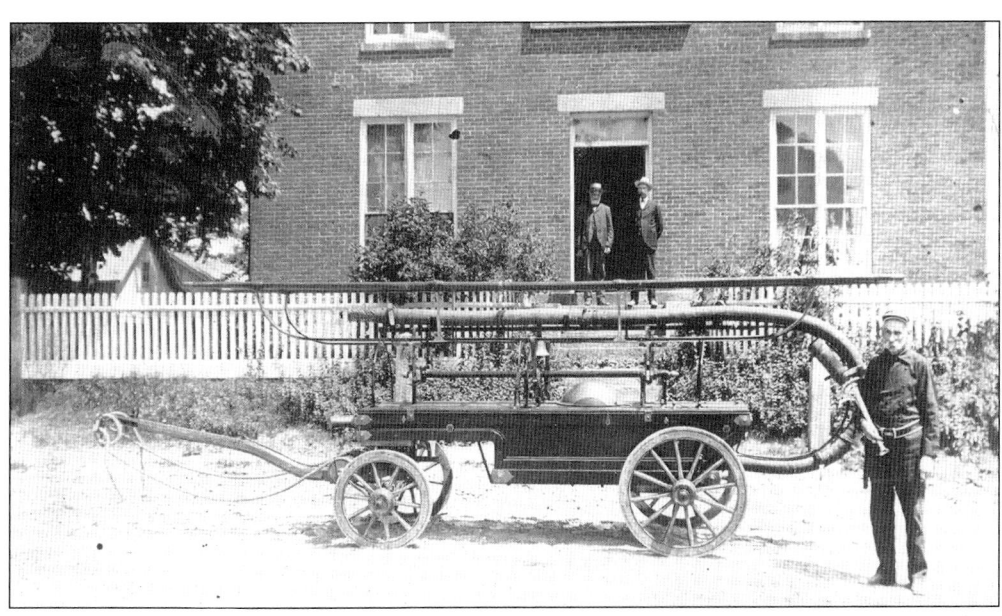

This photograph shows the "Water Witch," Greenville's first fire engine. It was purchased in July 1870 after a devastating fire broke out two months earlier, leaving one man seriously injured and two businesses destroyed. It disappeared while on loan to another community during World War II and has never been seen since. (HSS.)

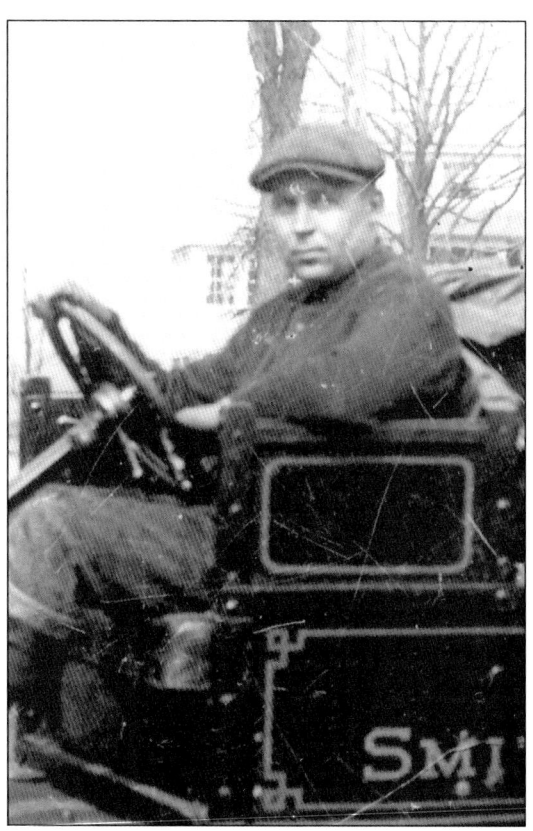

There was a time when the large siren on the roof of the Greenville Fire Station was used to call volunteers to answer an alarm. In October 1956, Raymond W. Segee of the Greenville Fire Company was running across Route 44 toward the fire station in response to an alarm when he suffered a heart attack. He died on October 7 at Roger Williams Hospital and became the first Smithfield firefighter to die in the line of duty. (SFD.)

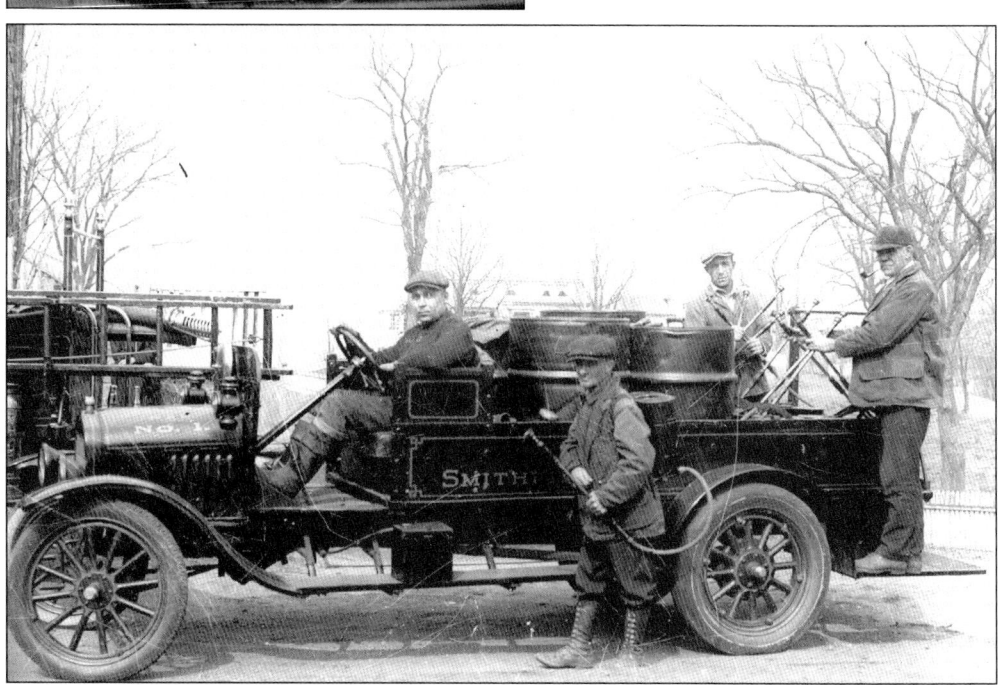

This photograph shows an early brush fire truck used by the department. Segee is sitting in the driver's seat. (SFD.)

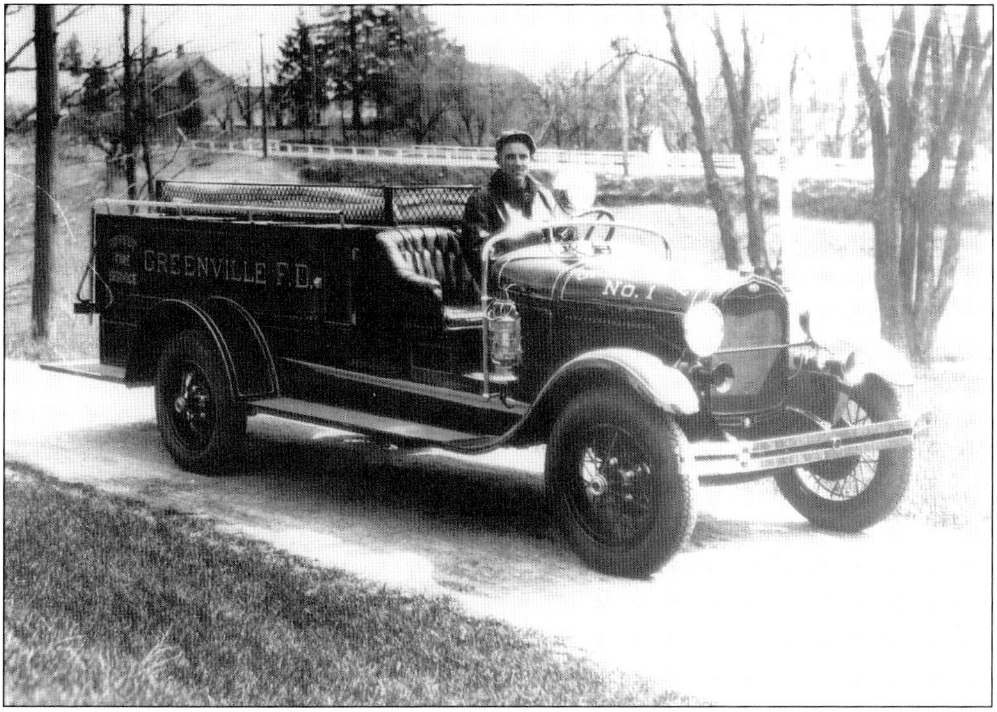

In 1928, a Ford Model A fire truck for battling forest fires was purchased. This truck could carry 300 gallons of water to a fire and is said to have been the first in Rhode Island to be able to do so. (SFD.)

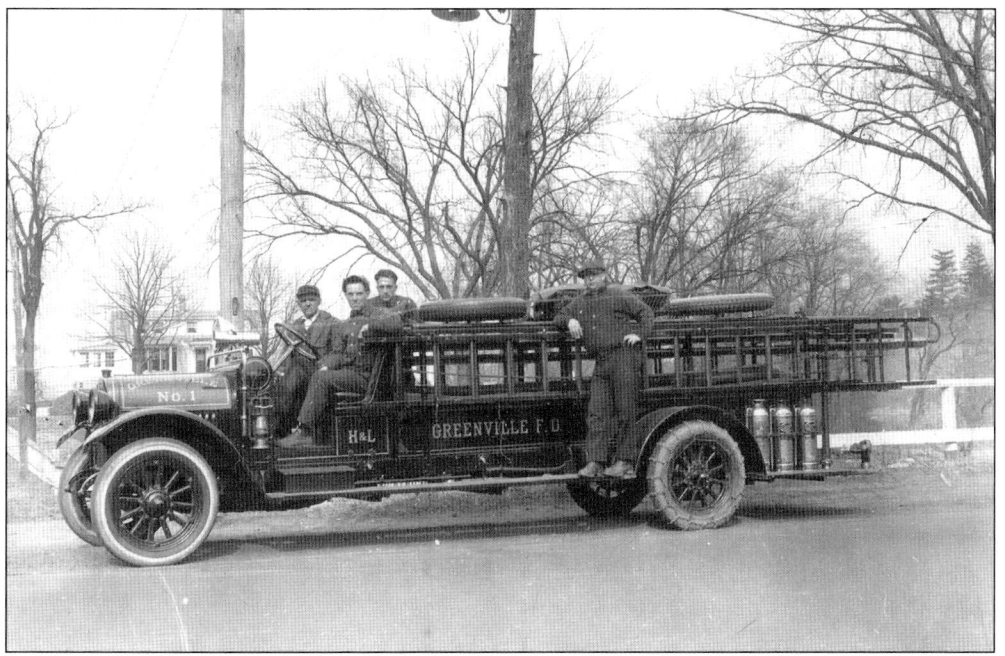

These men comprised the Greenville Fire Department hook and ladder company around 1930. Note the chains on the rear wheels for traction in snow and on muddy, unpaved side roads. (SFD.)

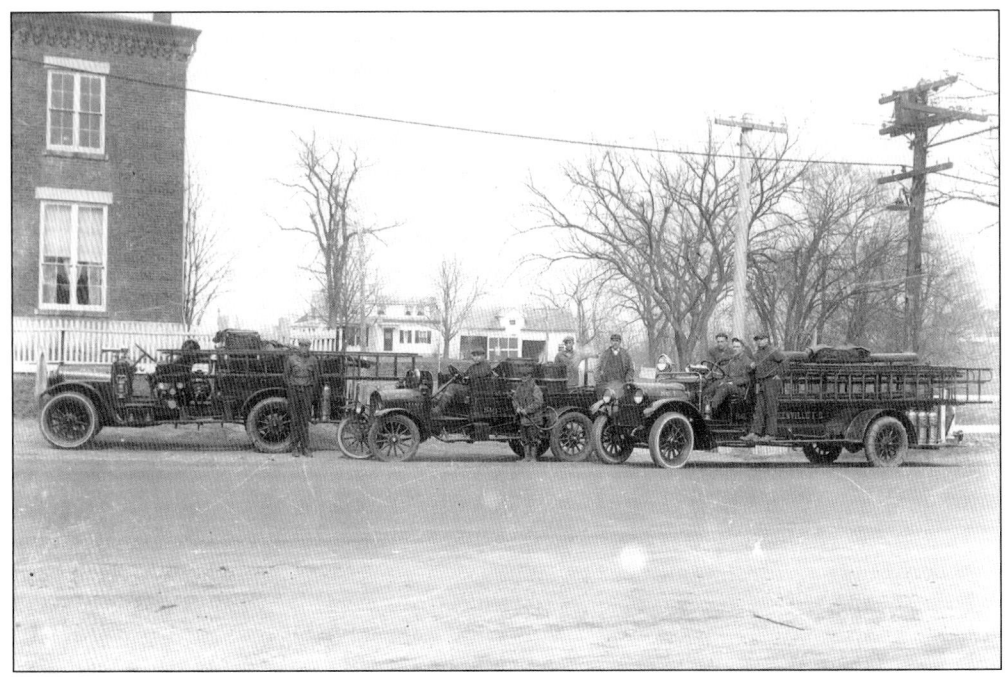

The Greenville Fire Company's trucks are lined up on Route 44 around 1930. (SFD.)

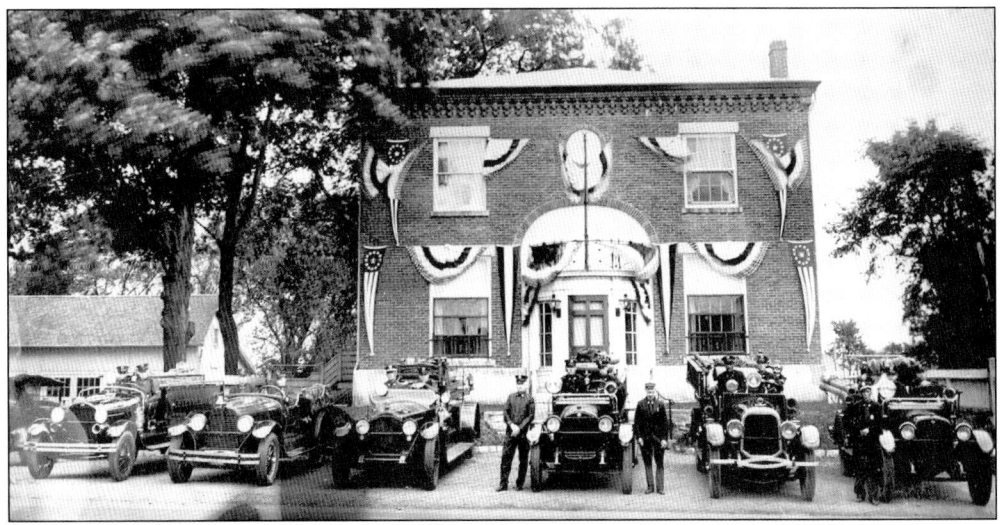

This photograph shows both Greenville and Georgiaville trucks lined up in front of the old Exchange Bank for the Smithfield bicentennial celebration of 1931. The first Greenville fire station was located in the basement of the bank. (KB.)

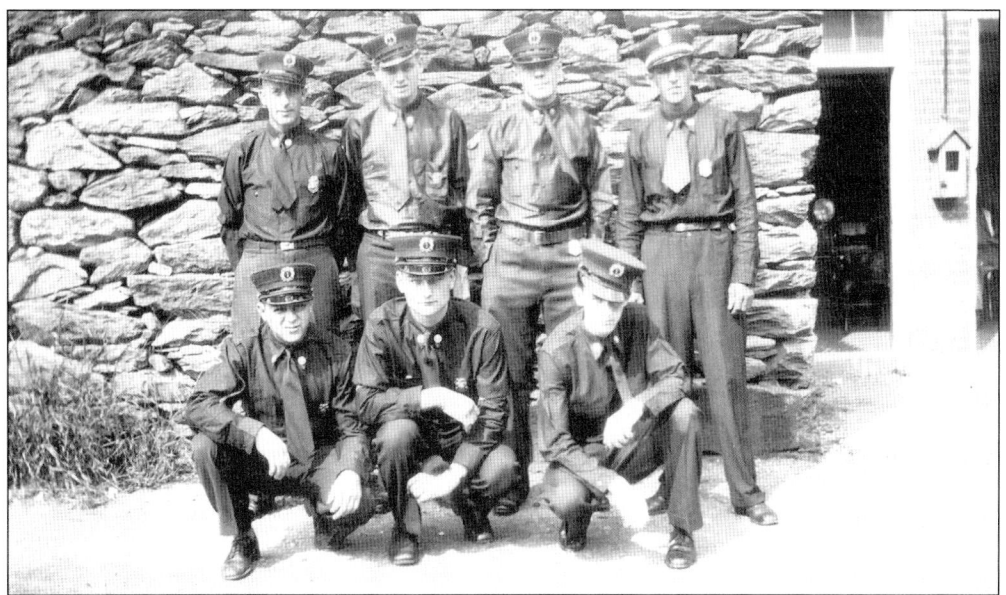
This photograph shows Greenville firefighters in 1932. (WK.)

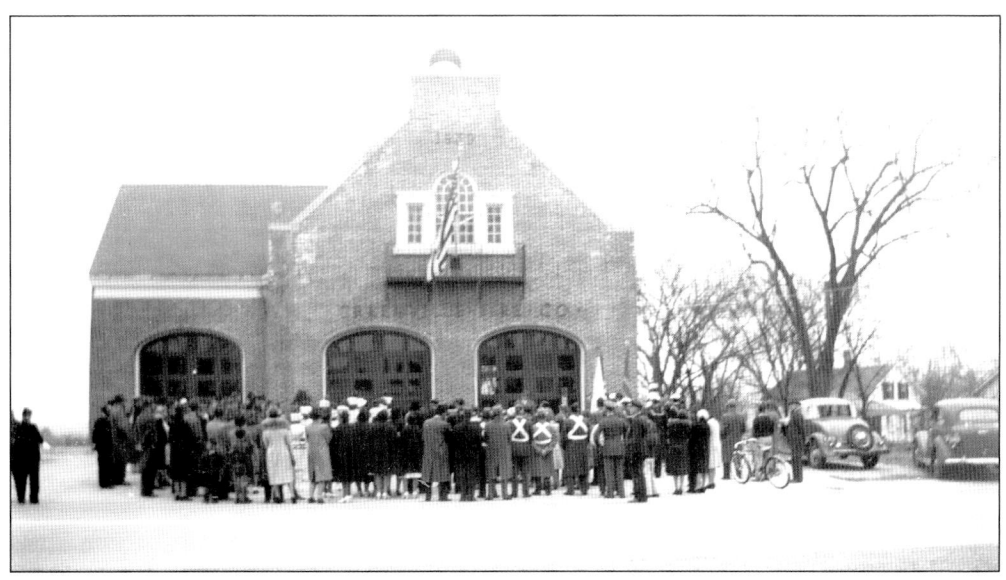
This photograph shows the new Greenville Fire Station dedication ceremony held in 1939. An addition was constructed on the east side of the building during the 1950s. (WK.)

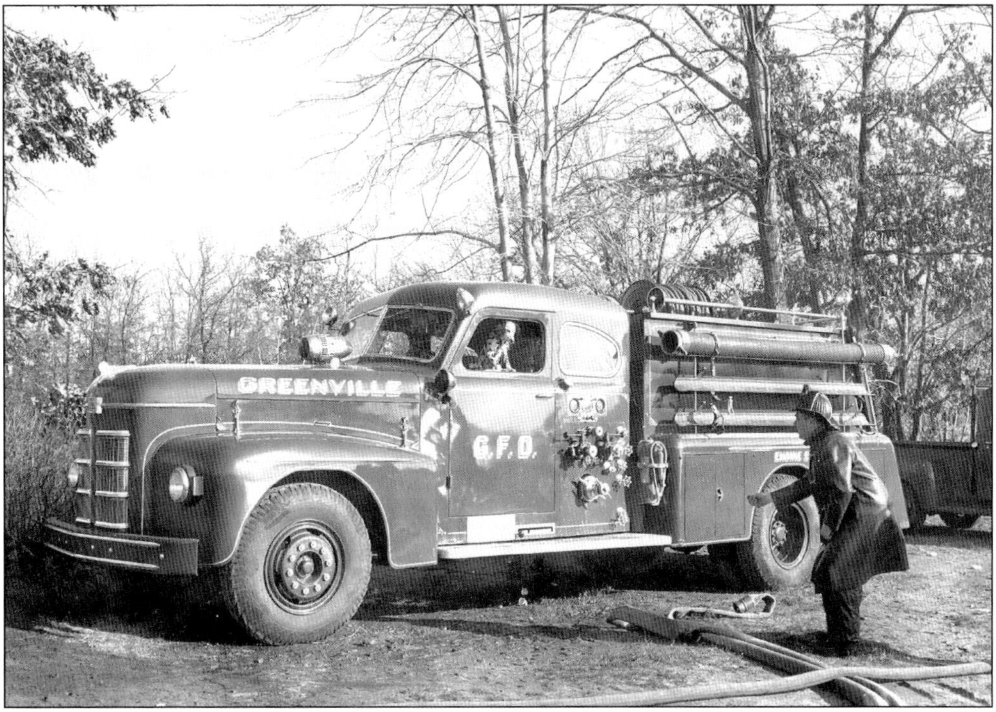

The company mascot looks on while a Greenville firefighter tries to coax him from the truck. (SFD.)

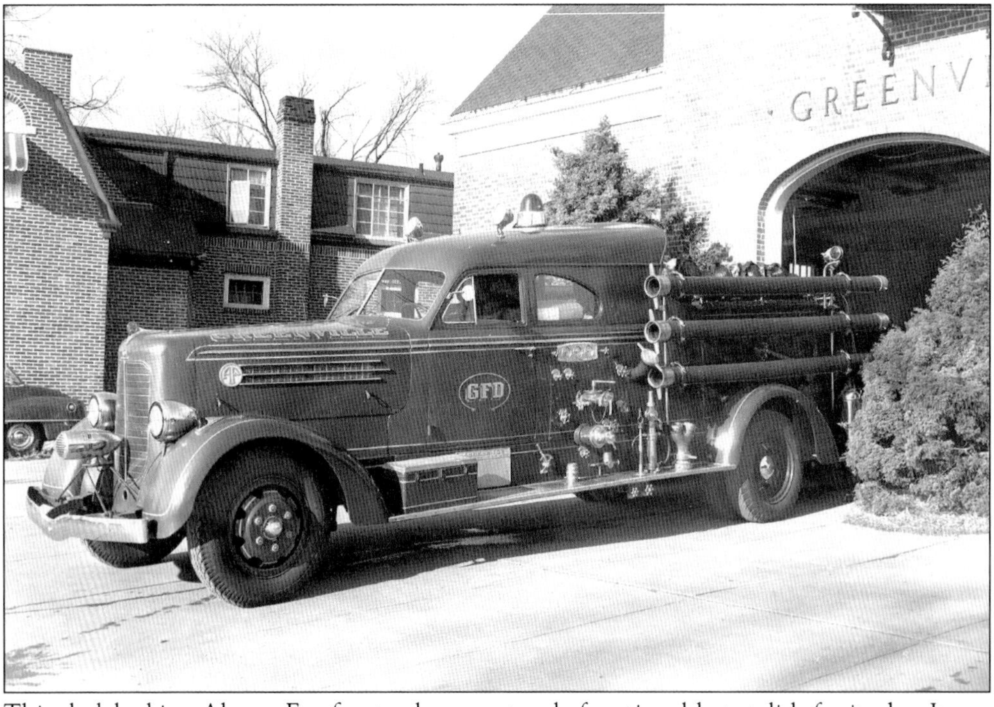

This sleek-looking Aherns-Fox fire truck was not only functional but stylish for its day. It saw service in Greenville for many years. (SFD.)

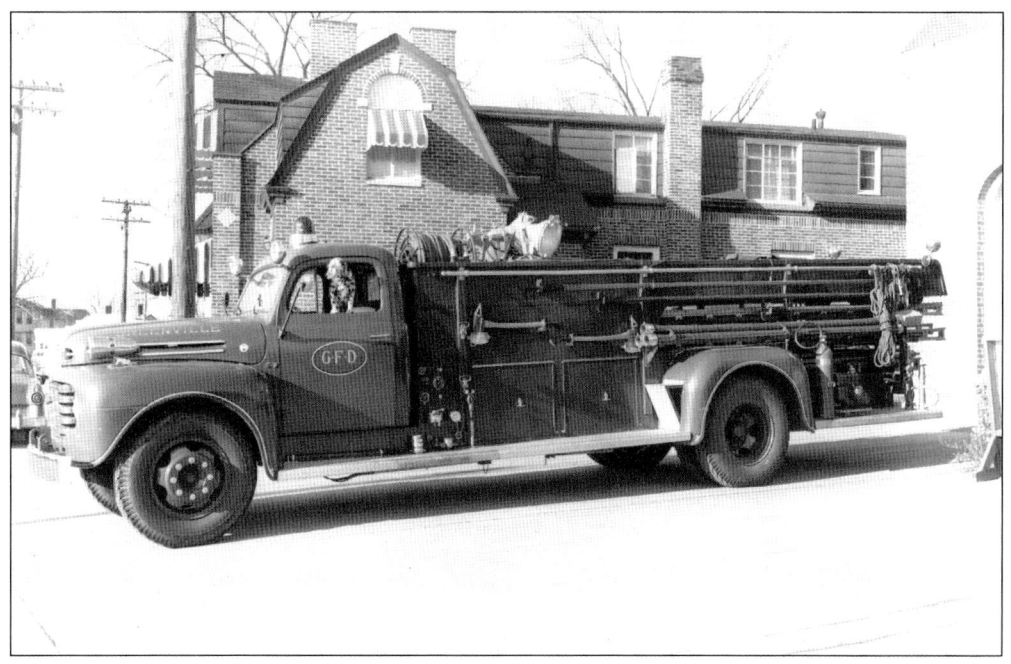

This Greenville hook and ladder truck was used in the 1950s. (SFD.)

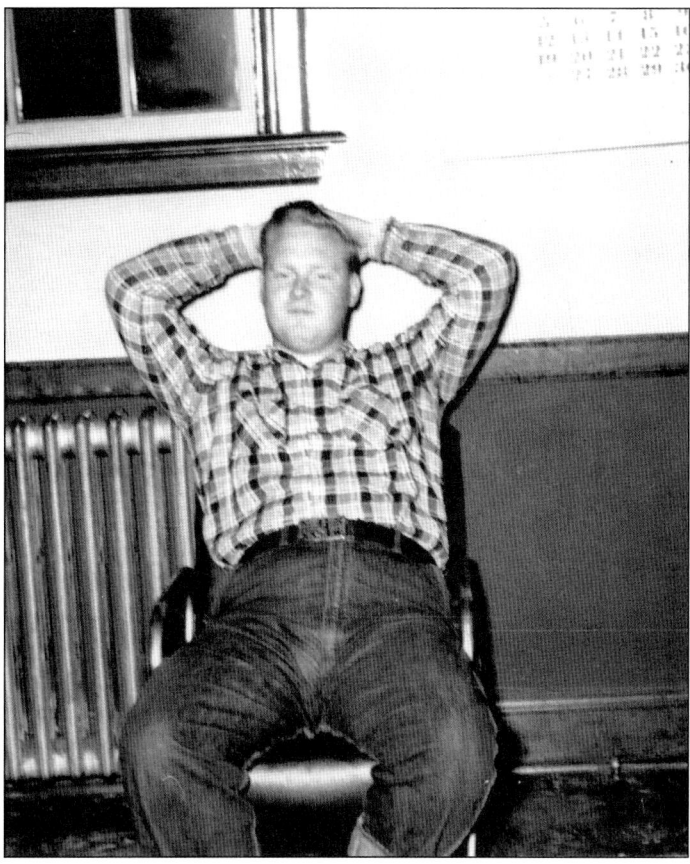

On October 29, 1979, Leo Kennedy Sr. of the Greenville Fire Company died in the line of duty when he suffered a heart attack during a training exercise. His son, Leo Jr., was also a member of the fire company and later joined the Cranston Fire Department where today he is a deputy chief. (SFD.)

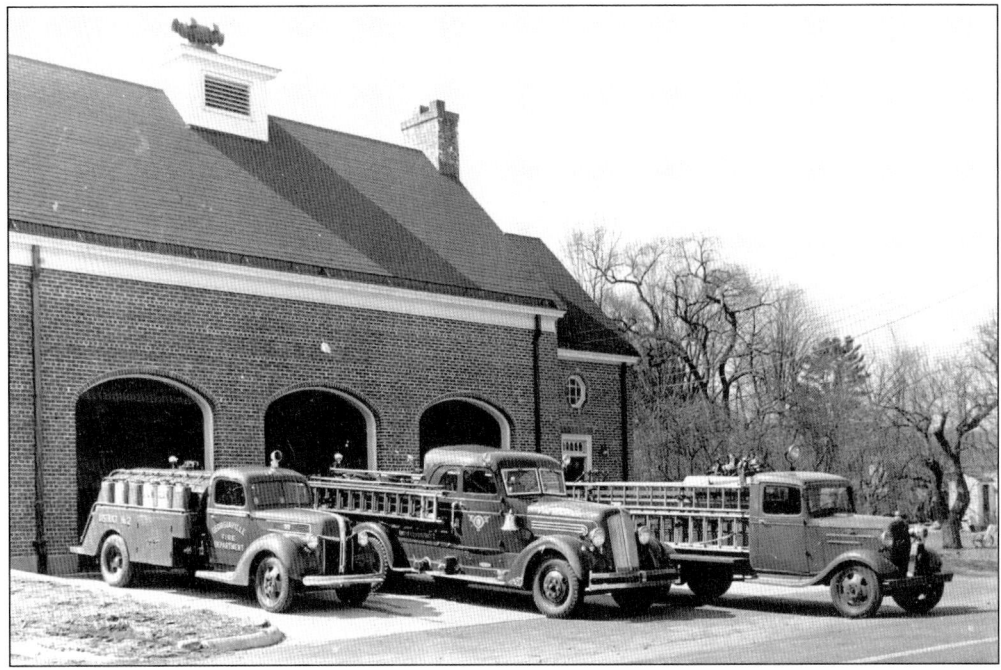

This photograph shows Georgiaville's fire trucks in 1941. The origin of the Georgiaville Fire Company was on April 26, 1915, when a meeting was held at Bernon Hall (owned by the Bernon Mill) to discuss organizing a volunteer fire company for that part of town. It was not until June 25, 1917, that the fire company was formally established as the Smithfield Fire Company No. 2. This information comes from original handwritten meeting records now in the possession of the Smithfield Fire Department. (KB.)

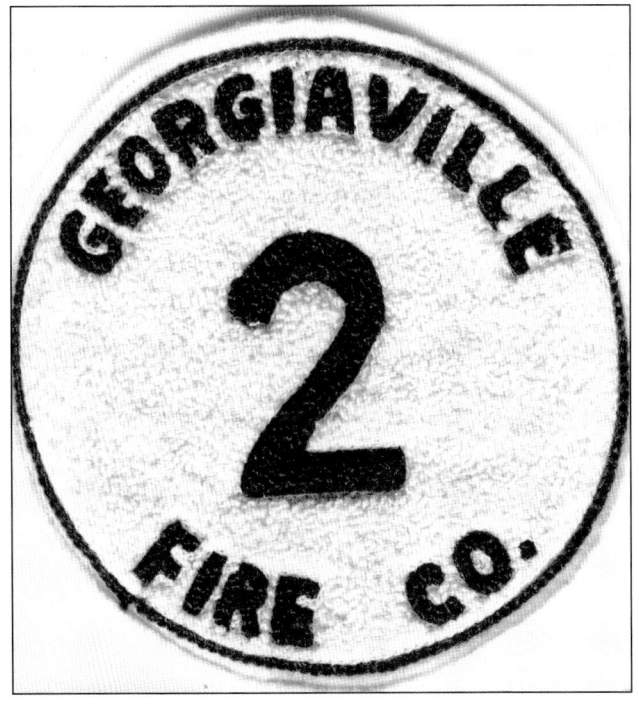

This is an early example of a company patch worn by members of the Georgiaville Fire Company on their jackets during the 1950s.

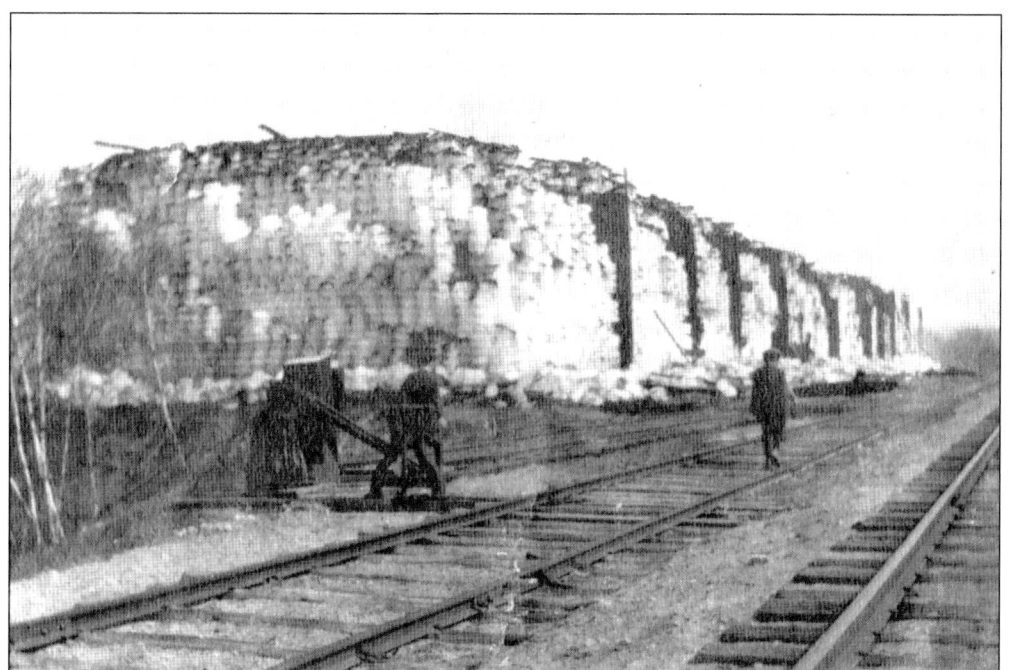

On April 20, 1919, two icehouses belonging to the Providence Ice Company burned to the ground along the shore of Georgiaville Pond with a monetary loss of $50,000. The buildings burned, but the ice did not. (AG.)

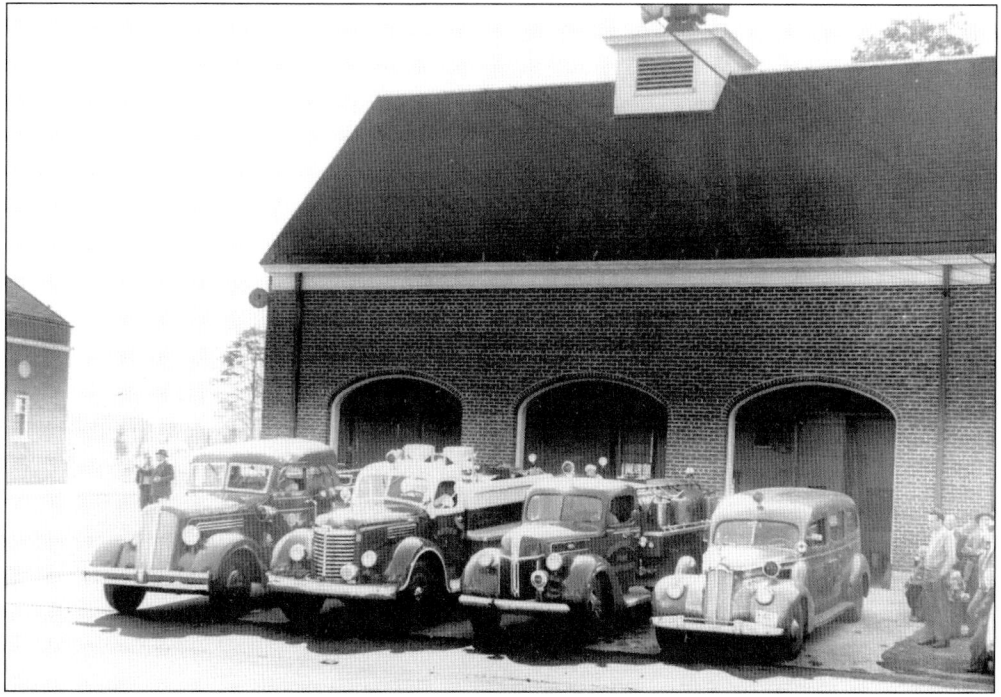

This photograph shows Georgiaville Fire Company apparatus in 1947. From left to right are a 1938 Seagraves pumper, 1947 International ladder truck, 1941 Ford tanker, and 1941 Packard ambulance. (KB.)

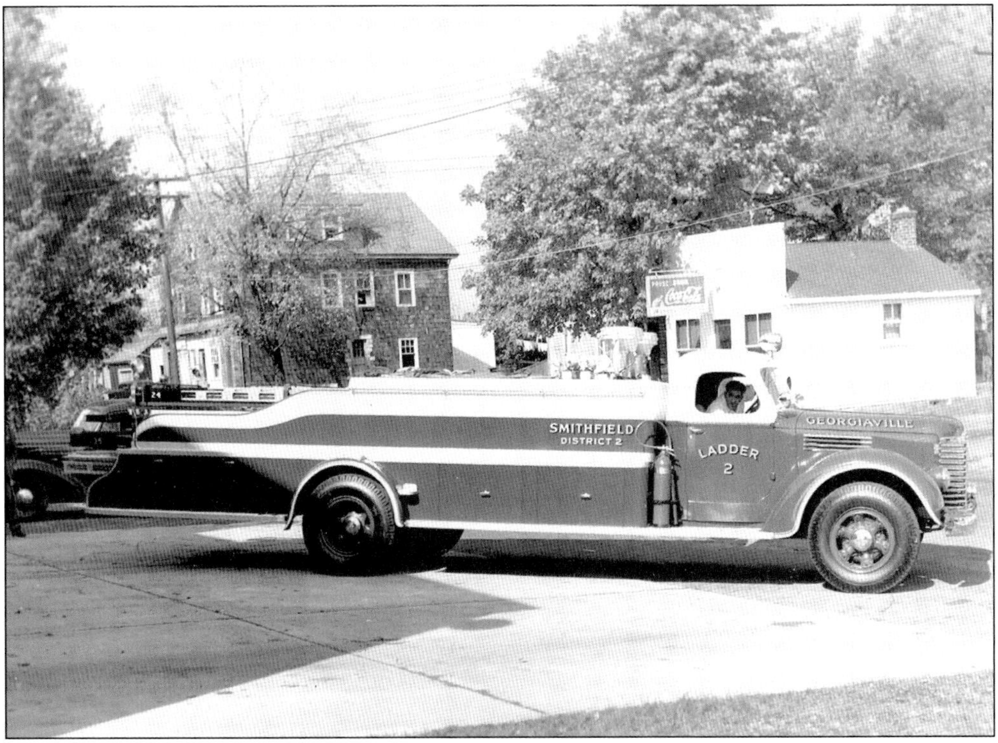

The Georgiaville Fire Company used this 1947 International ladder truck for many years. (KB.)

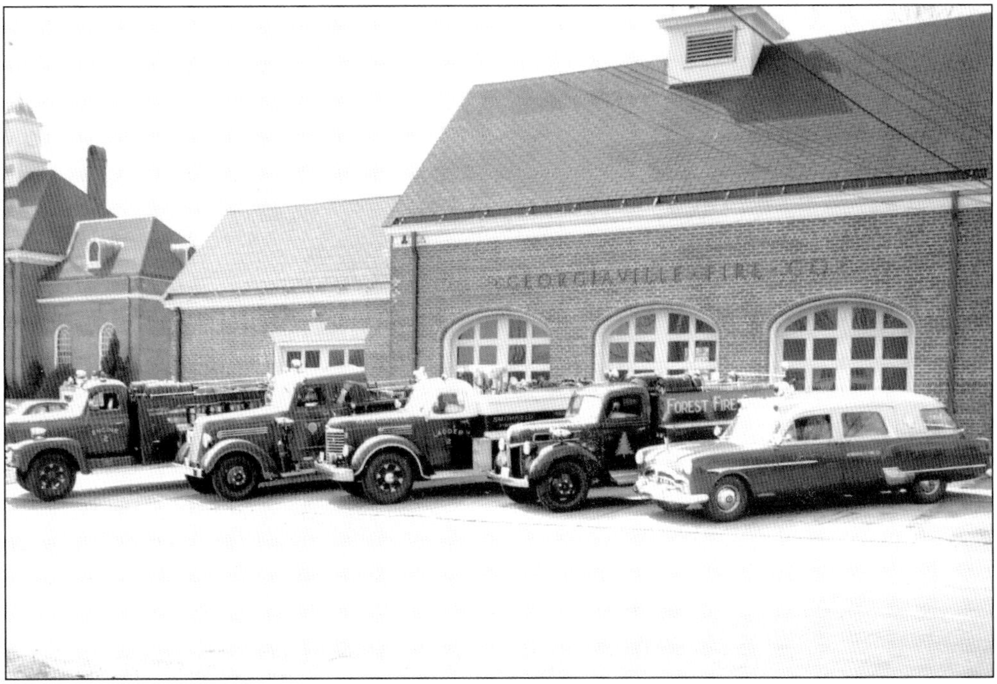

This photograph shows Georgiaville Fire Company apparatus in 1951. Note the Packard ambulance on the end. (KB.)

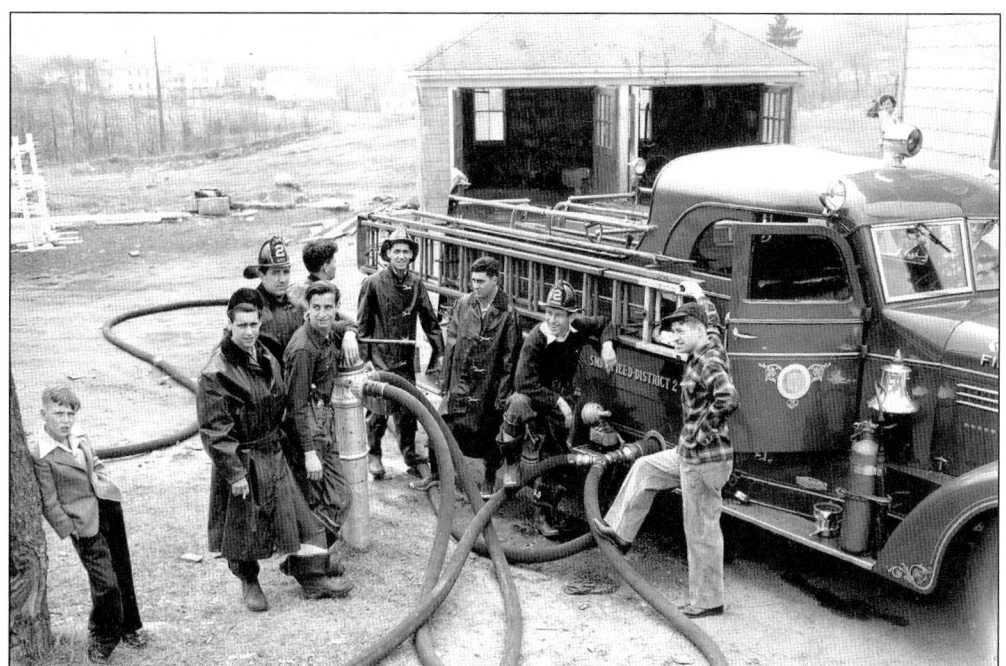

This is a photograph of Georgiaville firefighters training on Hill Street in the 1950s. The boy leaning against the tree is Robert D. Brown. When he was older, he joined the Georgiaville Fire Company. (KB.)

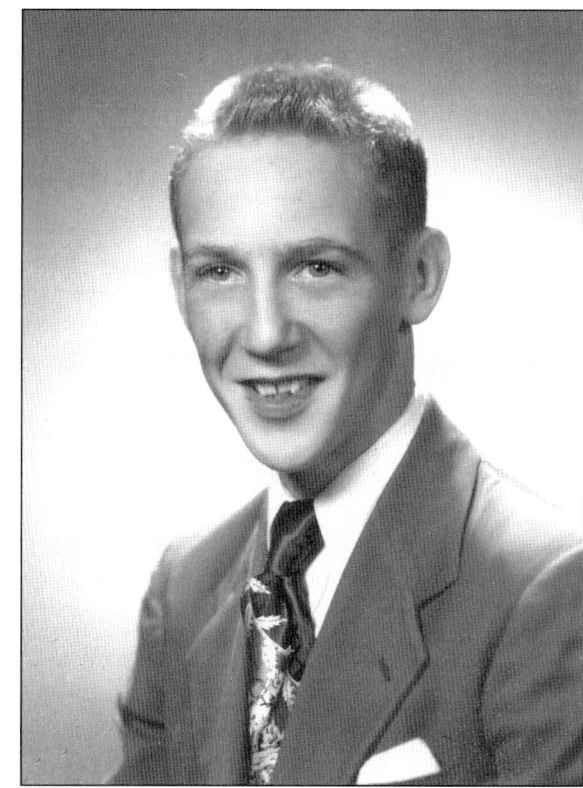

On April 2, 1960, Robert D. Brown fell from a moving fire truck while responding to a grass fire and suffered fatal injuries. He was promoted to lieutenant posthumously. (Brown family.)

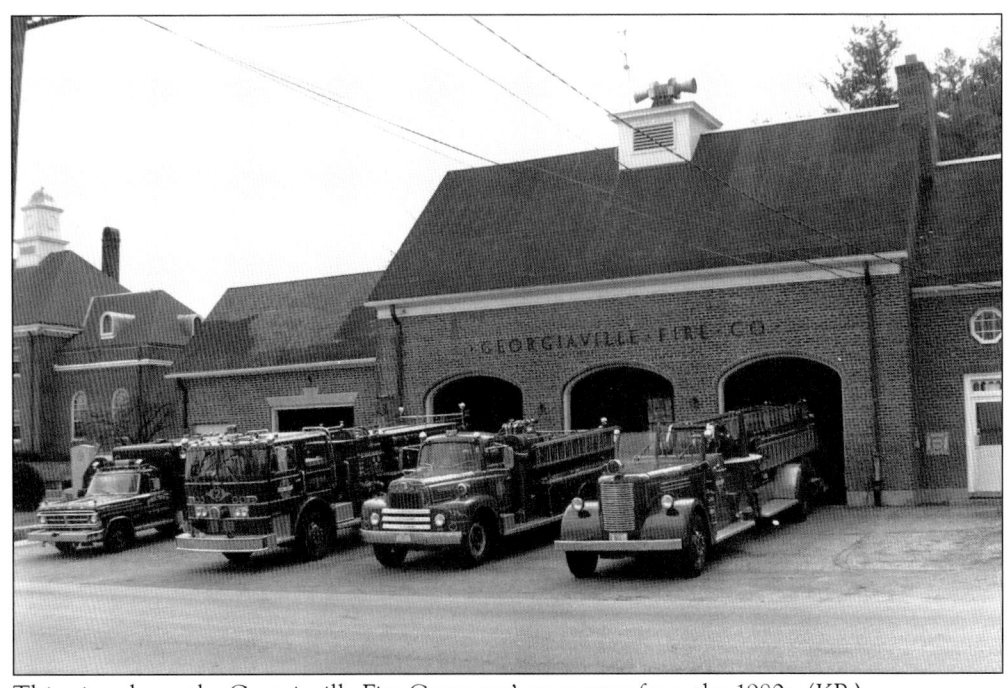

This view shows the Georgiaville Fire Company's apparatus from the 1980s. (KB.)

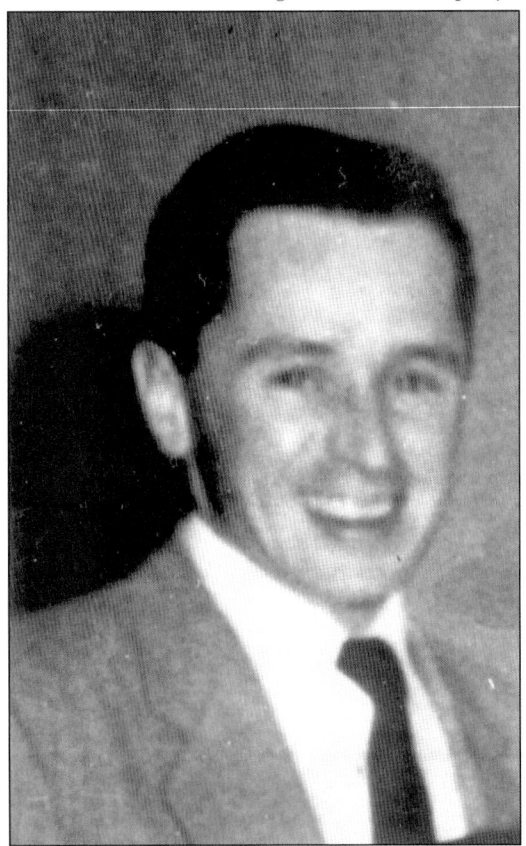

On September 6, 1964, Lt. Eugene E. Dorgan died when he fell from a moving fire truck while responding to a barn fire that was deliberately set. (DDB.)

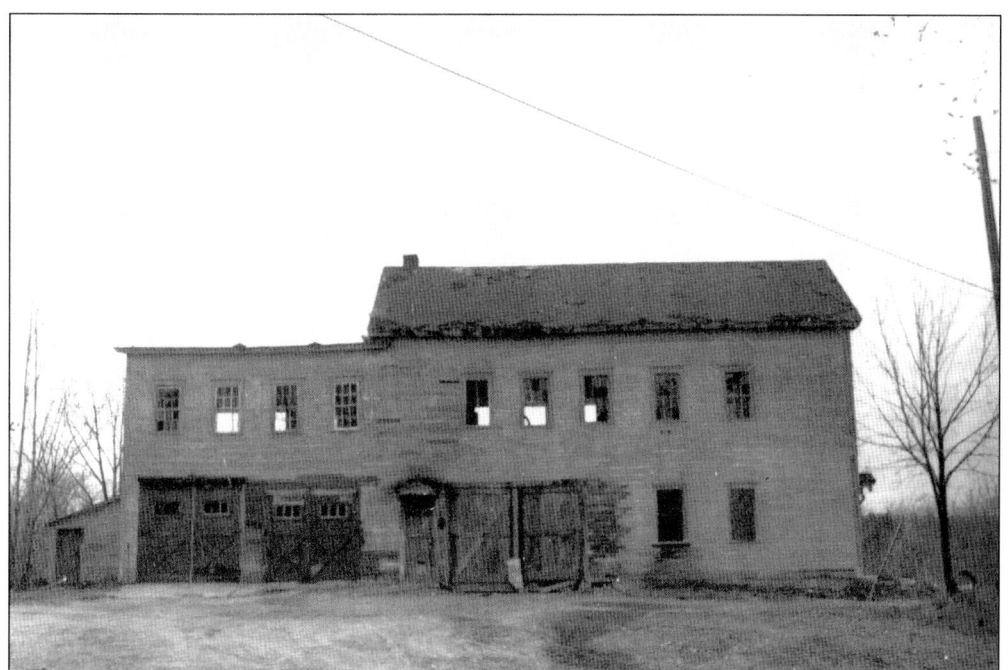

This building served as the Georgiaville School from 1850 to 1923. From 1927 to 1942, it was the headquarters for the Georgiaville Fire Company, then known as the Smithfield Fire Company No. 2. It later served as a town highway garage. It was burned for training by the fire department on May 8, 1961. (SFD.)

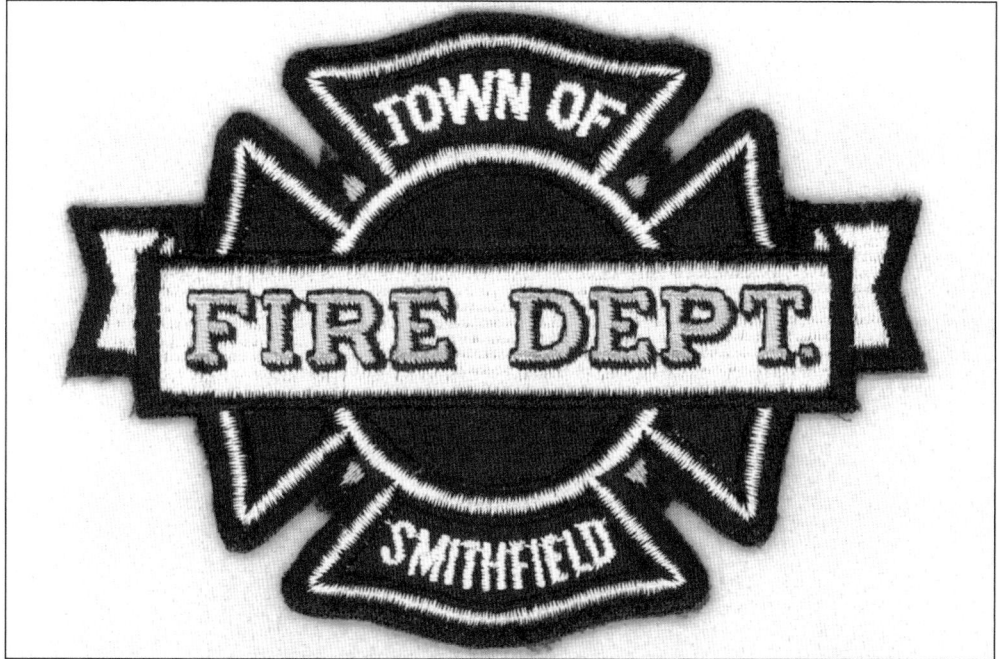

This is an early version of the uniform patch worn by the Smithfield Fire Department. Later versions have "Smithfield" across the top and "Rhode Island" across the bottom. The current issue has an American flag on it. (JI.)

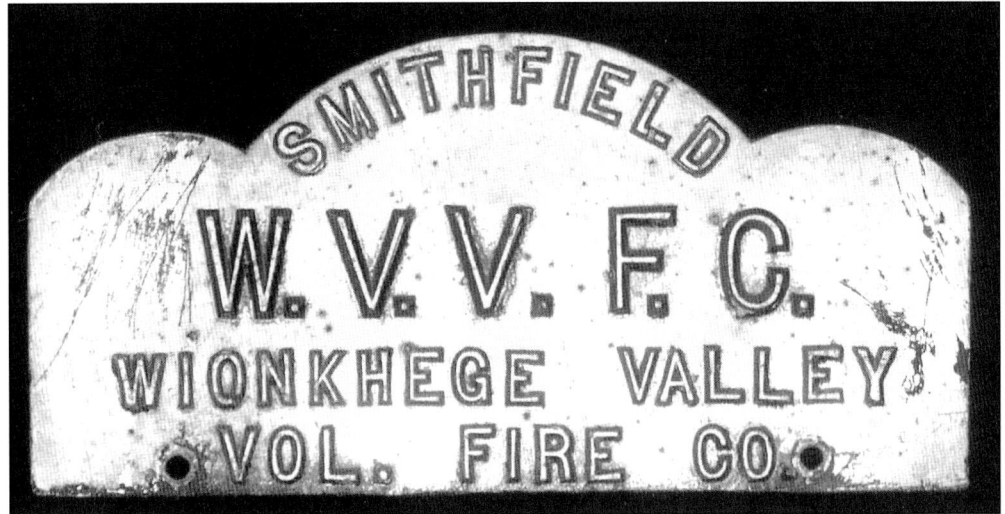

In September 1958, the Wionkhiege Valley Volunteer Fire Company was established in the northwest part of town. The new fire company held square dances to raise money and before long purchased a Ward LaFrance pumper truck. Fire company members also built their own tank truck that could carry 800 gallons of water. The company disbanded in 1962. (JI.)

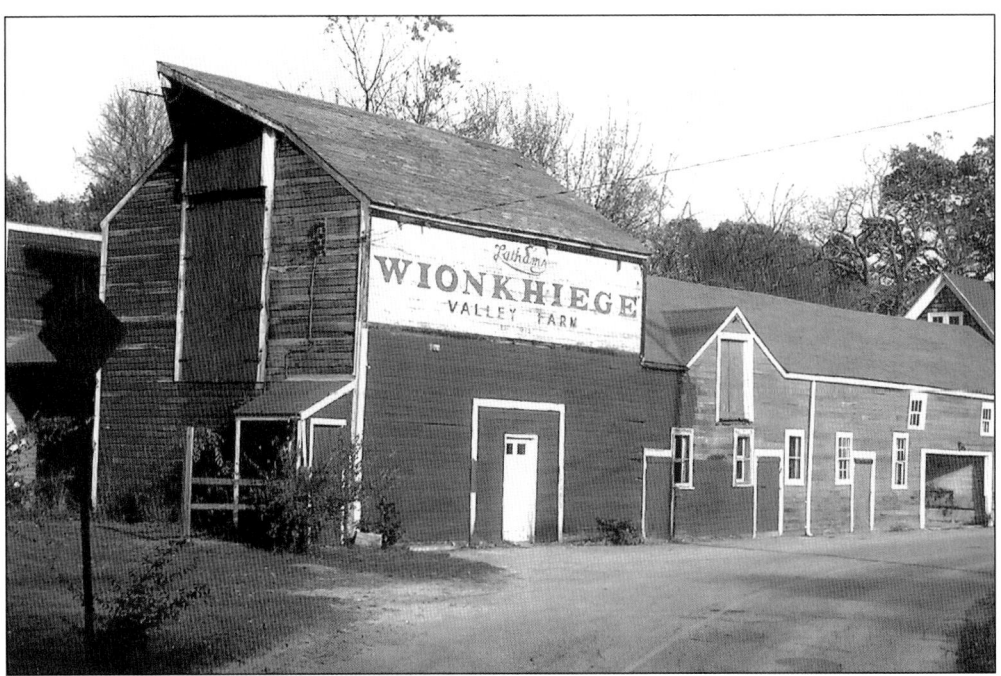

The Wionkhiege Valley Fire Company used this barn on Log Road as its first headquarters. Another barn just down the road was used later. (JI.)

Five
MILLS AND MILL VILLAGES

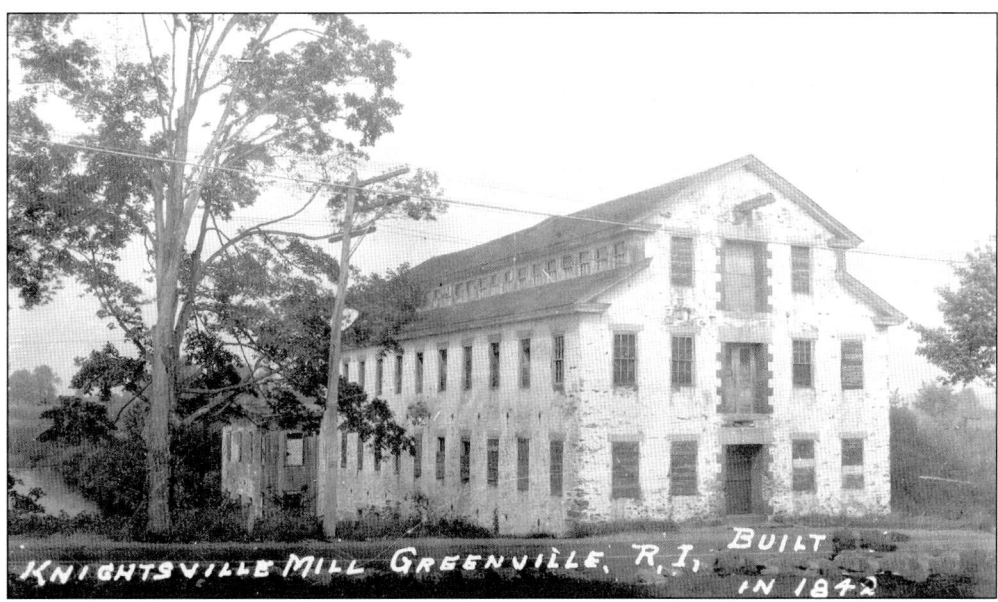

This photograph depicts the Knightsville Mill that once stood on the north side of Route 44 between Greenville Center and West Greenville Road. The origin of the mill's name is unknown as there are no areas of town known as Knightsville. (HSS.)

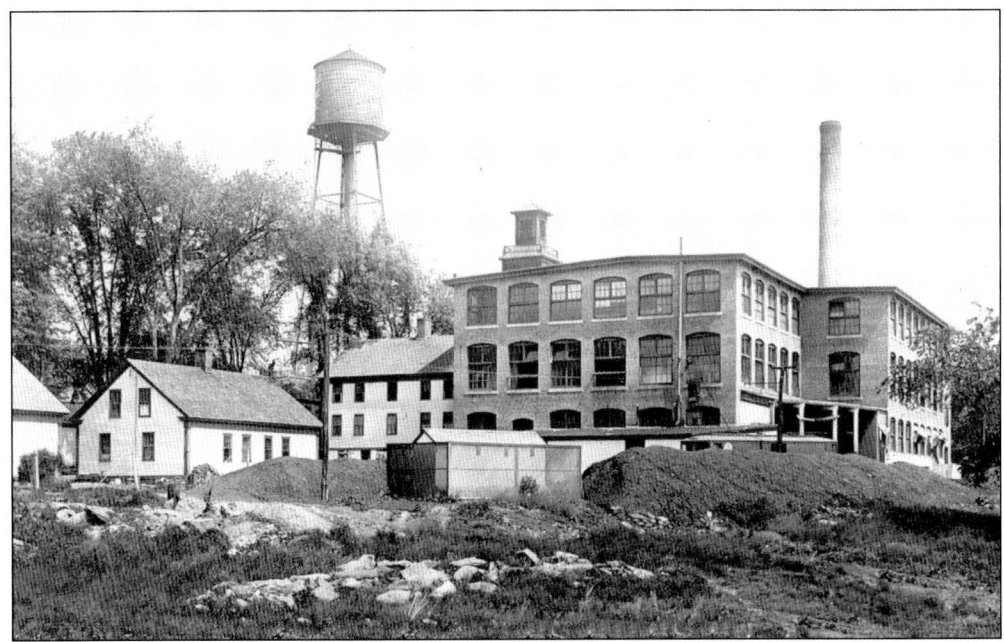

This is an early view of the old Greenville Finishing Mill on Route 44. It was originally a woolen mill owned by Poor and Steere Company and dates from the early 1800s. (WK.)

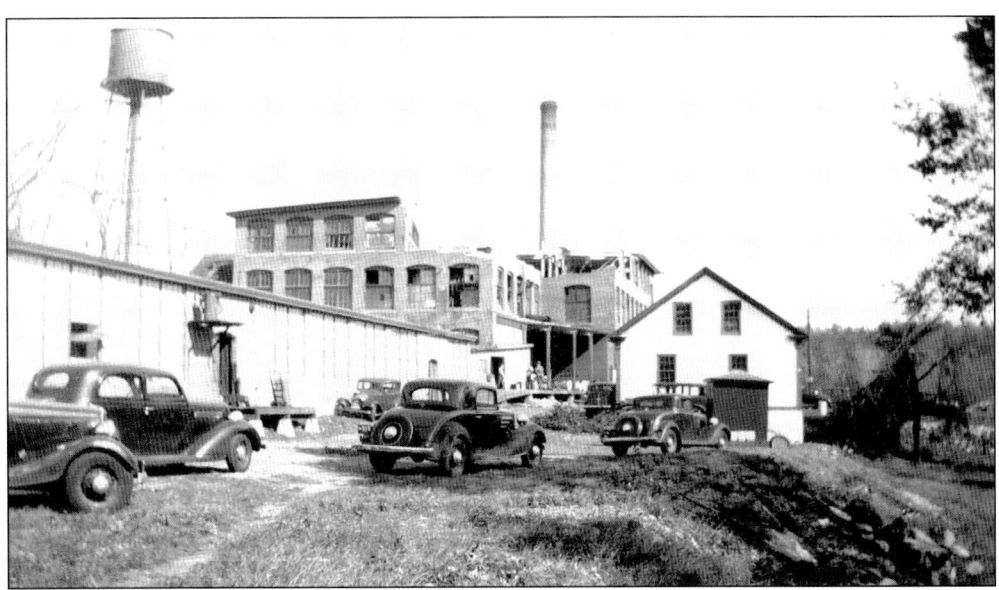

In a later view than the image above, this photograph shows damage done to the mill by the Hurricane of 1938. Note that the house has been relocated and an addition has been constructed on the front of the building. (WK.)

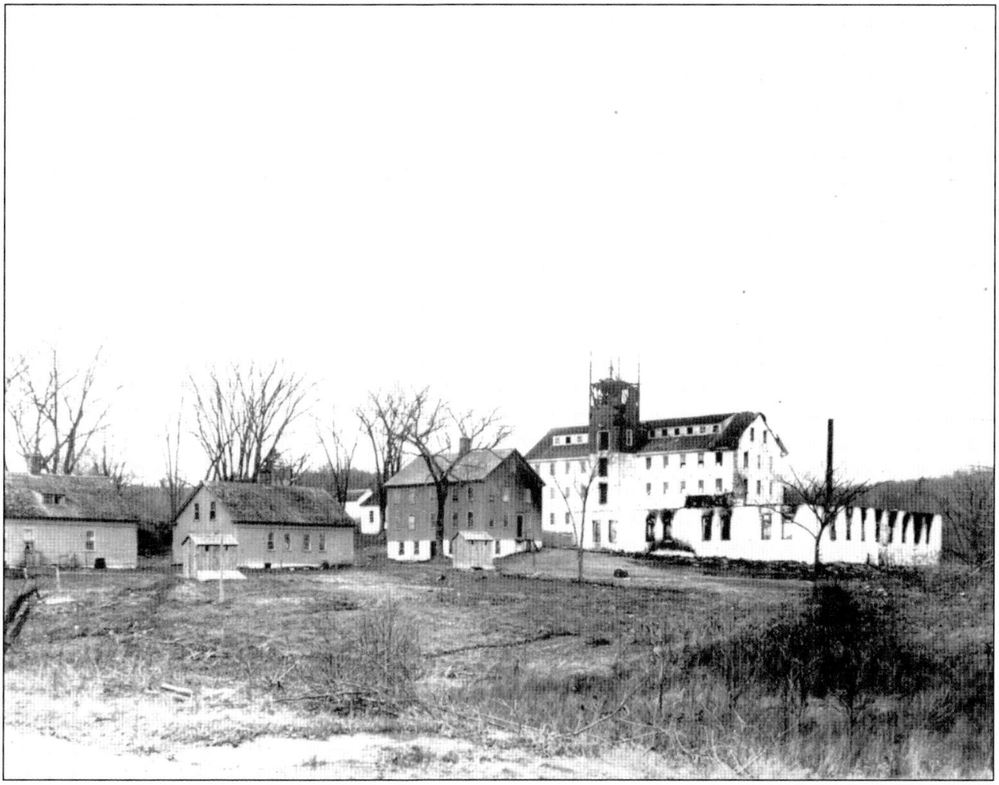

This view of the Poor and Steere Mill, taken about 1890, shows that the building has survived at least one fire. (PH.)

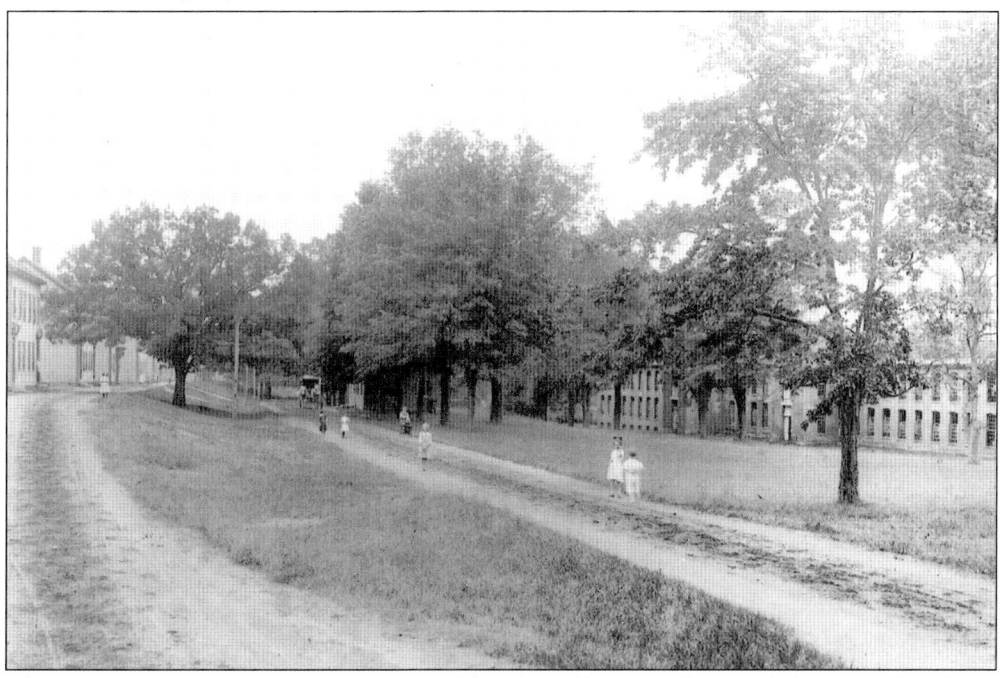

This is a view of Stillwater Road in front of the old Stillwater Mill around the 1880s. (JE.)

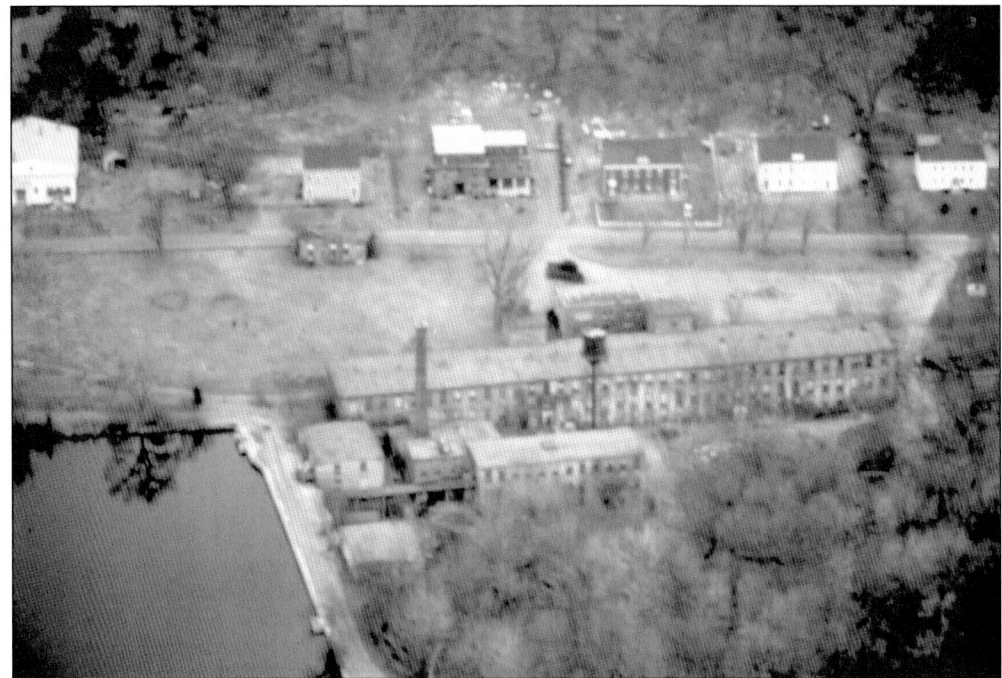

This view shows the Stillwater Mill as it looked in 1974. Several mills have stood on this site since 1824, and all were destroyed by fire. The mill pictured here was built in 1871. (HSS.)

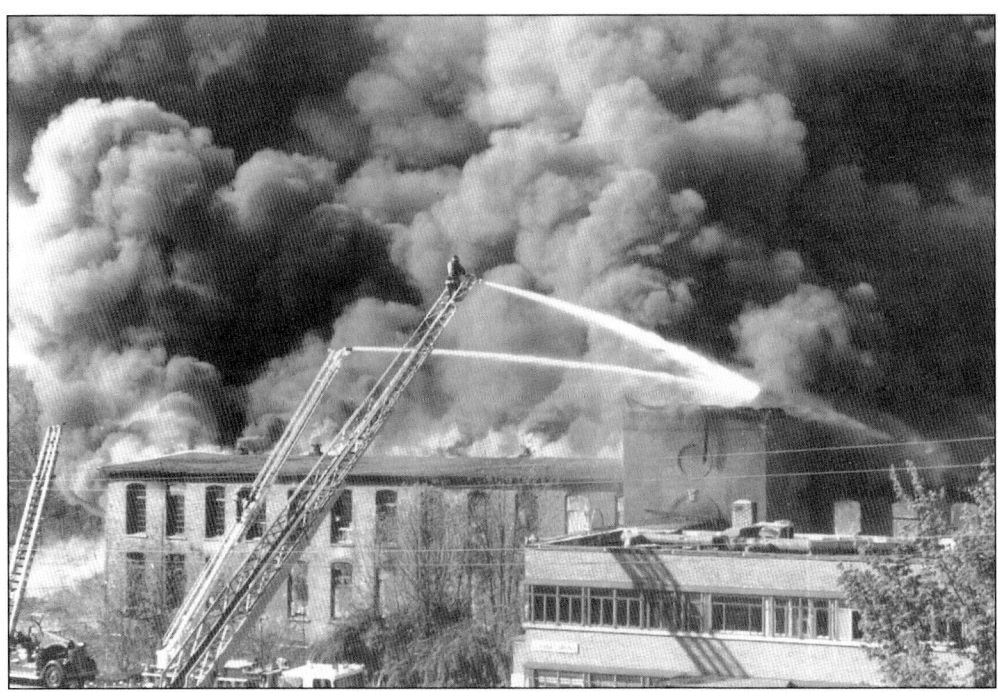

On May 17, 1984, the Stillwater Mill burned to the ground in what was one of Smithfield's most spectacular fires. The smoke could be seen for miles. (KB.)

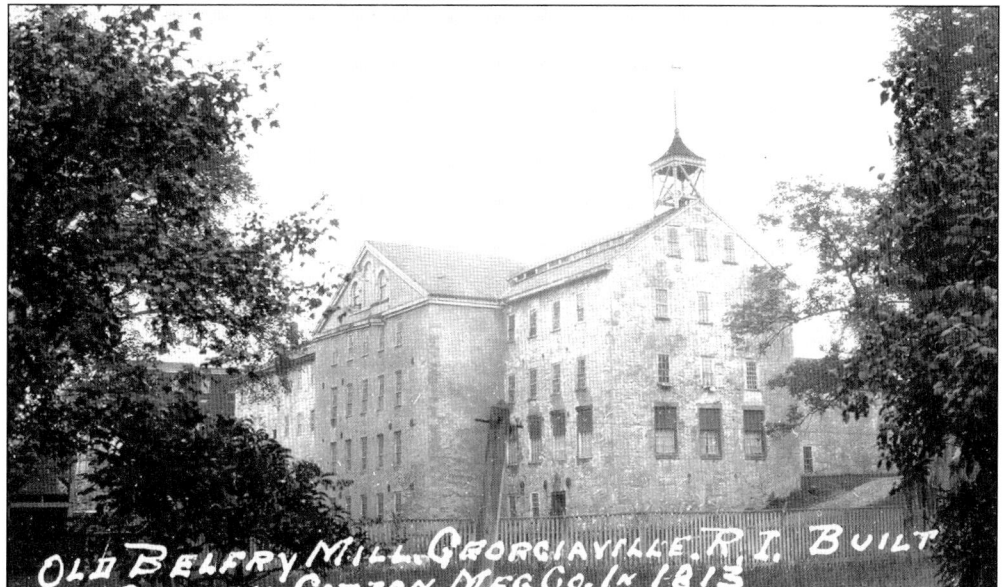

The Georgiaville Cotton Mill was built in 1813, and this photograph shows how it looked about 1900 when it was known as the Bernon Mill. In later years it was the Homestead Mill. Today it is a housing complex. (HSS.)

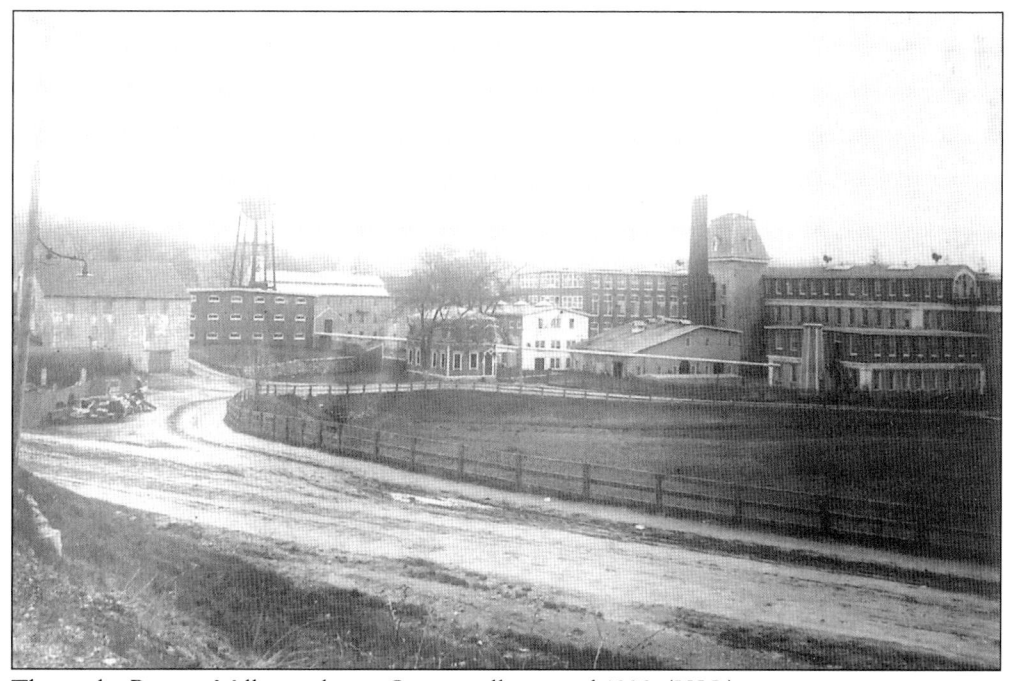

This is the Bernon Mill complex in Georgiaville around 1890. (HSS.)

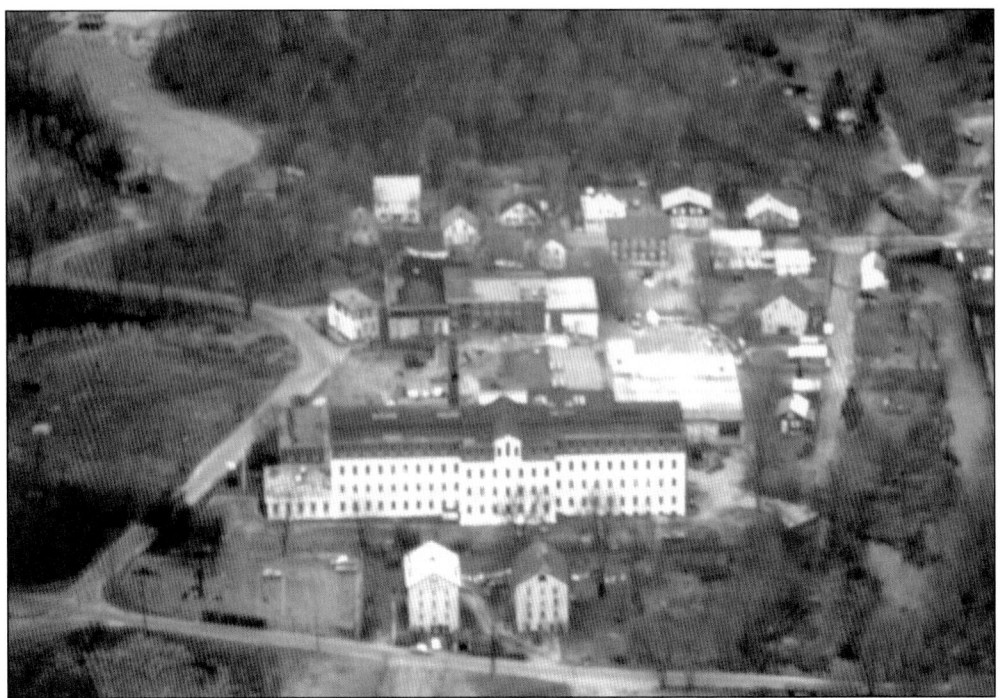

This aerial view of the Homestead Mill complex in Georgiaville was taken in 1974. Georgiaville got its name from the Georgia Cotton Manufacturing Company that built a mill there in 1813. (HSS.)

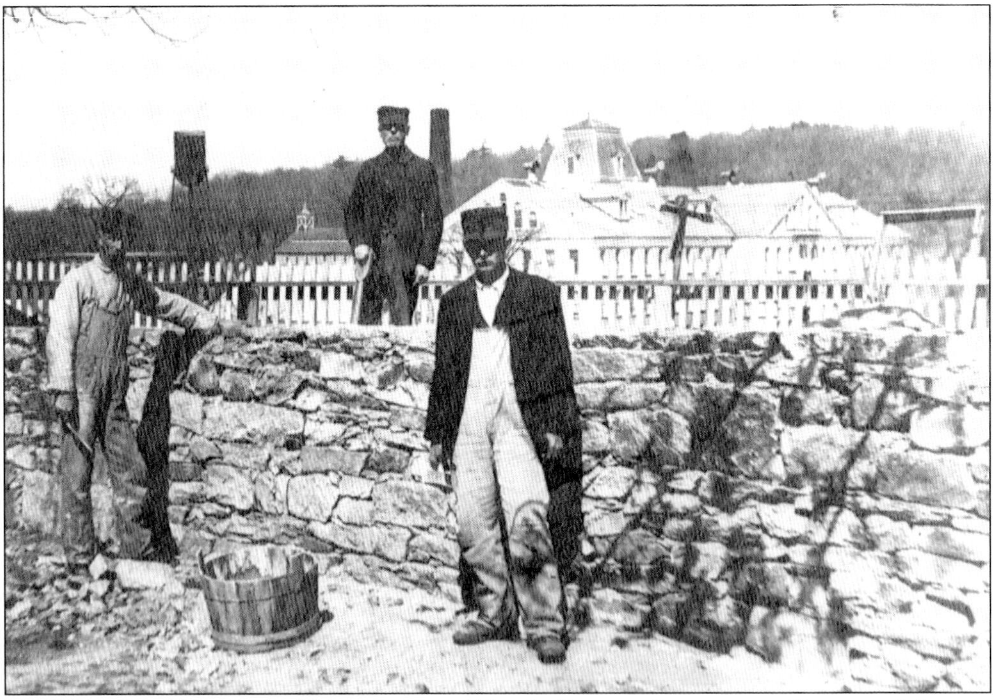

This view shows laborers building a stone wall for the Farnum Cemetery on Homestead Avenue with the Bernon Mill in the background around 1890. (JE/TM.)

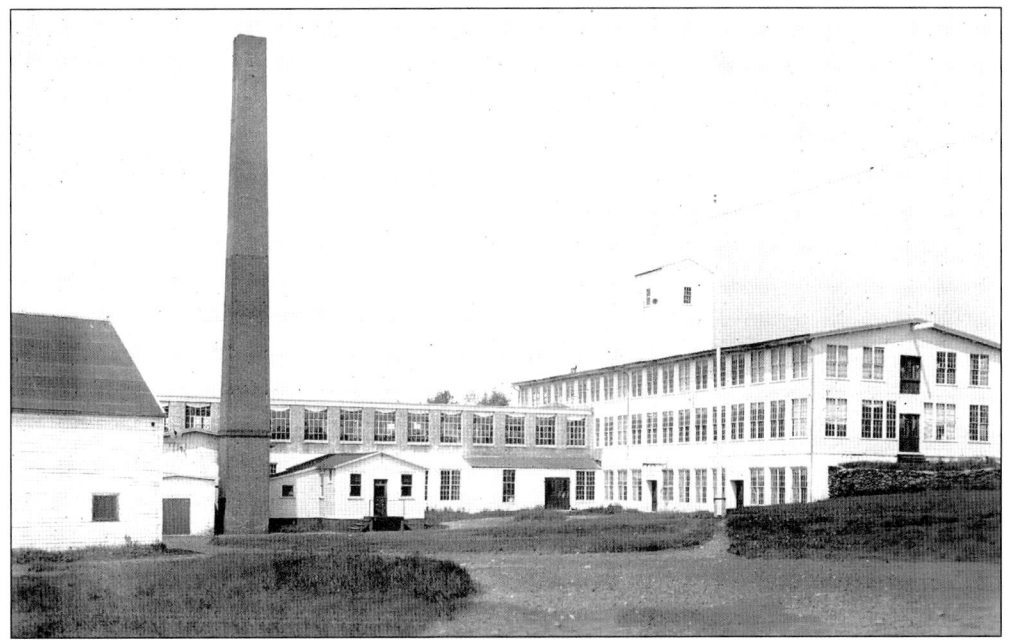
This view is of the Stillwater Worsted Company, also known as the Levie Mill, on Austin Avenue in Greenville as it looked about 1910. (WK.)

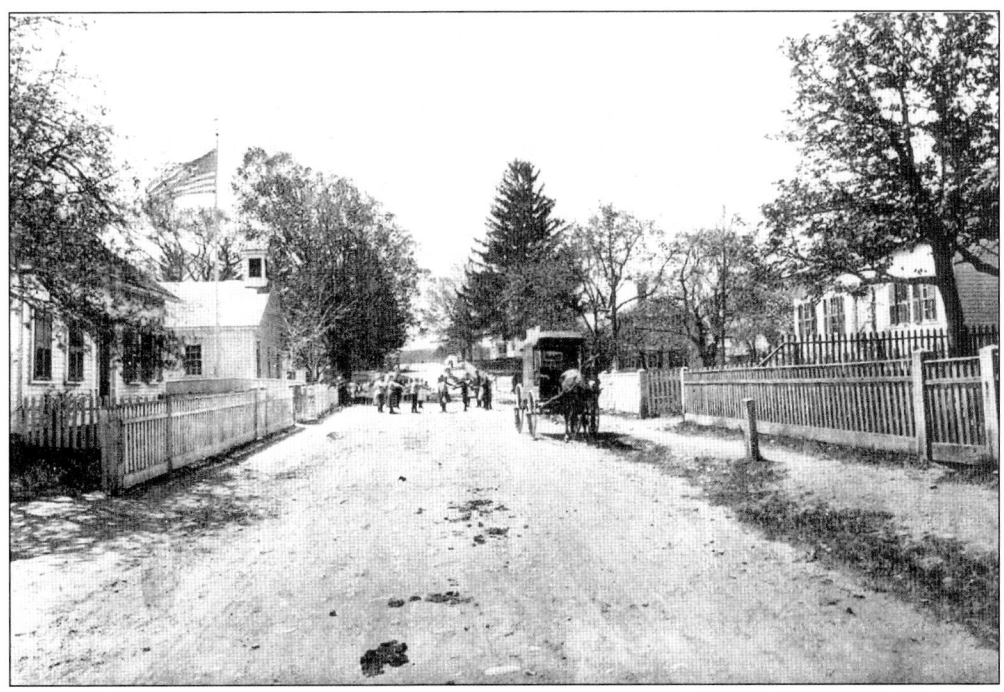
This is an early view of Esmond Street looking south. (HSS.)

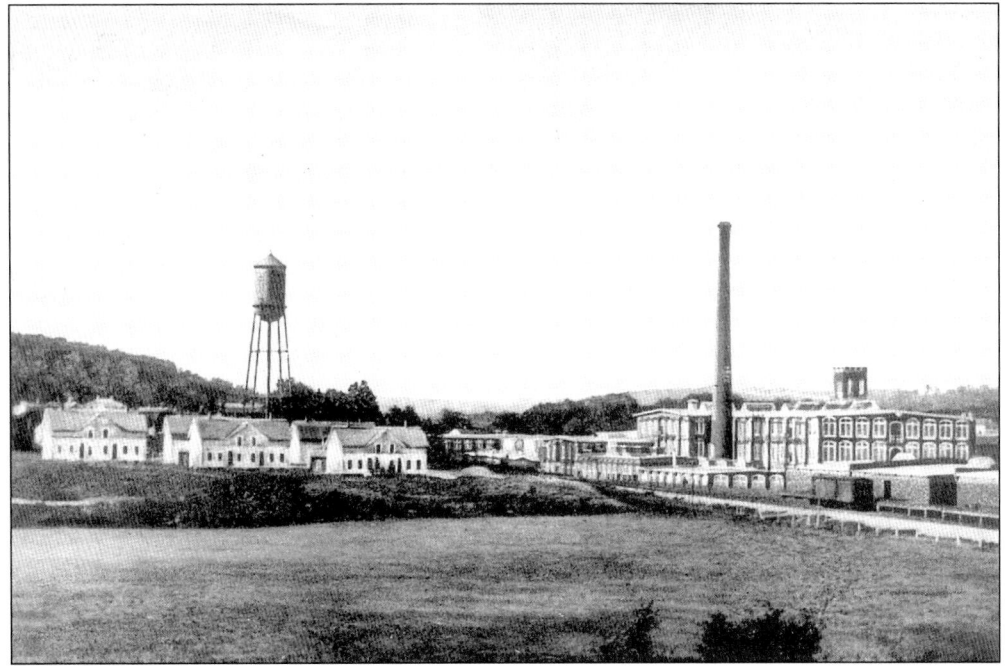

This postcard view by H. G. Thornton of the Esmond Mills dates from about 1910. Esmond was originally called Allenville, named for ex–Rhode Island governor Phillip Allen who purchased land there in 1813. In 1881, the first post office was established there and the name was changed to Enfield. The name was changed to Esmond about 1906. (TM.)

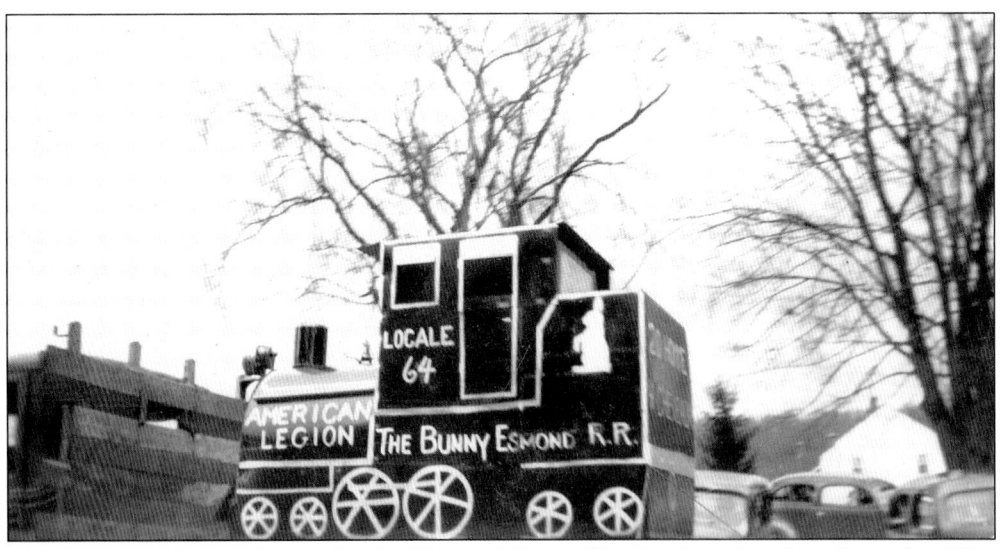

The Esmond Mills was famous for the "Esmond Bunny Blankets" produced in the early 1900s. This photograph was taken in November 1934. (AS.)

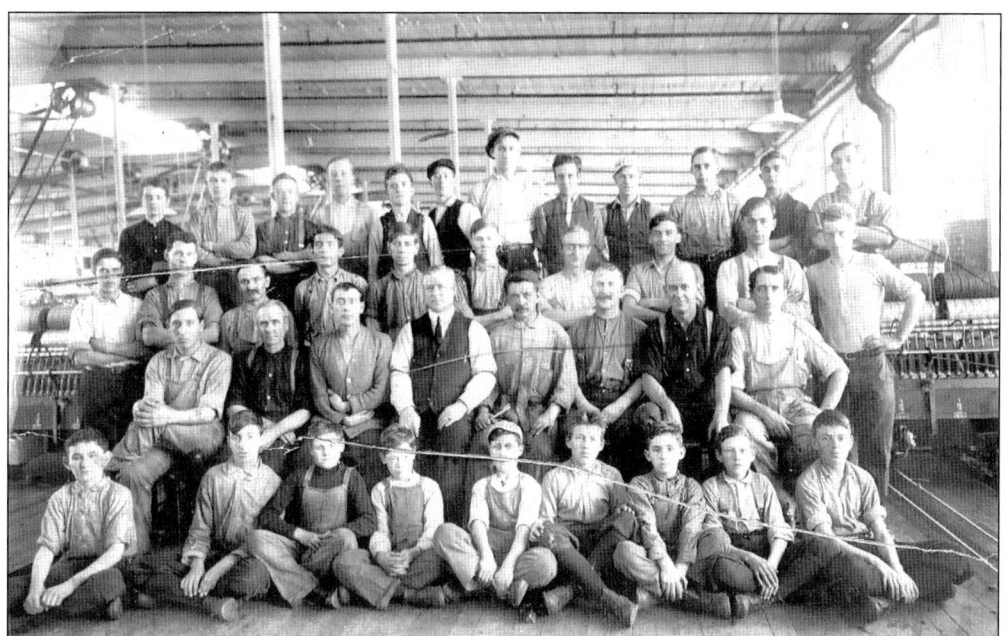

This photograph shows a group of workers from the "mule room" at the Esmond Mills. The Esmond Bunny became the official logo for the mill and was painted on the mill's water tower, printed on boxes and labels, sewn onto blankets, and appeared on athletic jackets worn by sports teams sponsored by the mill. In addition, there were even official Esmond Bunny story and coloring books. (AS.)

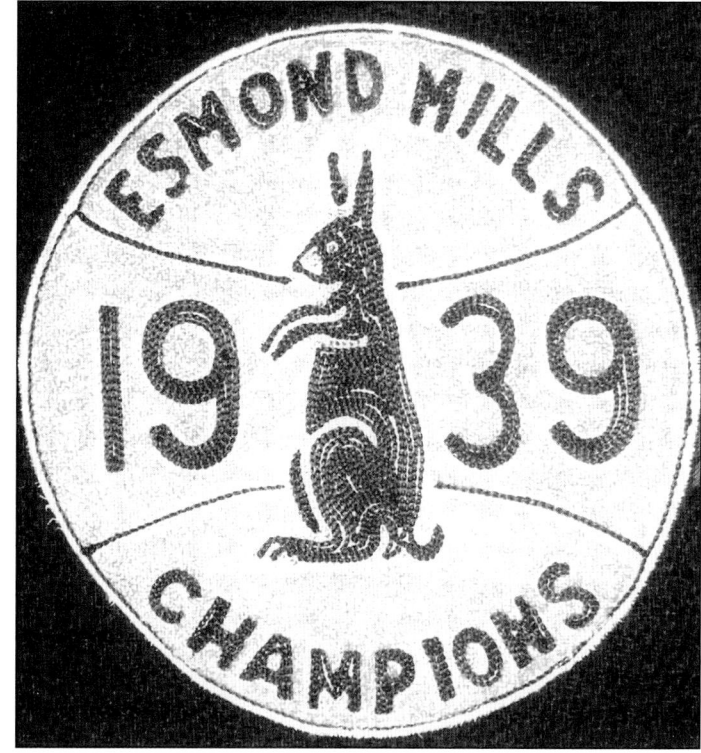

This emblem, worn on the jackets of a baseball team sponsored by the Esmond Mills in 1939, clearly shows the famous Esmond Bunny logo. (HSS.)

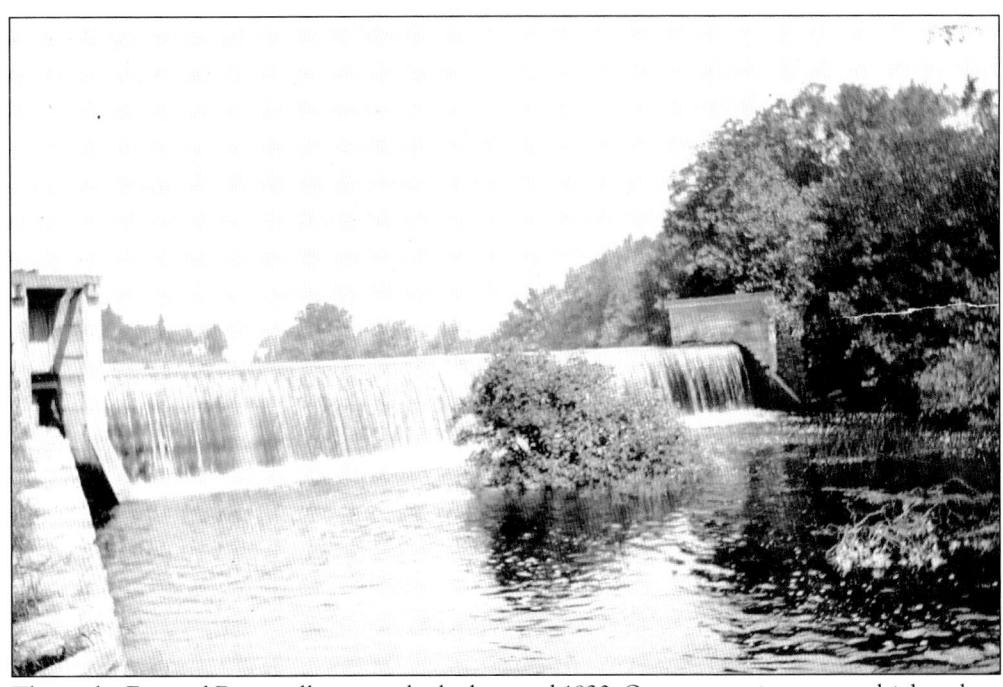

This is the Esmond Dam spillway as it looked around 1930. One can see it was once higher than it is today. At one time, children could be seen cooling off on a hot summer day in the water at the base of the dam. (FF.)

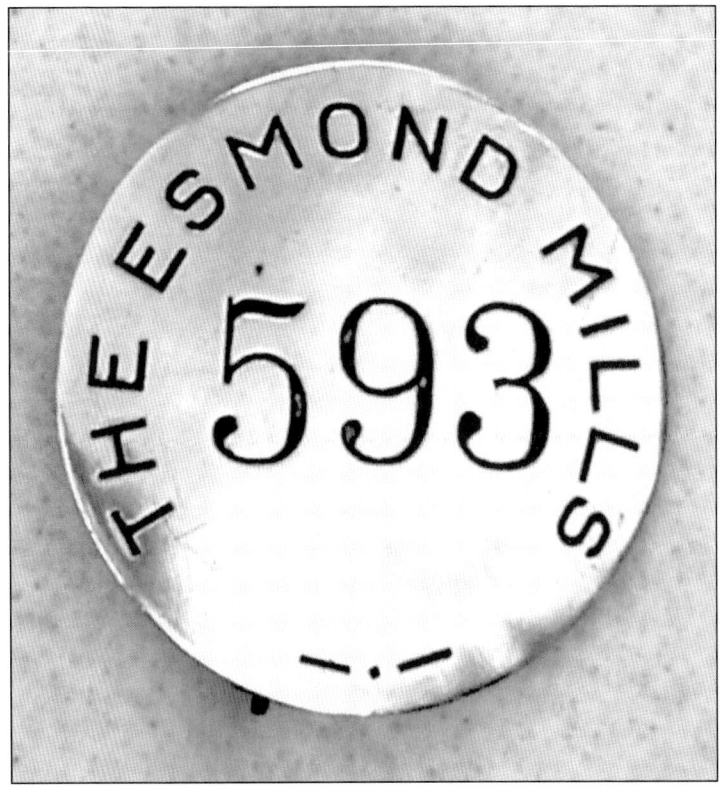

Workers at the Esmond Mills wore brass badges like this one for easy identification and security reasons. The mill employed hundreds of people. (KB.)

Six
Early Smithfield Schools

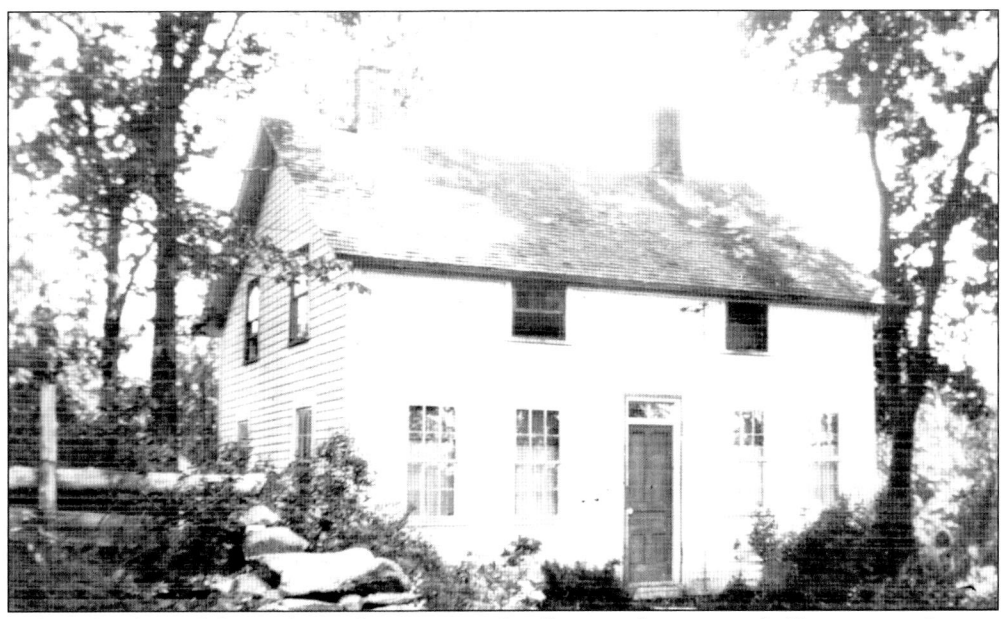

Before the days of the traditional one-room schoolhouse, classes were held in private homes. This house once served as a school for the children of Stillwater. In 1800, the Rhode Island General Assembly enacted a law providing free schooling for children. At that time, Smithfield appointed a committee to establish school districts within the town. By 1834, the number of school districts was 24, and by 1840, it had risen to 35. The districts were small by today's standards because schools had to be located within walking distance, which was considered to be about two miles. (HSS.)

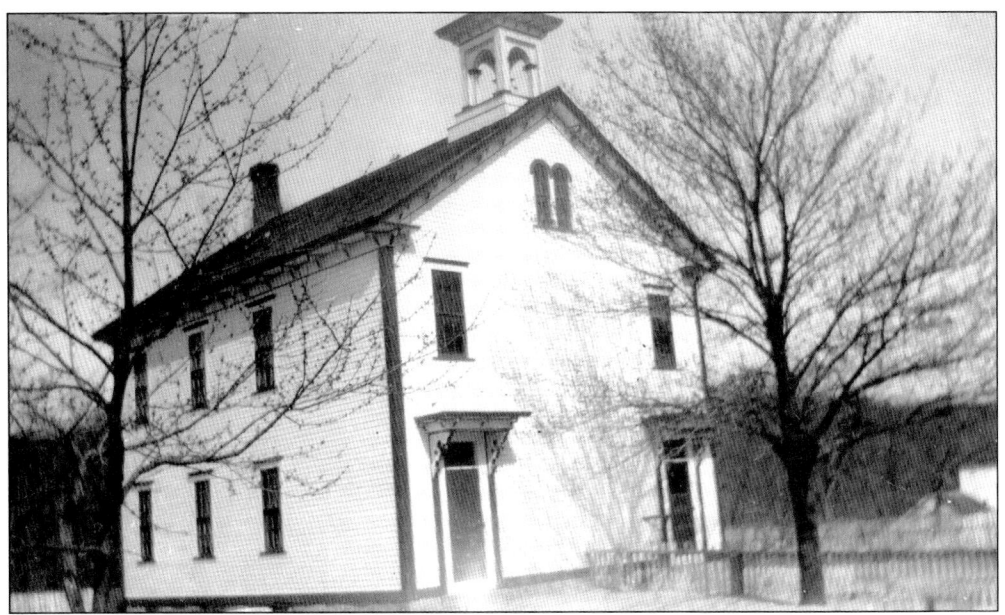
The Stillwater School was built in 1869 and served the village into the 1930s. (HSS.)

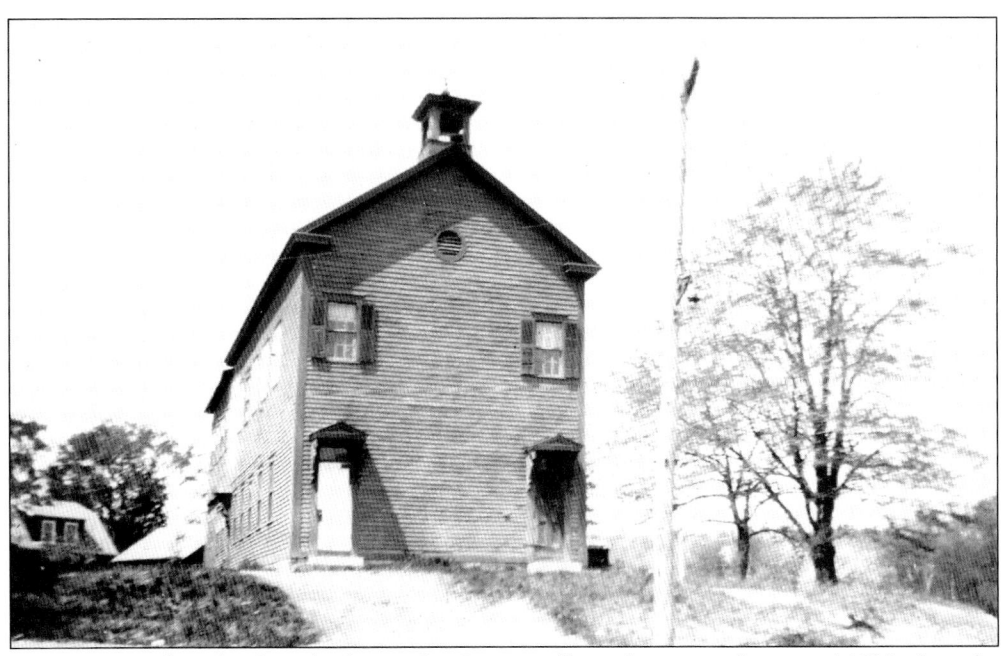
The Georgiaville School was built in 1850. Georgiaville students went here until 1923 when the Cook School was built. Afterward the building served as a fire station and a highway garage. It was burned for training by the fire department in 1962. (HSS.)

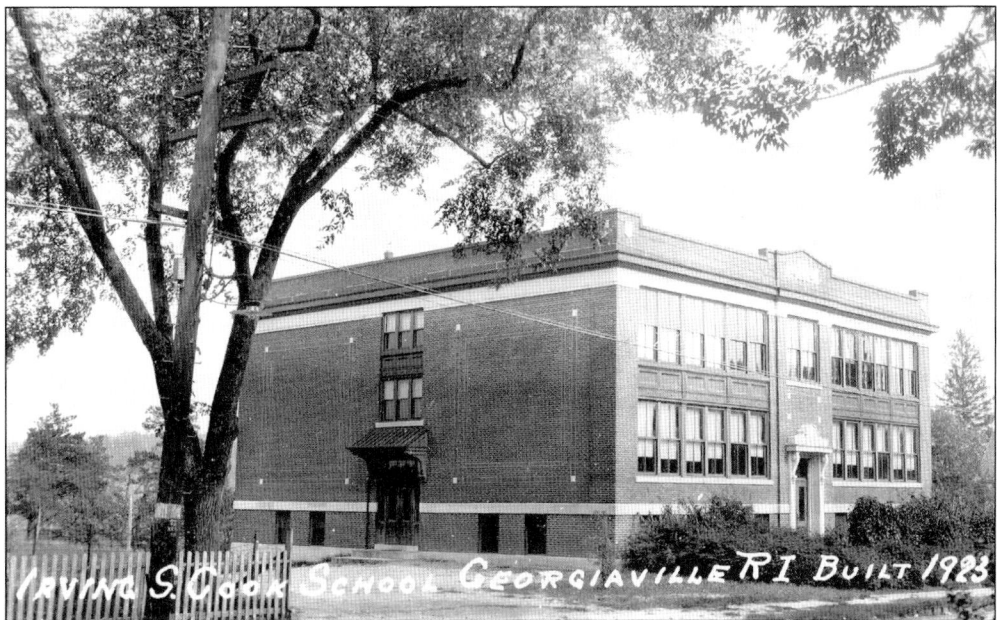

What was once the Irving S. Cook School now serves as the Smithfield school department's administrative building. From 1800 to 1840, each school district was supervised by a taxpayer who was appointed by the town. This changed in 1840 when the state passed a law requiring school committees for each town. (HSS.)

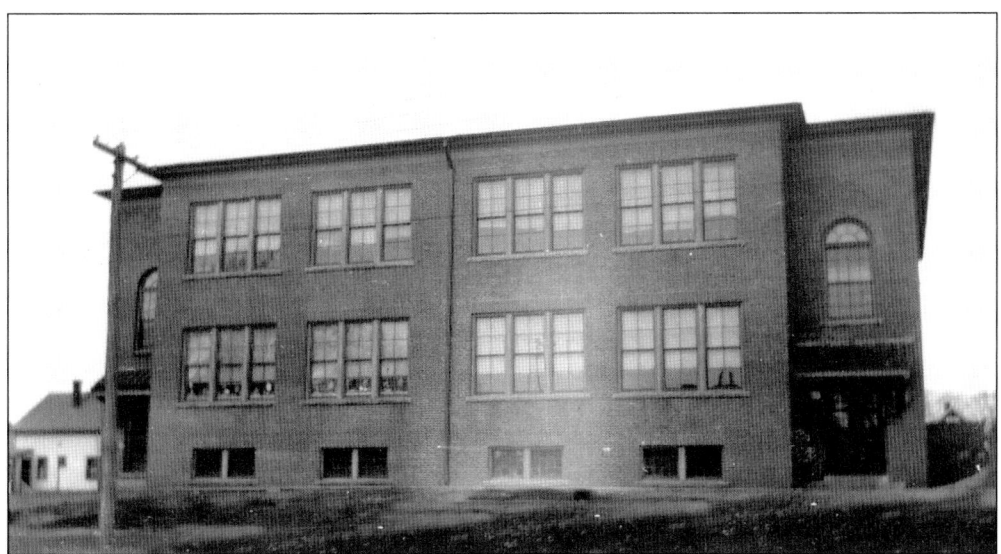

This photograph shows the Dorothy T. P. Dame School in Esmond as it looked in 1931. Today it is the home of the East Smithfield Public Library. (HSS.)

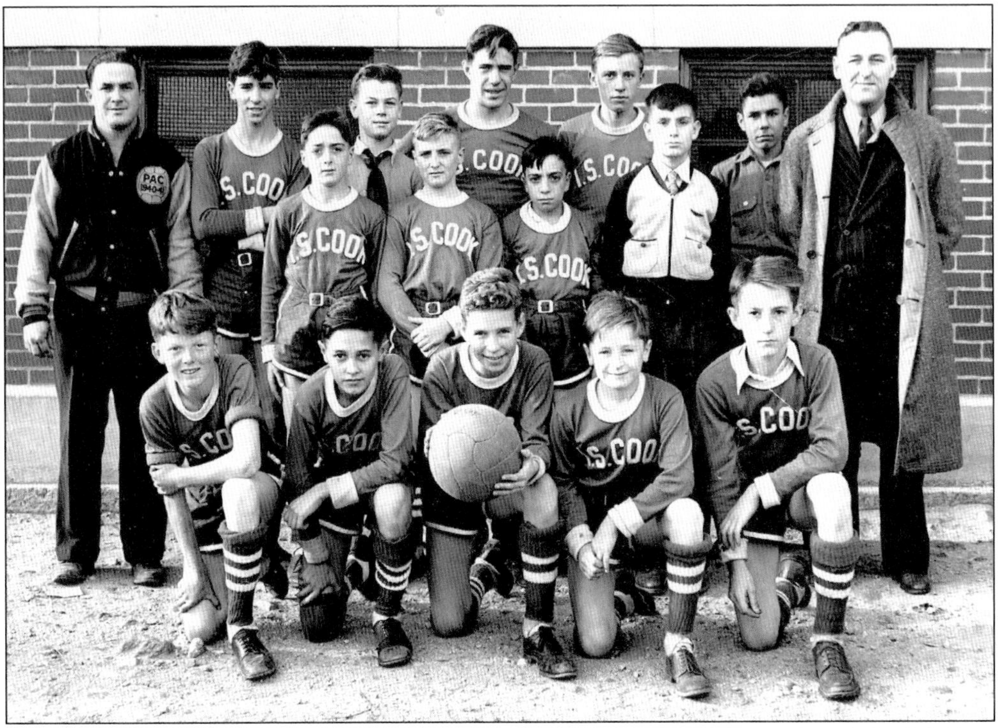

This photograph shows the Irving S. Cook School boys' basketball team in the 1940s. (TM.)

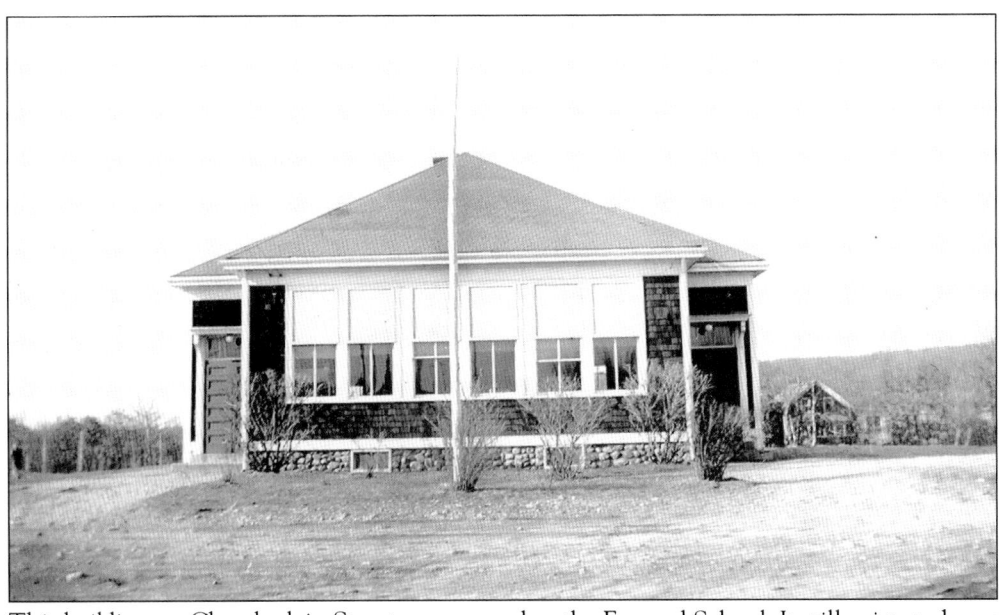

This building on Chamberlain Street once served as the Esmond School. It still exists today as a private residence. (PH.)

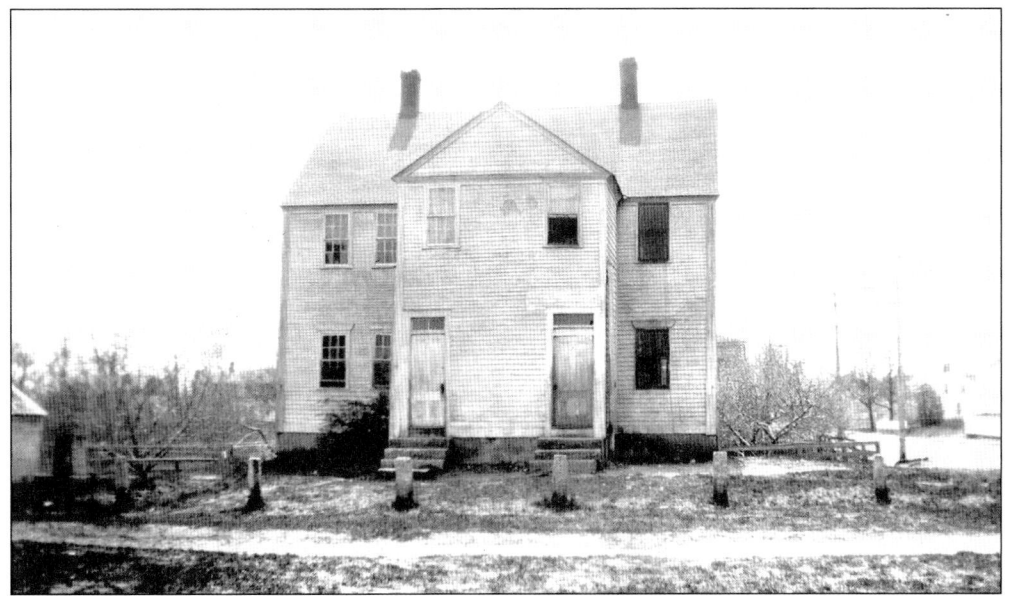

This is the old Greenville Academy, a school that stood on Austin Avenue near the present-day Greenville Post Office. It was built in the early 1800s and moved to Smith Avenue in 1874. It was torn down in 1938. (HSS.)

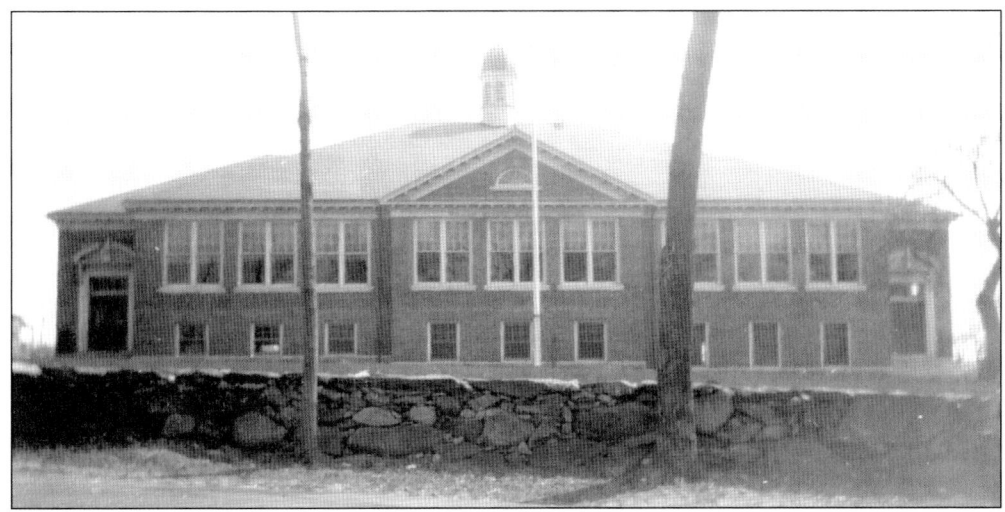

The William Winsor School is seen as it looked in 1930. By the 20th century, the local population had grown enough to make the traditional one-room schoolhouse obsolete. School districts were consolidated, and modern schools as known today were built. (HSS.)

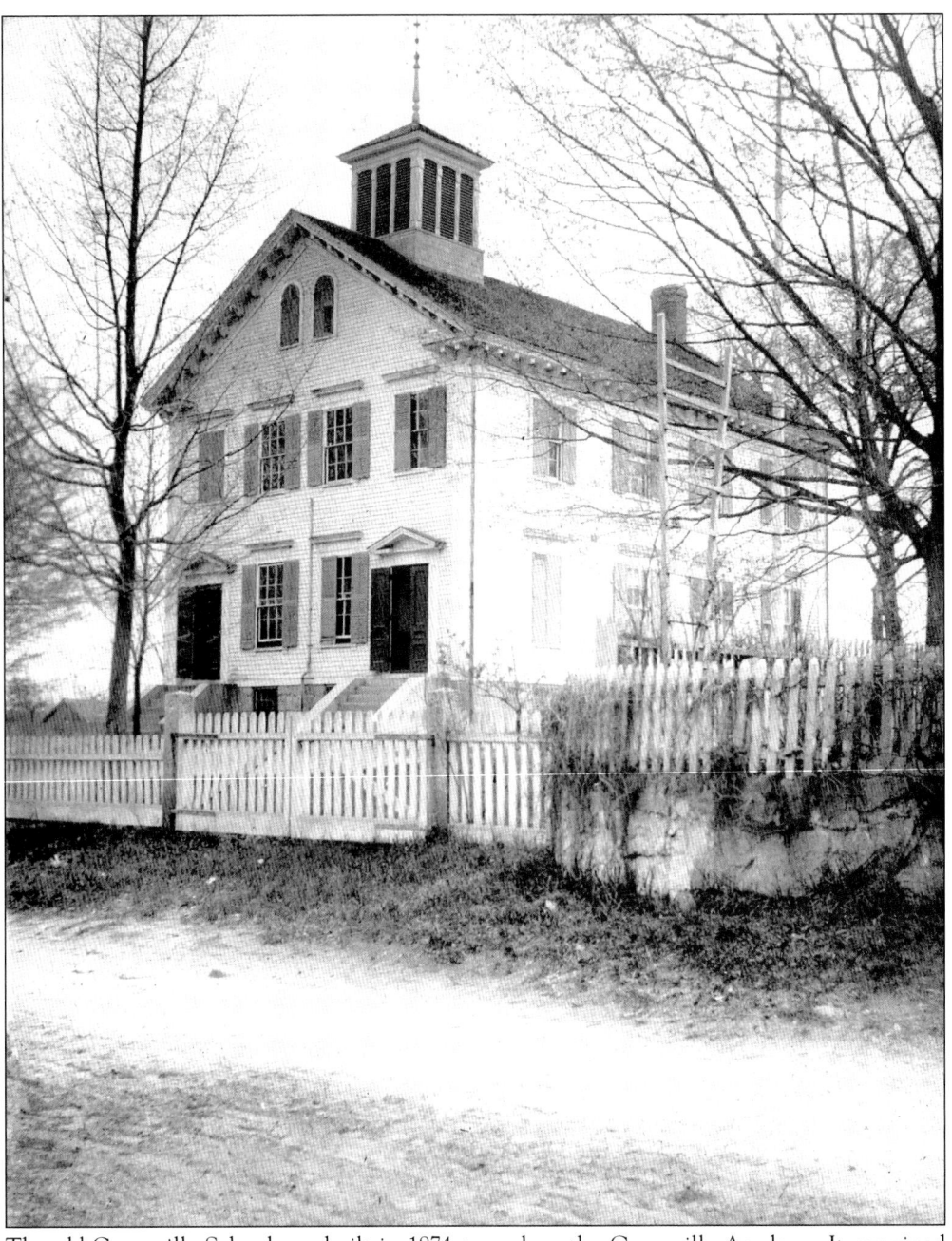

The old Greenville School was built in 1874 to replace the Greenville Academy. It remained open until 1930, when the Winsor School on Route 44 was completed. In 1939, the building was acquired by the Greenville Grange No. 37. The building was torn down in the 1980s. (PH.)

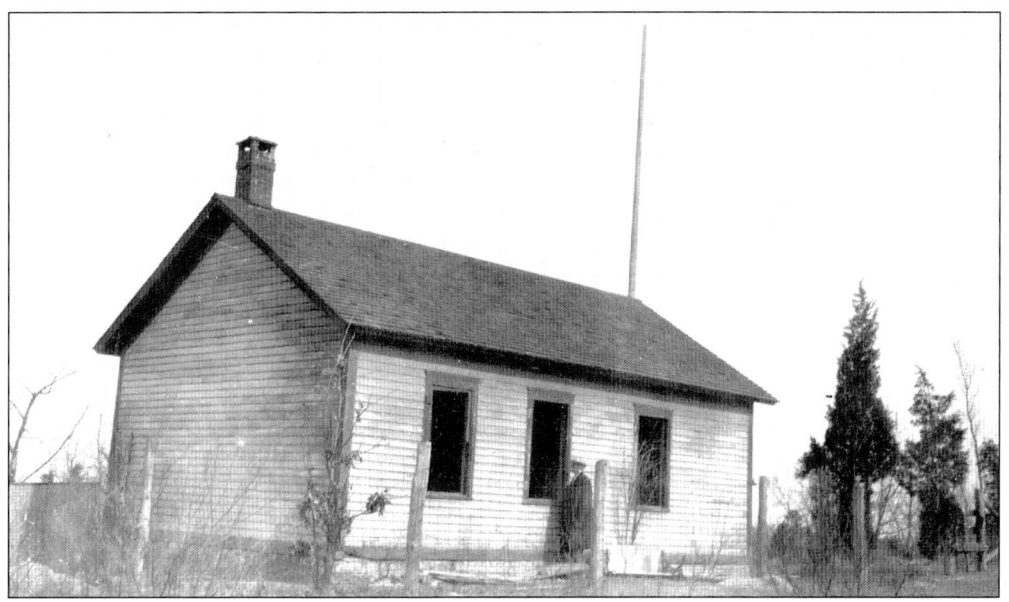

This is the one-room schoolhouse in Spragueville as it looked in 1933. Classes often ranged from late fall after the harvest was done to early spring when planting season came about. Some school districts held classes during the summer after crops were planted. (HSS.)

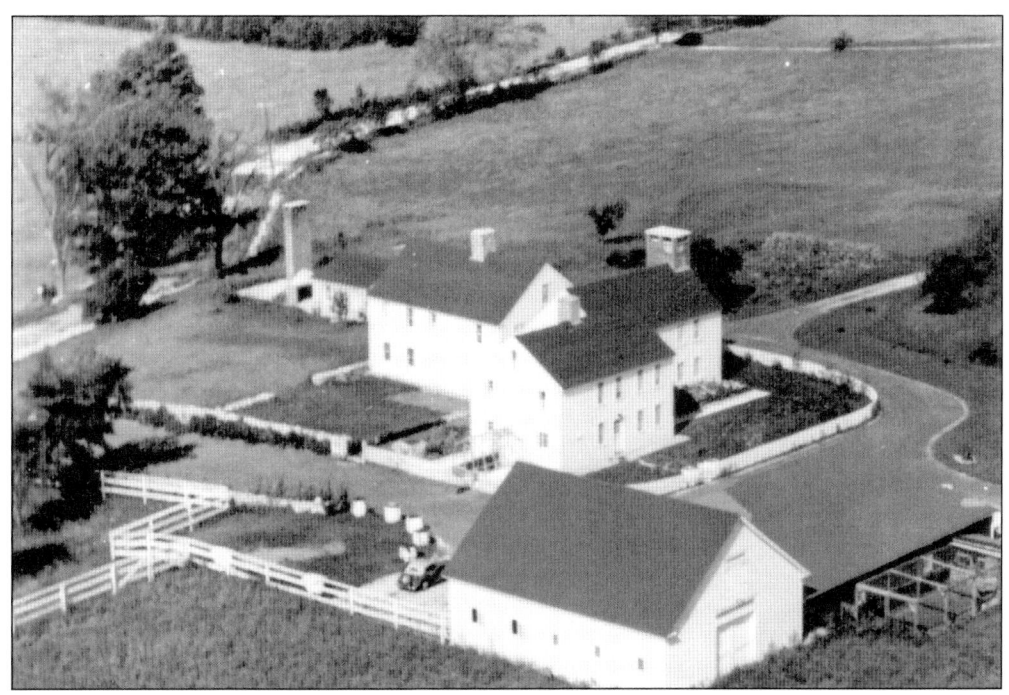

These buildings stood where the Bryant University Unistructure stands today. (HSS.)

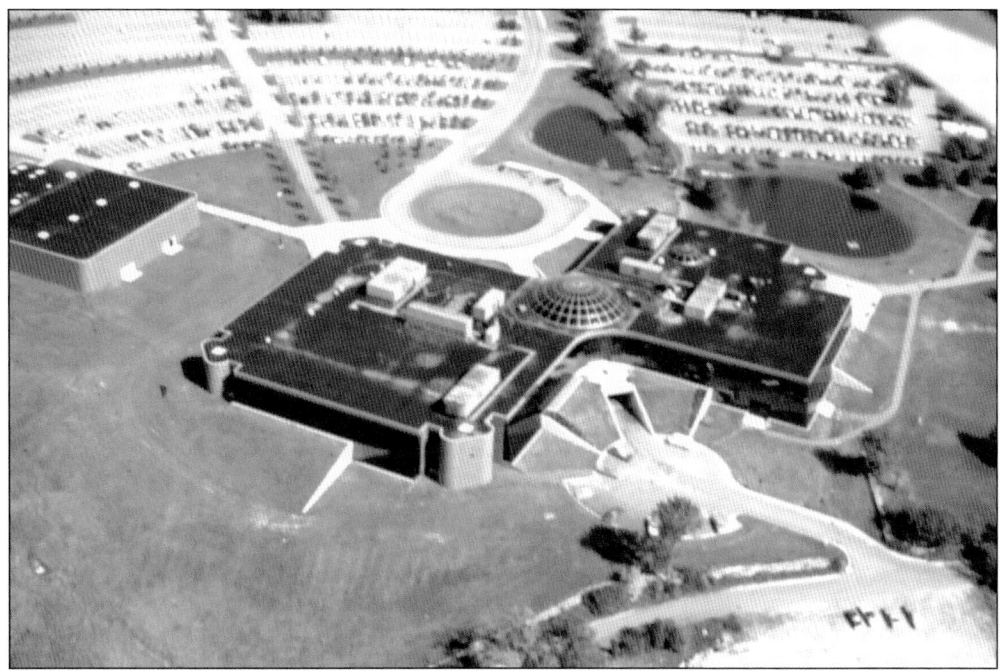

In 1971, Bryant College moved from Providence to its present location on Route 7 in Smithfield. The above photograph shows the campus Unistructure as it looked in 1975. Since this photograph was taken, the Unistructure has had some major additions to it. A library and a student center now occupy the two parking lots. The college became a university in 2004. (HSS.)

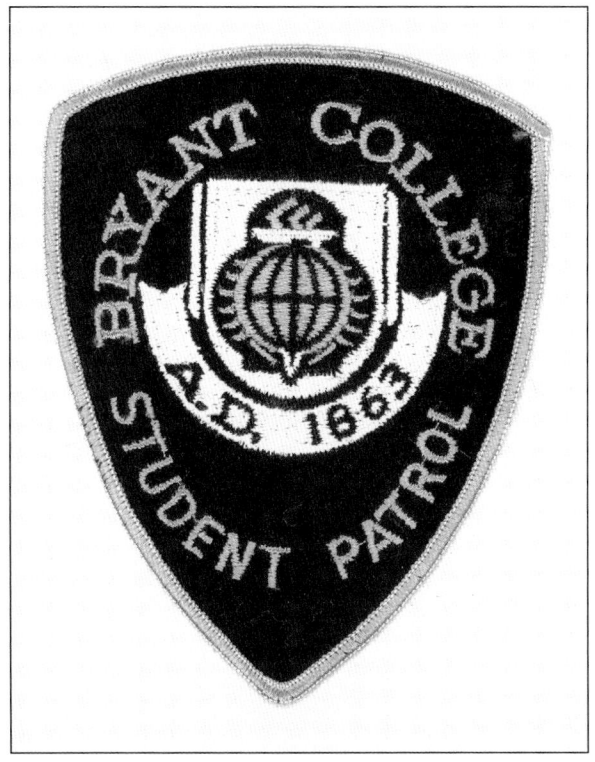

The Bryant University Department of Public Safety had its beginnings as the Bryant College Student Patrol in the 1970s. The student patrol was primarily made up of Bryant students majoring in criminal justice who were supervised by several full-time employees. Their uniforms were modeled after those worn by the Smithfield police at the time. The uniform patch shown here was the first to be worn by the department, and it depicts an old symbol for the university. (JI.)

Seven
Stagecoaches, Taverns, Trains, and Planes

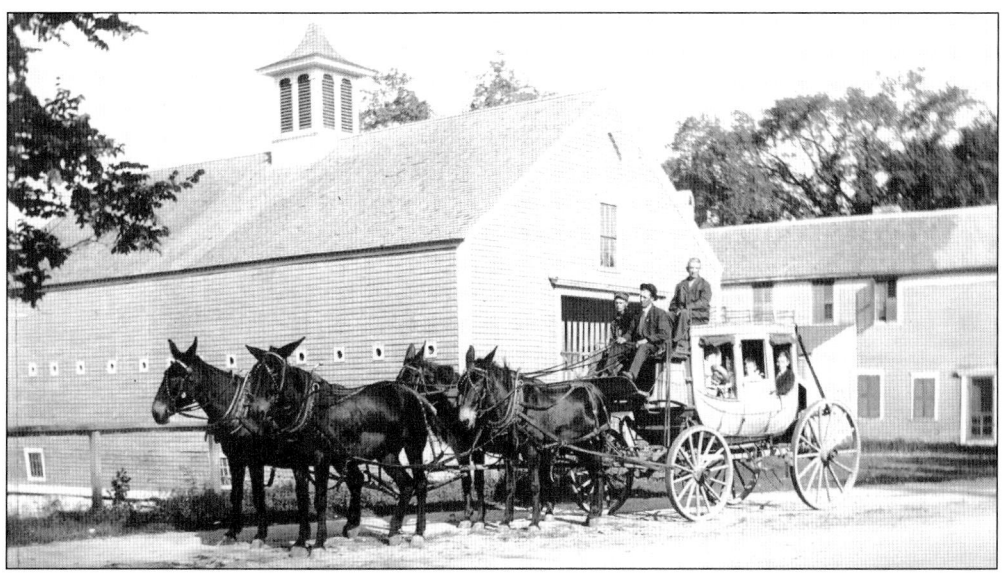

The above photograph shows the stagecoach that ran from Centerdale to Harmony. Stagecoaches and taverns seem to go together, for it seems one could not operate without the other. The taverns were the way stations, rest stops, hotels, and restaurants of early America. Most had a large barn where horses could be fed and watered and any needed repairs could be made to the stagecoach. The arrival of a stagecoach was eagerly awaited as the stage meant news and mail, as well as business for the local tavern owner. (HSS.)

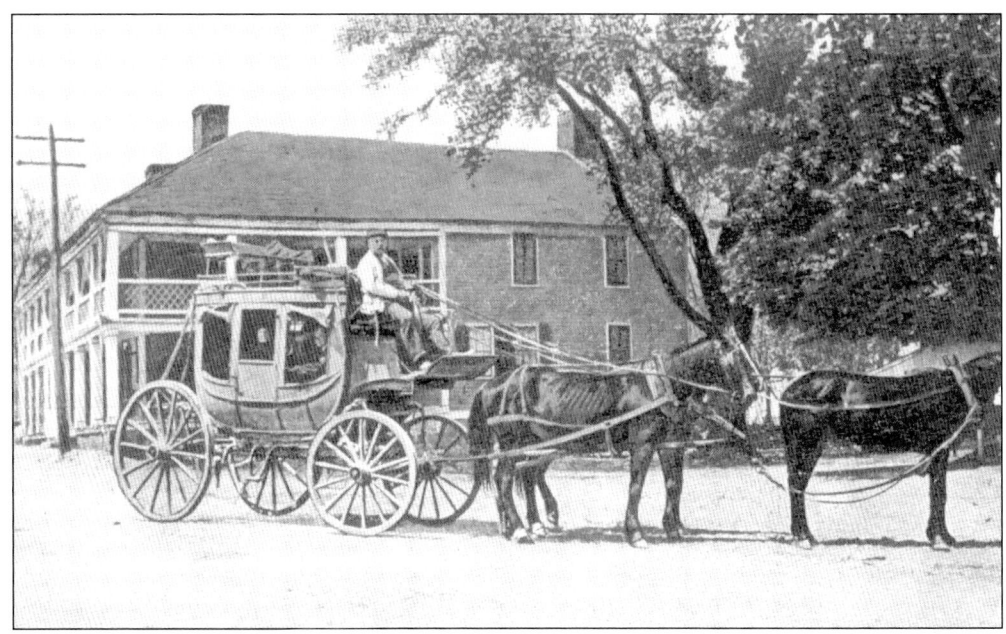

This postcard view depicts the Greenville Stage standing in front of the Waterman Tavern. (HSS.)

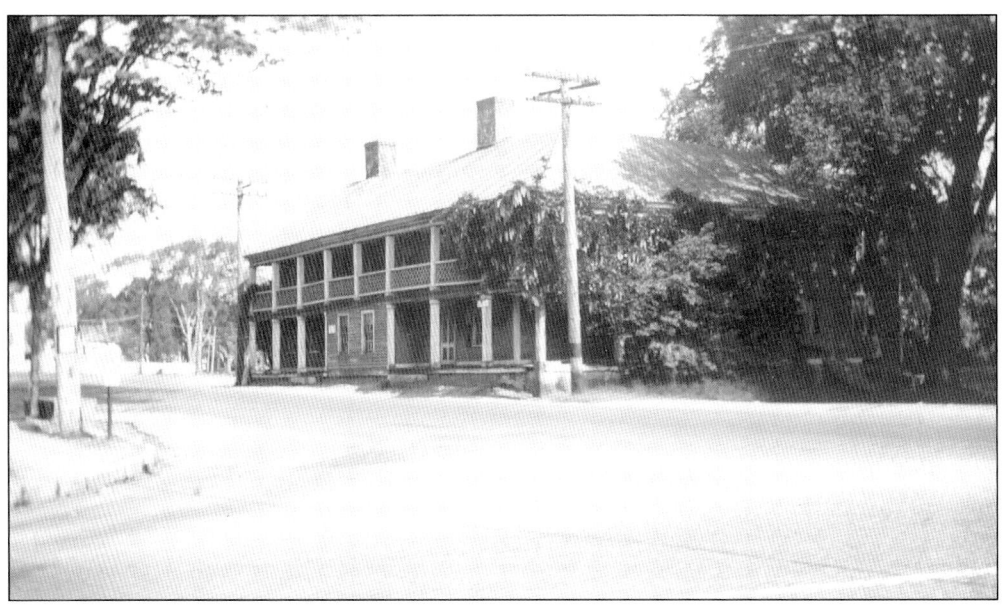

The Waterman Tavern was built by Resolved Waterman in 1730. In 1936, the front portion was removed for the widening of Route 44. All that remains today is the back ell that dates from the 1850s. (HSS.)

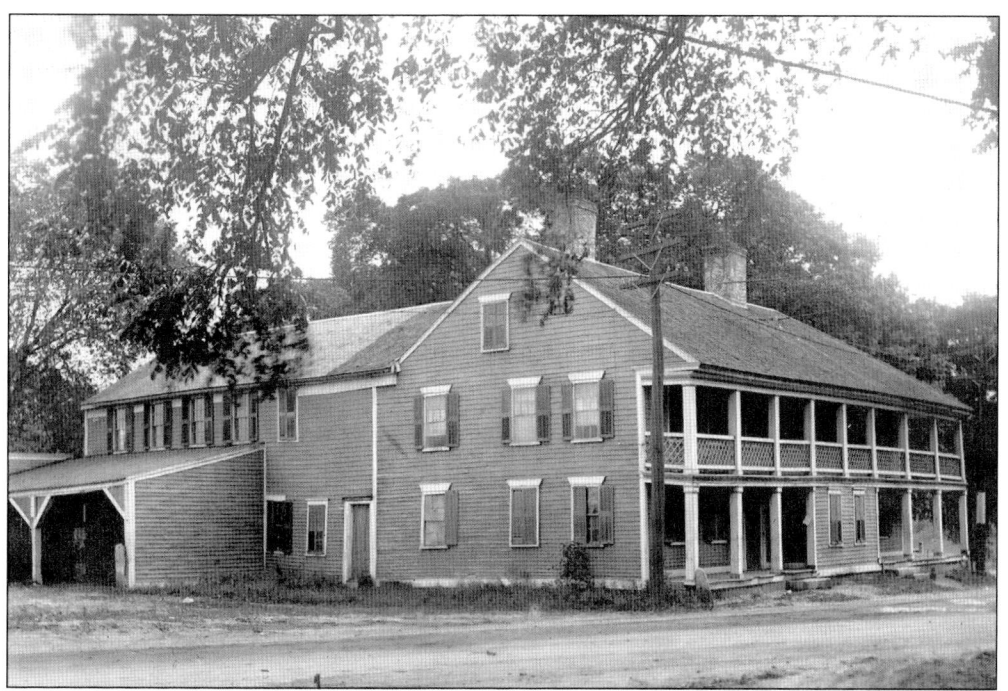

This view shows the west side of the old Waterman Tavern. (WK.)

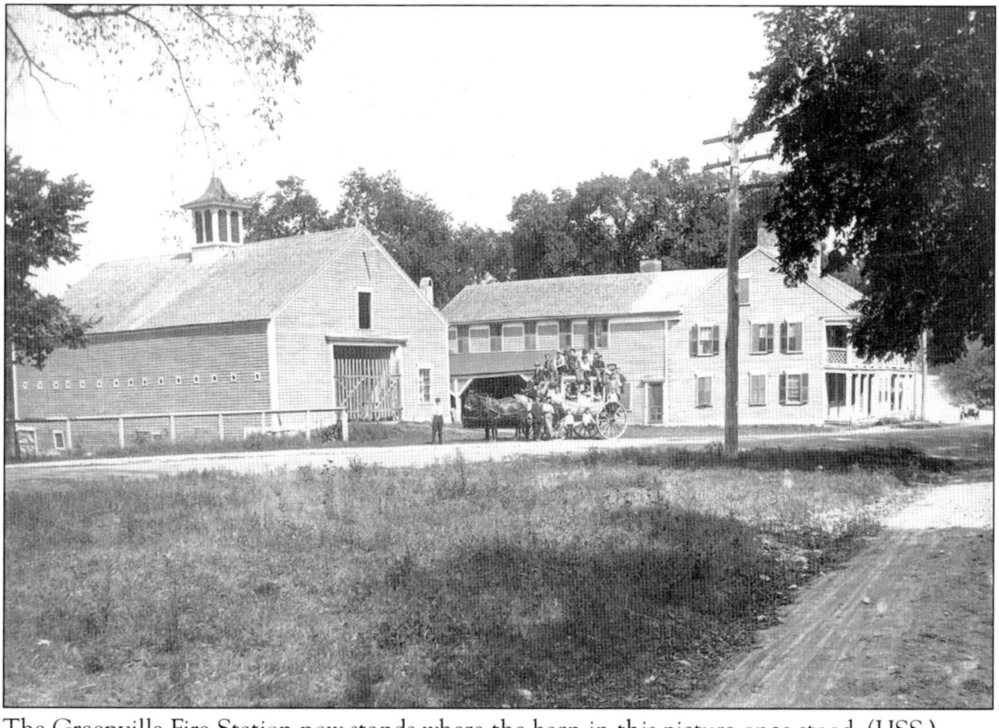

The Greenville Fire Station now stands where the barn in this picture once stood. (HSS.)

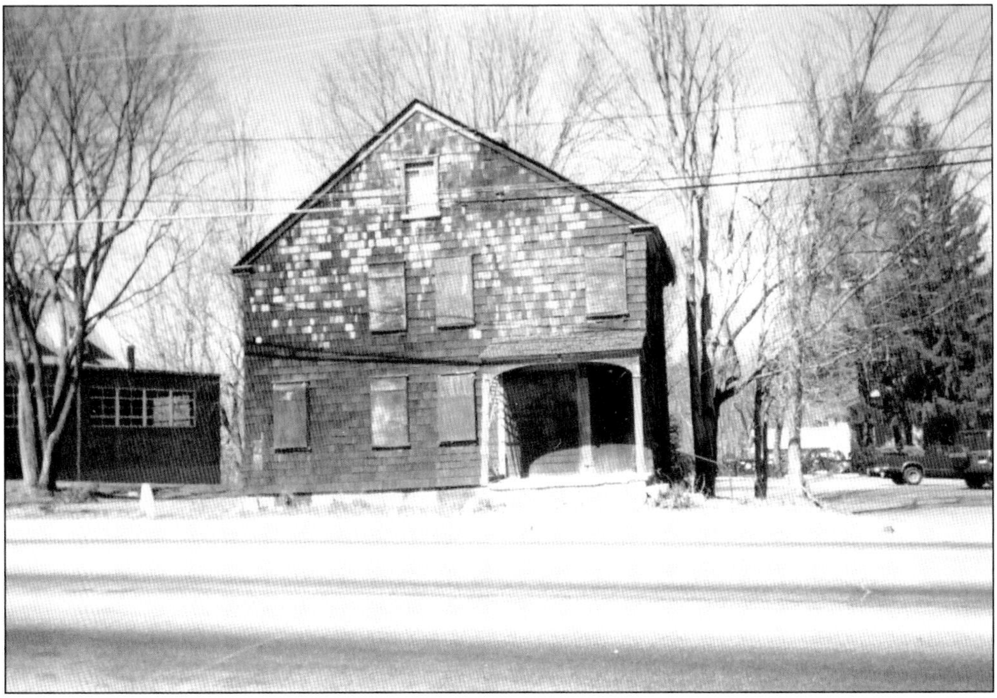

This picture of the back ell of the Waterman Tavern was taken in the 1980s. (HSS.)

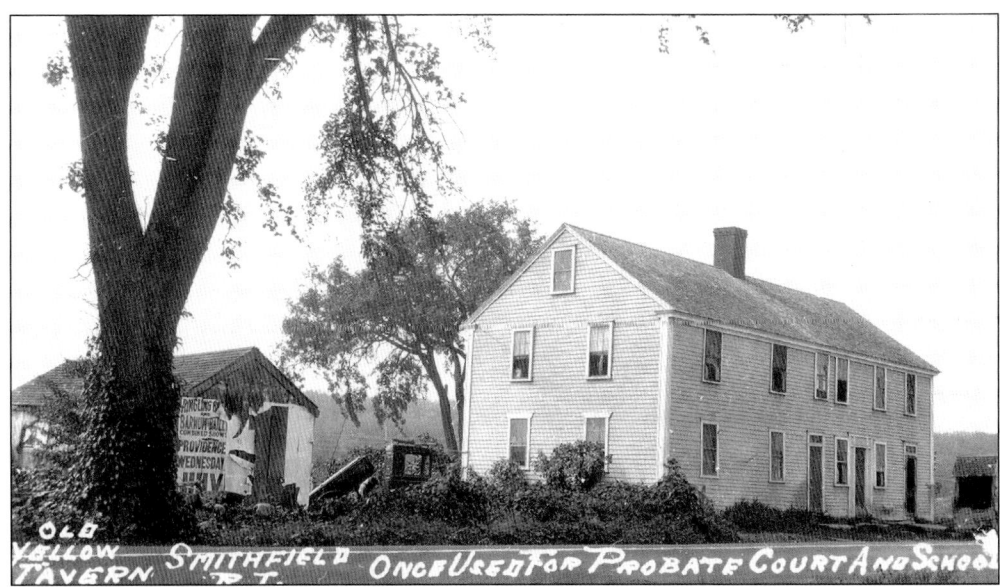

The Yellow Tavern is seen as it looked in 1931. Located on Route 104 at Old Forge Road, this building dates from the late 1700s and has served as a tavern, an inn, and even a school. Today it is a private residence. (HSS.)

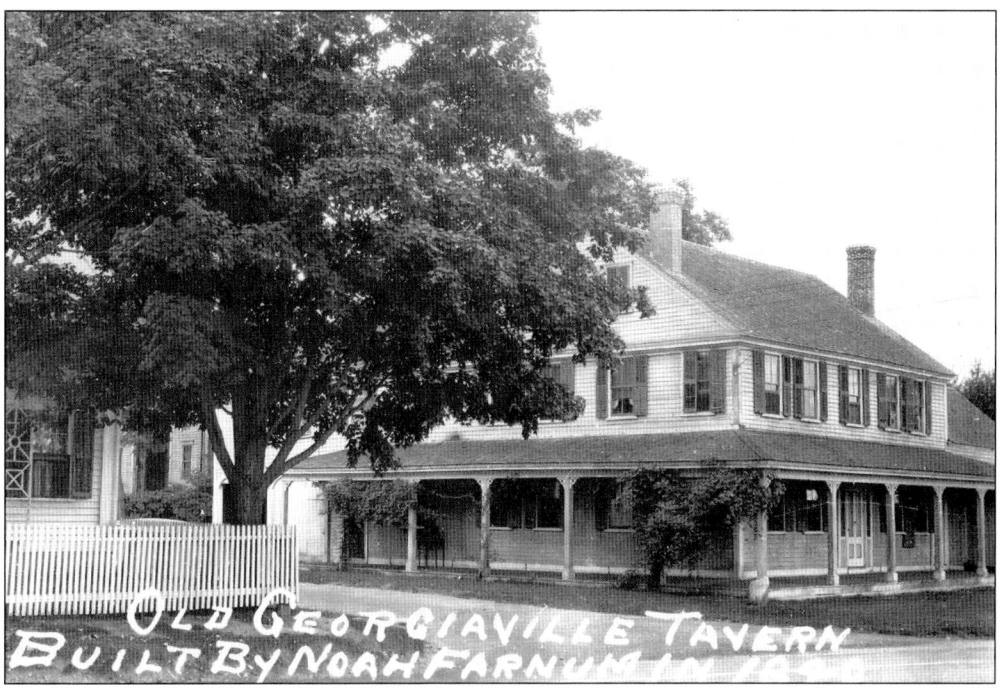

The Georgiaville Tavern was located at the intersection of Wolf Hill Road and Route 104. The building still exists today; however, the porch has been removed, the exterior vinyl sided, and the interior turned into apartments. (HSS.)

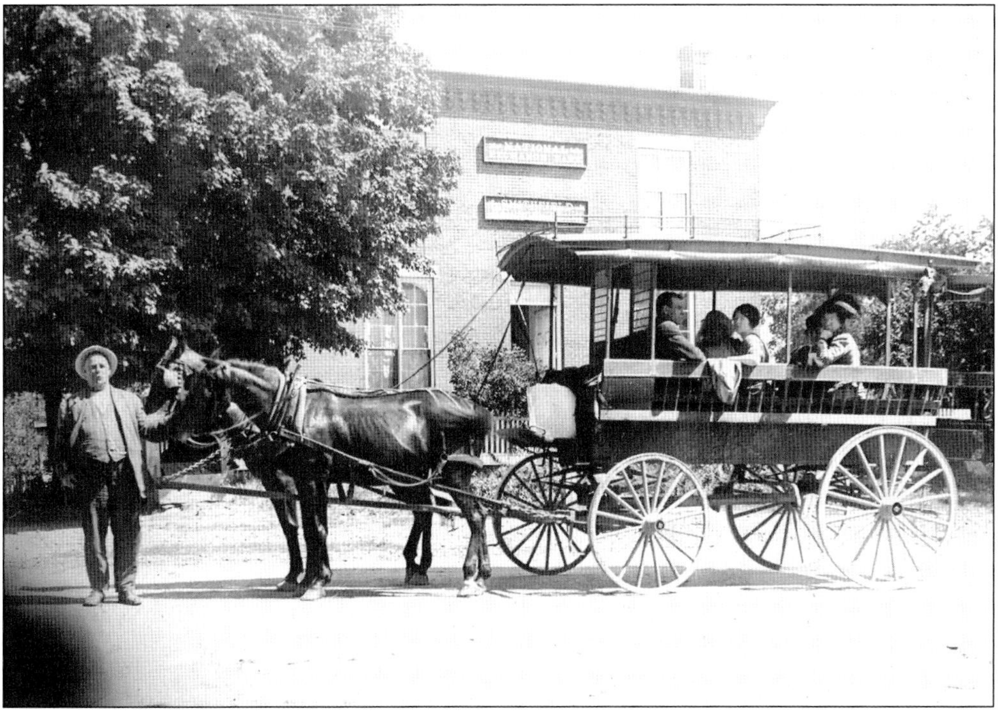

This open-air coach was obviously only used in nice weather and most likely only for local routes. Note the old Exchange Bank in the background. (PH.)

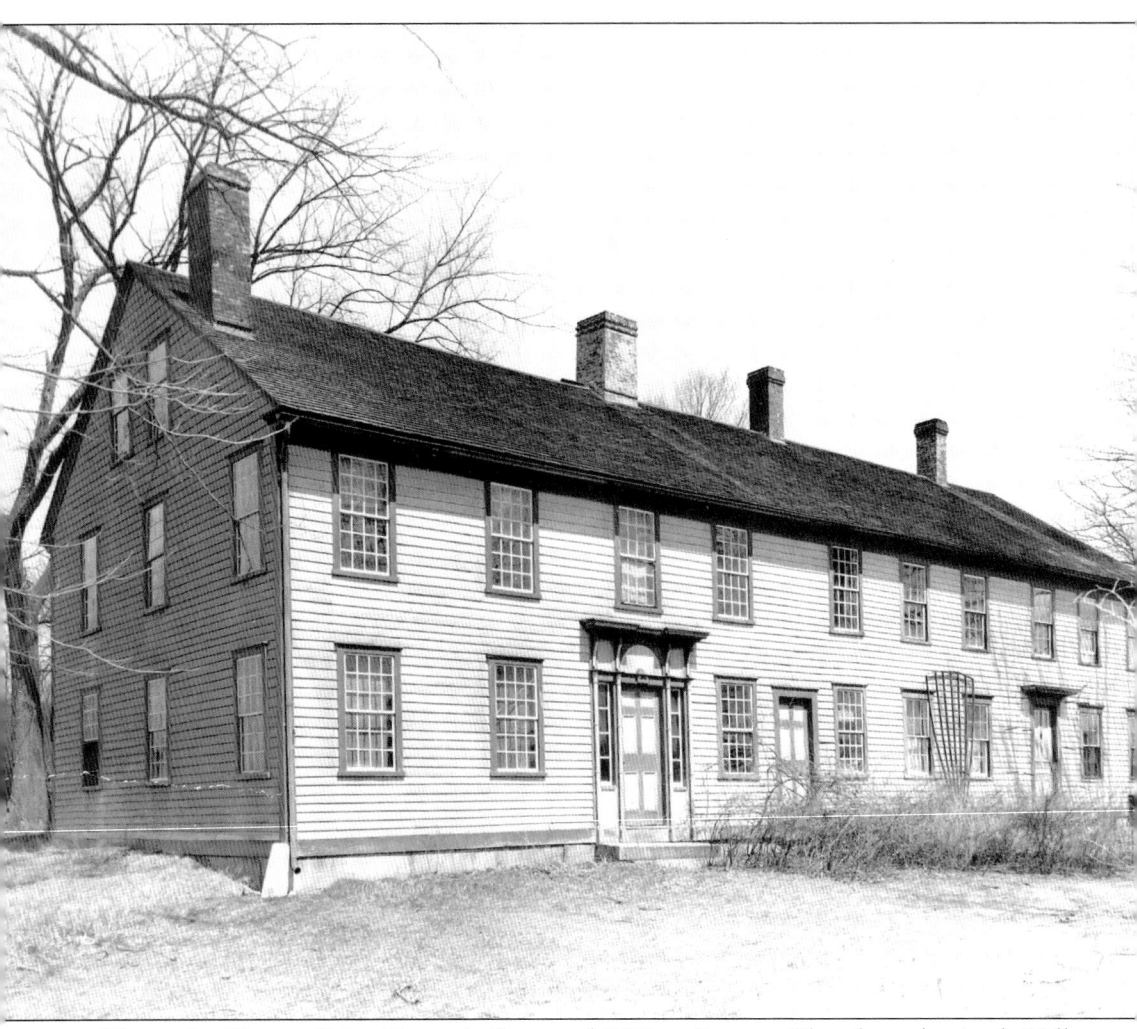

This is the Thomas Paine Tavern built around 1790 on Putnam Pike where the Apple Valley Mall stands today. The word *pike* is short for *turnpike*, which means "toll road." A turnpike was actually a gate that blocked a roadway. Individual travelers and stagecoaches were expected to stop at the gate and pay a toll before being allowed to proceed. The money collected was supposed to go to the gatekeeper, who was charged with fixing and maintaining the portion of road that fell under his responsibility. (HSS.)

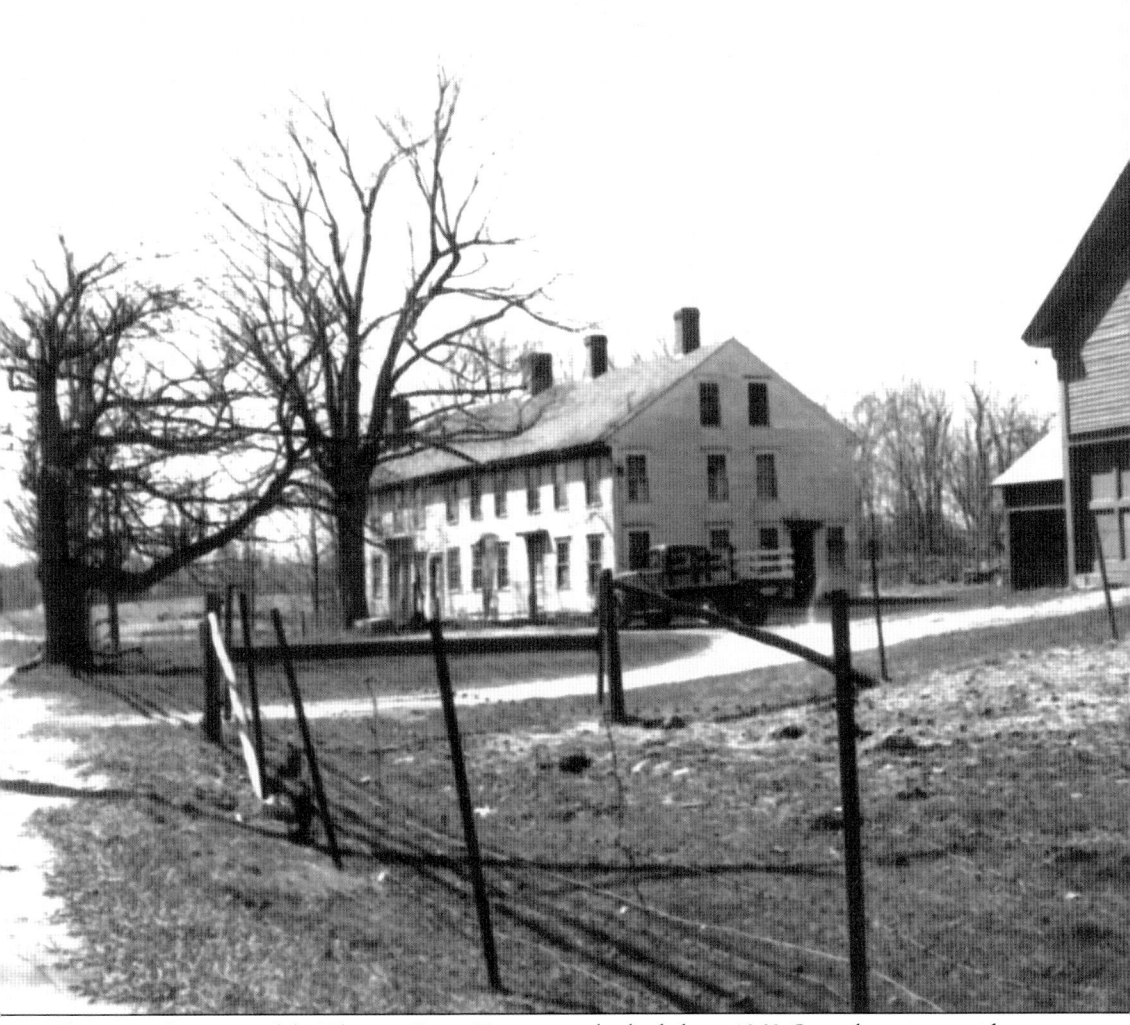
This is another view of the Thomas Paine Tavern as it looked about 1960. Some longtime residents of the town may remember that the Brown University mascot—a large brown bear—was once kept here in a pen by a Mr. Walcott who owned the property. (WK.)

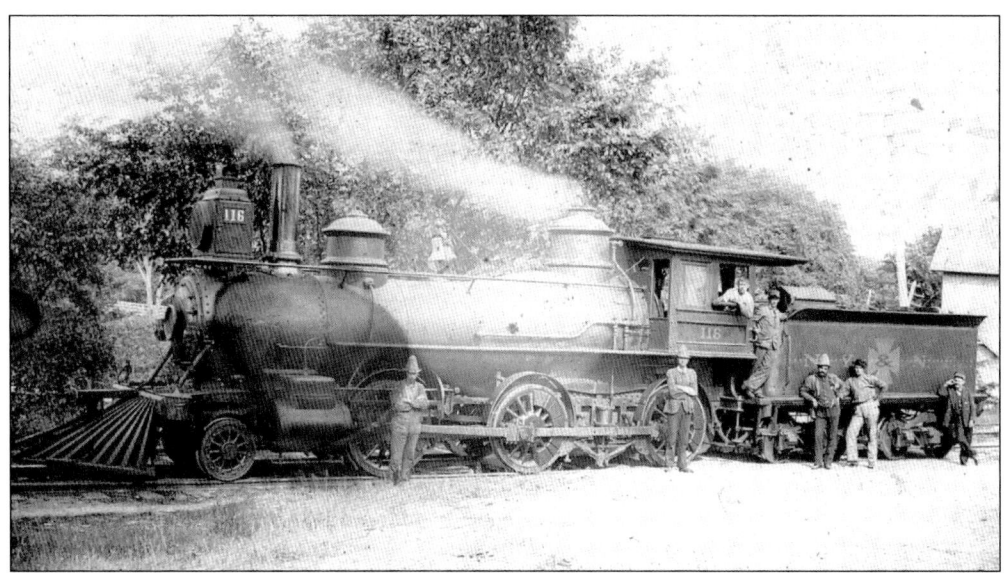

The Providence to Pascoag line of the Providence and Springfield Railroad opened on August 11, 1873, and stopped at four stations in Smithfield. (JC.)

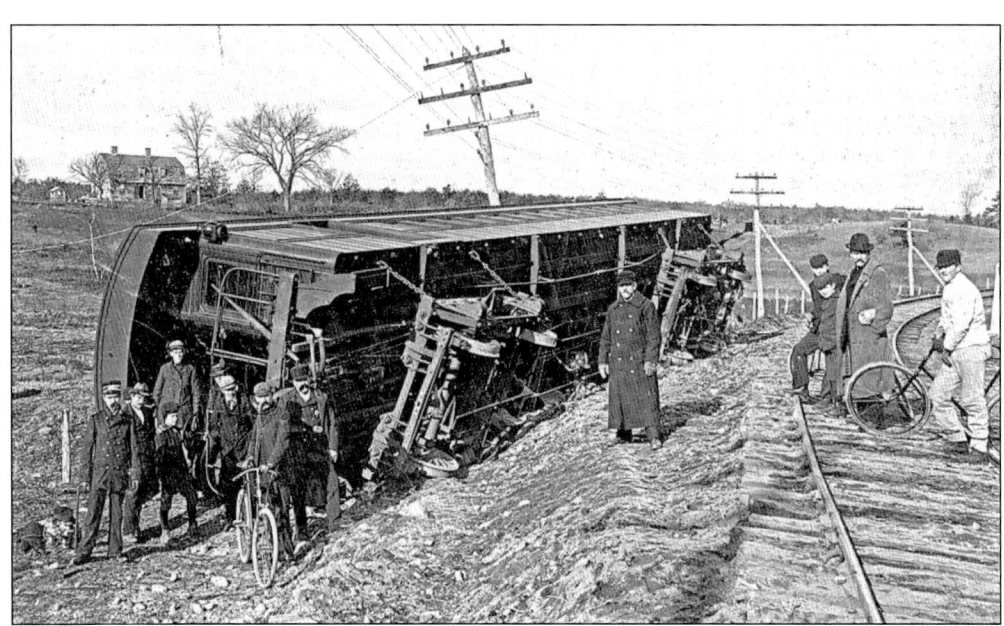

There is some debate as to exactly when and where this accident happened in Smithfield. Some say it was in Esmond, and others say farther north along the line, between 1906 and 1910. (JC.)

Trains for Enfield

Via New York, New Haven & Hartford Railroad.

Leave Providence, Union Station, at 6.40, 8.45, 11.45 a. m.; 3.55 and 6.30 p. m. (11.20 p. m. Saturdays only.) Twenty-three minutes ride.

Leave Pascoag at 5.33, 7.51 a. m.; 12.55 and 7.51 p. m.

Leave Southbridge at 6.45 a. m. and 3.25 p. m.

Trains Leave Enfield

For Providence at 6.08, 8.26 a. m.; 1.30, 5.06 and 8.26 p. m. Twenty-three minutes ride.

For Pascoag at 7.03, 9.08 a.m.; 12.08, 4.18 and 6.53 p. m. (11.43 p. m. Saturdays only.)

For Southbridge at 9.08 a. m. and 4.18 p. m.

Electric Cars between Providence and Centredale

NOTE:—The Rhode Island Company now run cars between Providence and Centredale; they have nearly completed an extension to Greystone and have a franchise from Greystone through Enfield to Georgiaville.

Via Smith Street

Leave Providence, Market Sq., at 6.45 a. m. and every 20 minutes until midnight.

Leave Centredale for Providence at 6.15 a. m. and every 20 minutes until midnight. Thirty minutes ride.

Via Olneyville

Leave Providence, Market Sq., at 6.32 a. m. and every 30 minutes until 11.32 p. m.

Leave Centredale for Providence at 5.47 a. m. and every 30 minutes until 12.17 midnight. Forty-five minutes ride.

This Smithfield train schedule is from 1905. (HSS.)

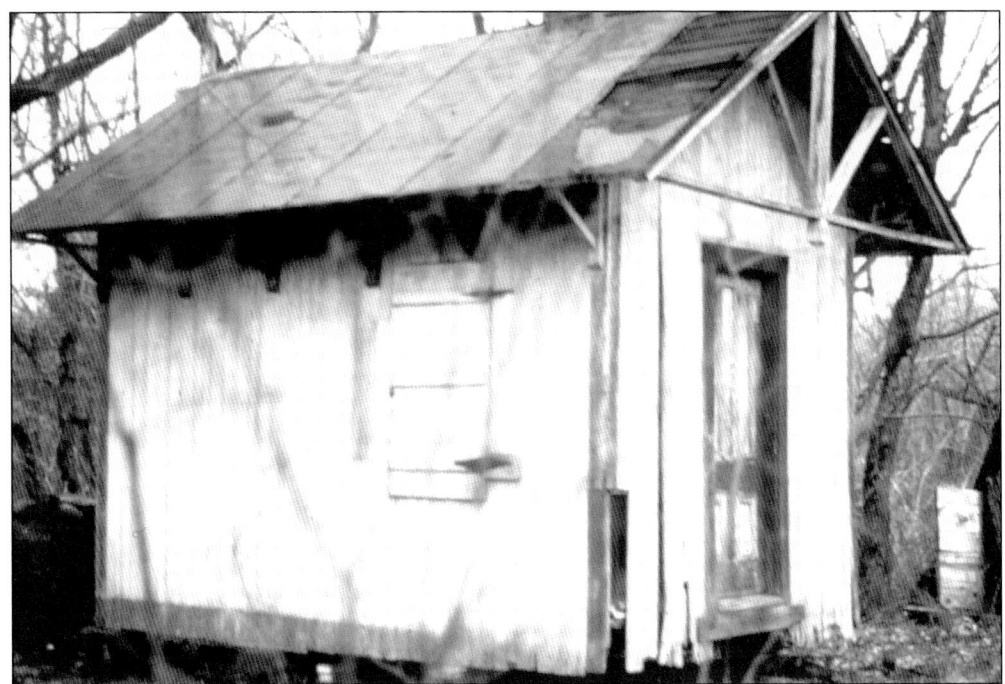

Smithfield had four train stations: Esmond, Georgiaville, Stillwater, and Smithfield station, which was located on Brayton Road near Farnum Pike. Only the Smithfield station survives today, thanks to the efforts of the Historical Society of Smithfield. It was built in the 1870s and utilized until the 1930s. In 1975, the historical society bought it for $300 and restored it. It can be seen today at the Smith-Appleby House Museum. (HSS.)

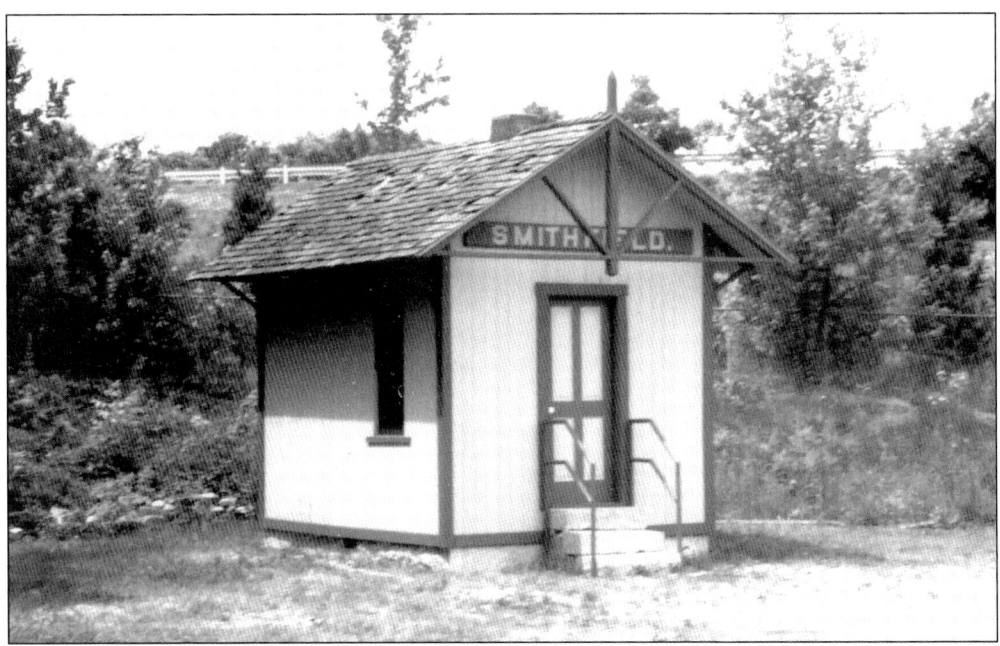

This is the Smithfield station as it looks today after restoration. It is Smithfield's only surviving train station. (HSS.)

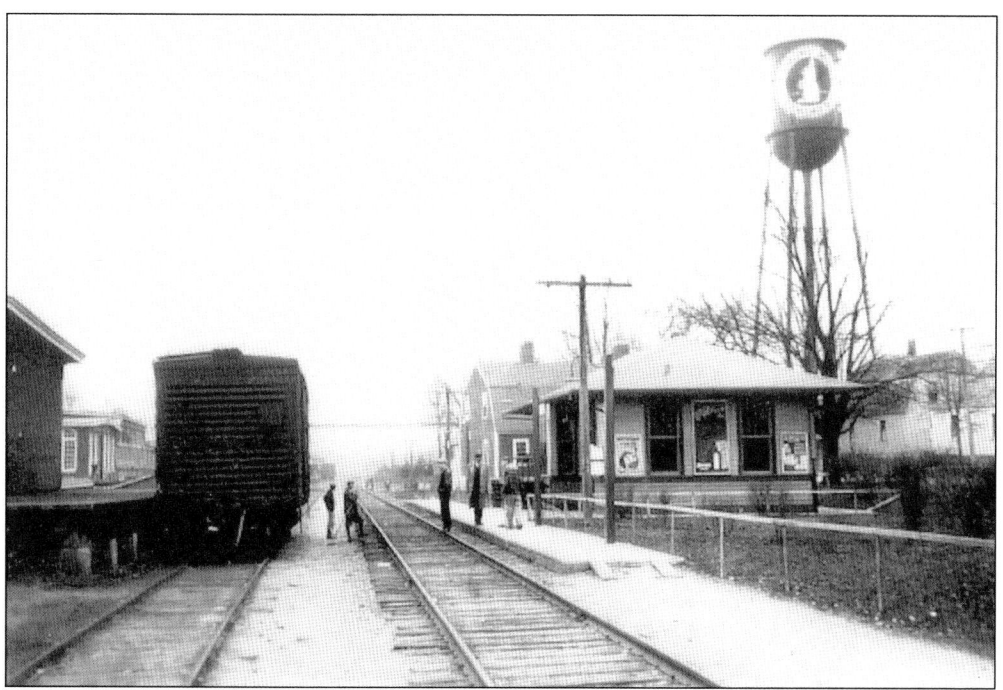

The Esmond train station was located at Esmond Street and Maple Avenue. This photograph was taken around 1930. (AS.)

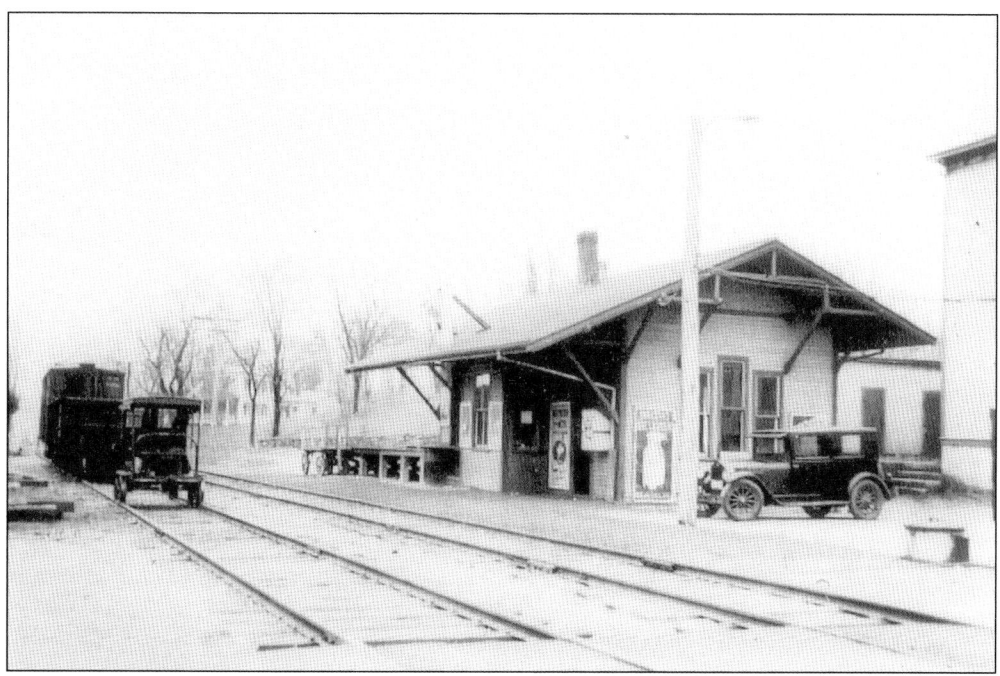

The Georgiaville train station stood on present-day St. Michael's Way. This photograph dates from about 1930. (AS.)

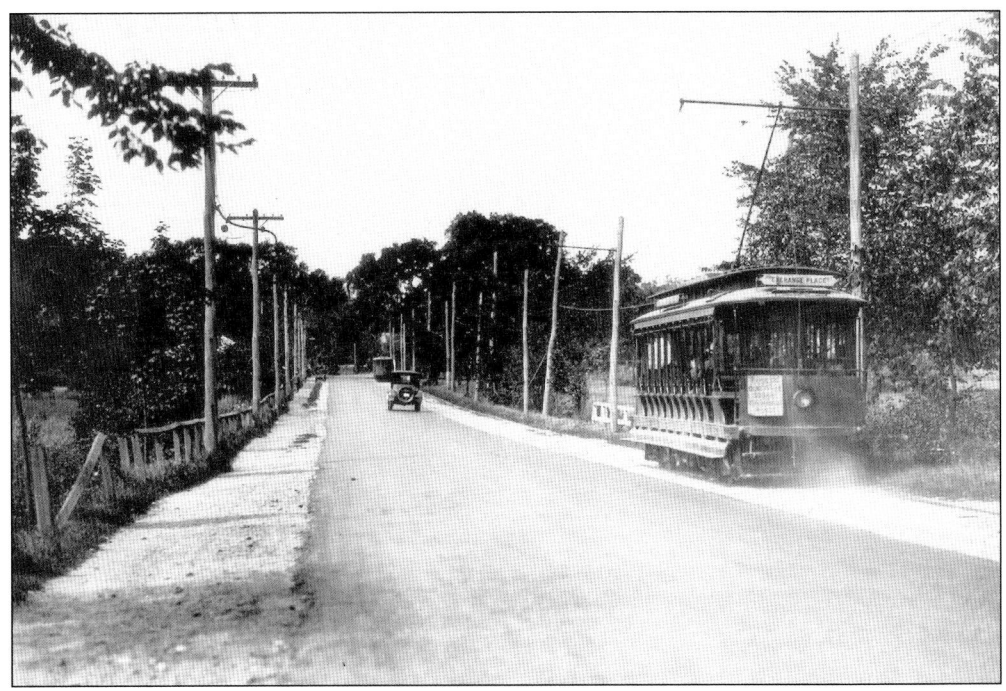

Smithfield's other railroads of sorts were the trolley lines that operated on Waterman Avenue and Route 44 between 1895 and 1935. (AS.)

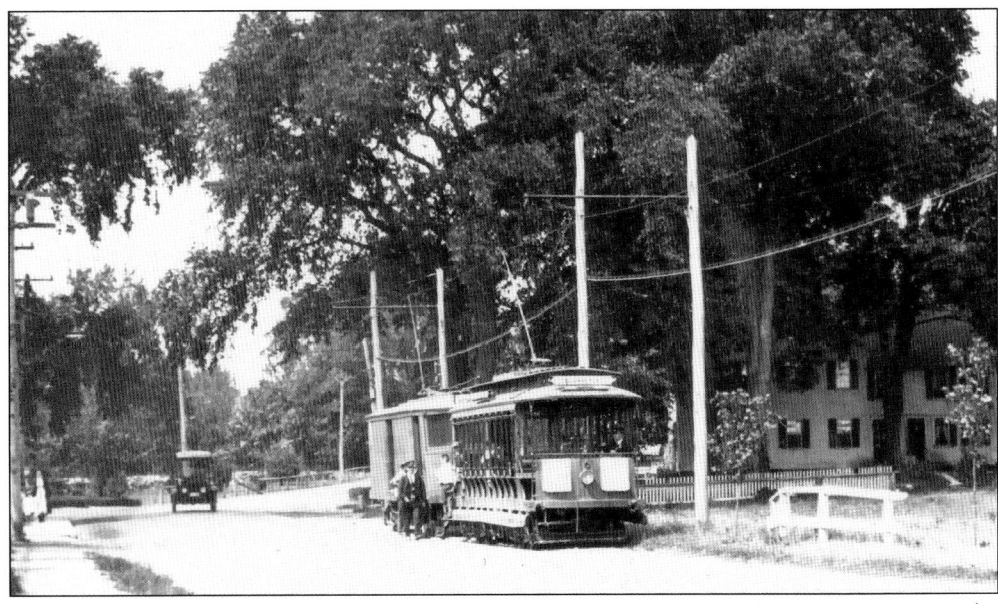

The trolleys were operated by a succession of companies that offered an alternative to the noise and soot of the trains. This photograph was taken at Waterman Avenue and Esmond Street. (AS.)

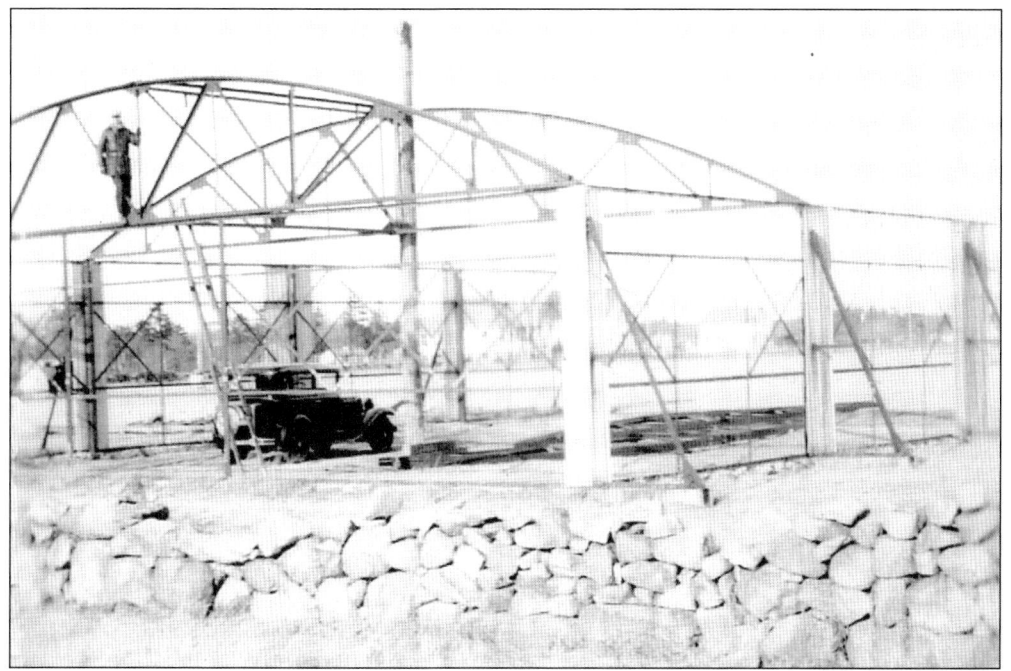

Smithfield's first airport was located where Bryant University is today. It opened in 1932 when John Emin Sr. cleared a cornfield and built a hangar for his airplane. (JE.)

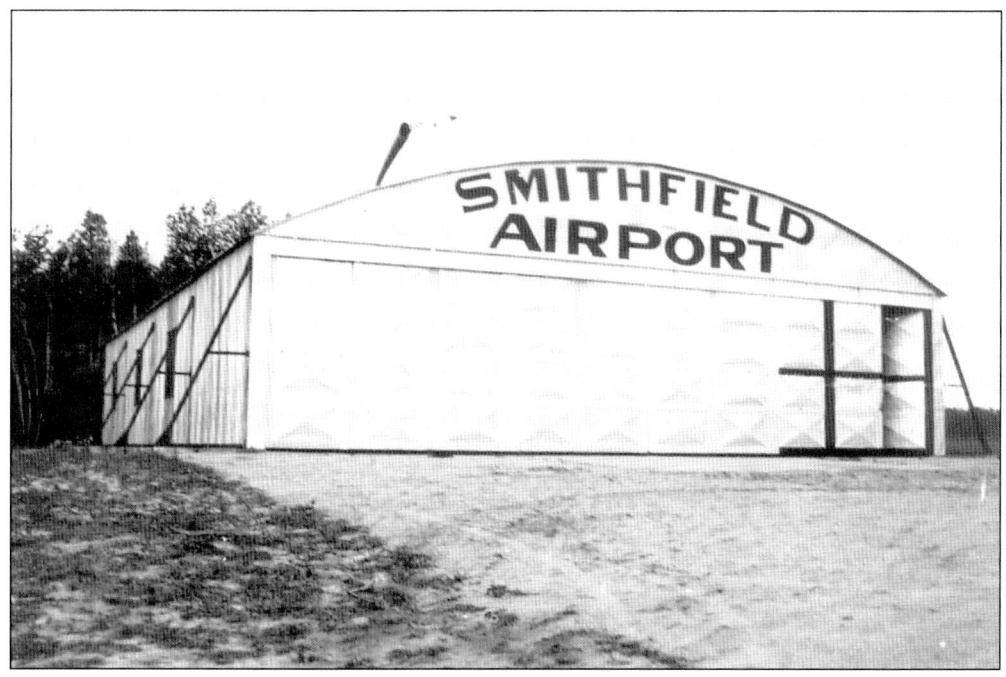

This view shows the completed hangar for Smithfield's first airport. (JE.)

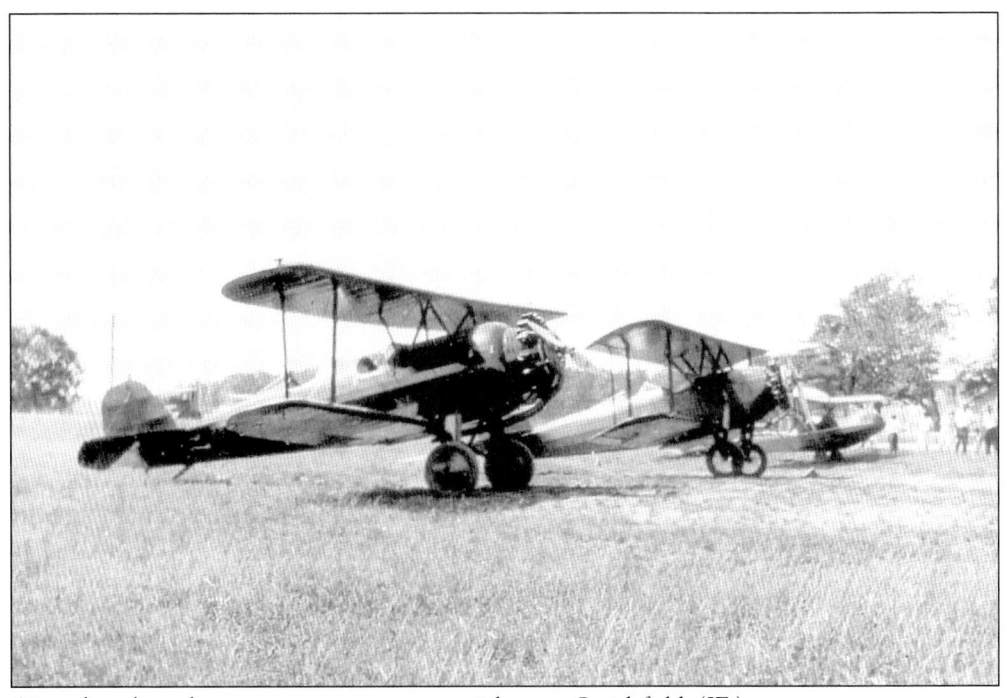
Aircraft such as these were once a common sight over Smithfield. (JE.)

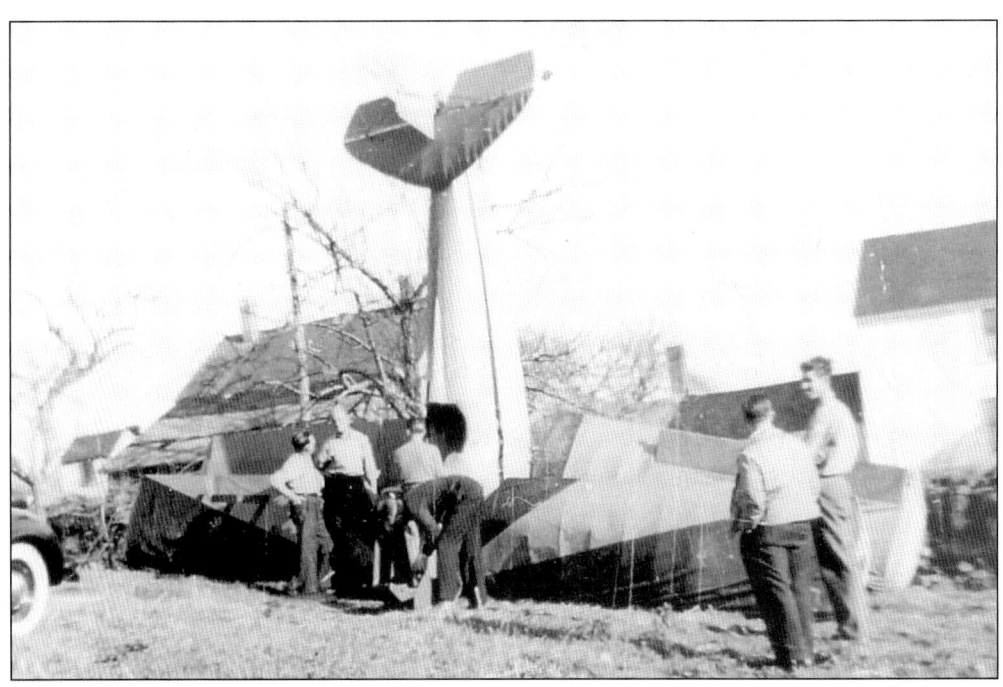
This accident happened on Route 7 near the present entrance to Bryant University. (JE.)

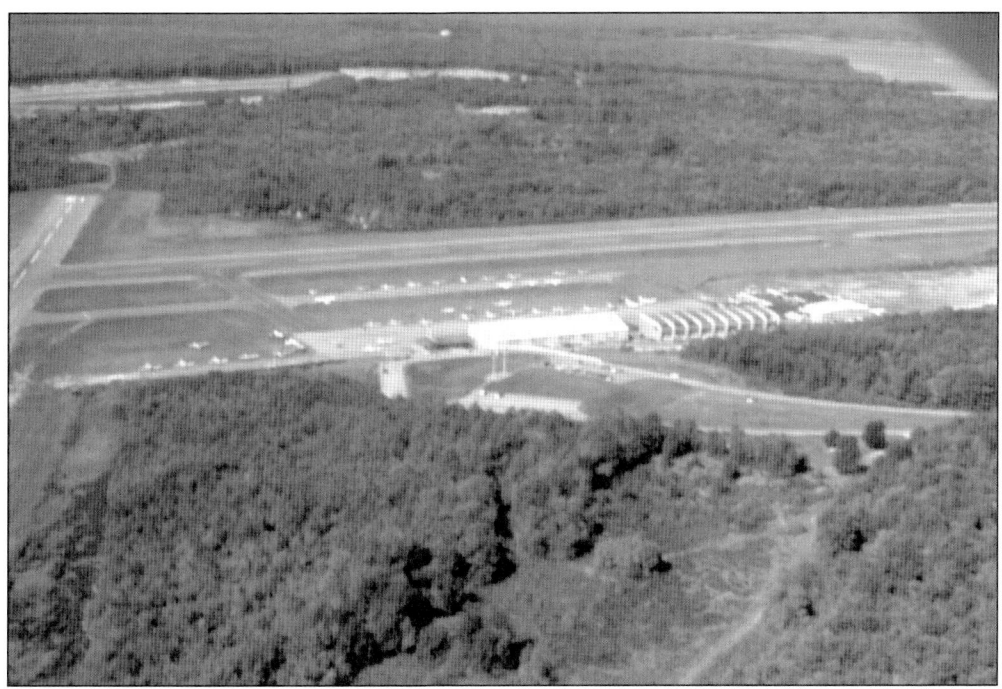
This aerial view of North Central State Airport was taken in 1974. At one time it was thought North Central might become as active as T. F. Greene in Warwick. (HSS.)

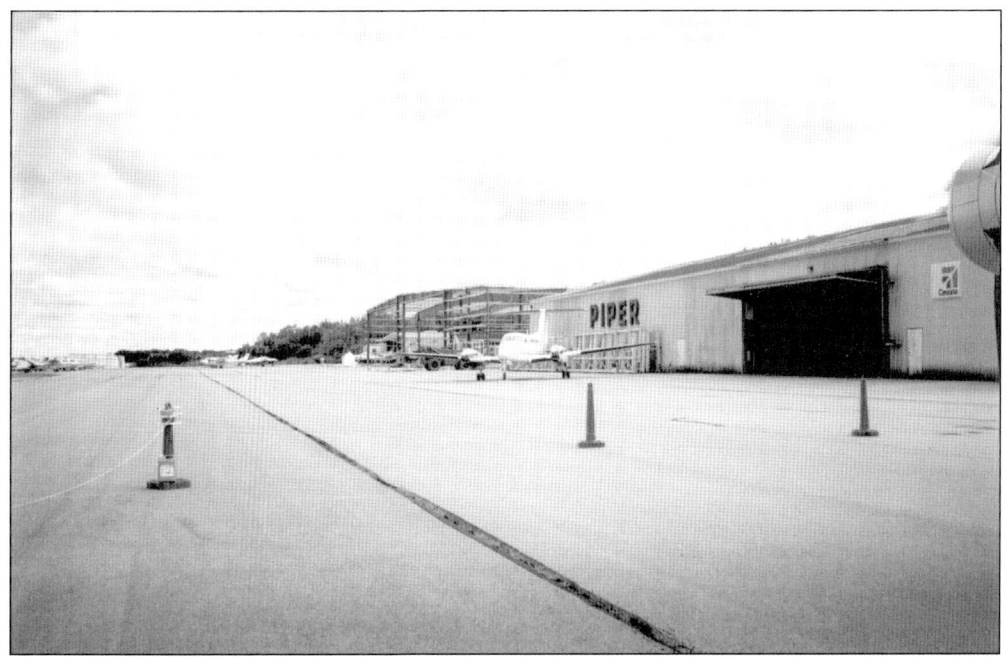
This view shows a new hangar under construction in 2004. (JI.)

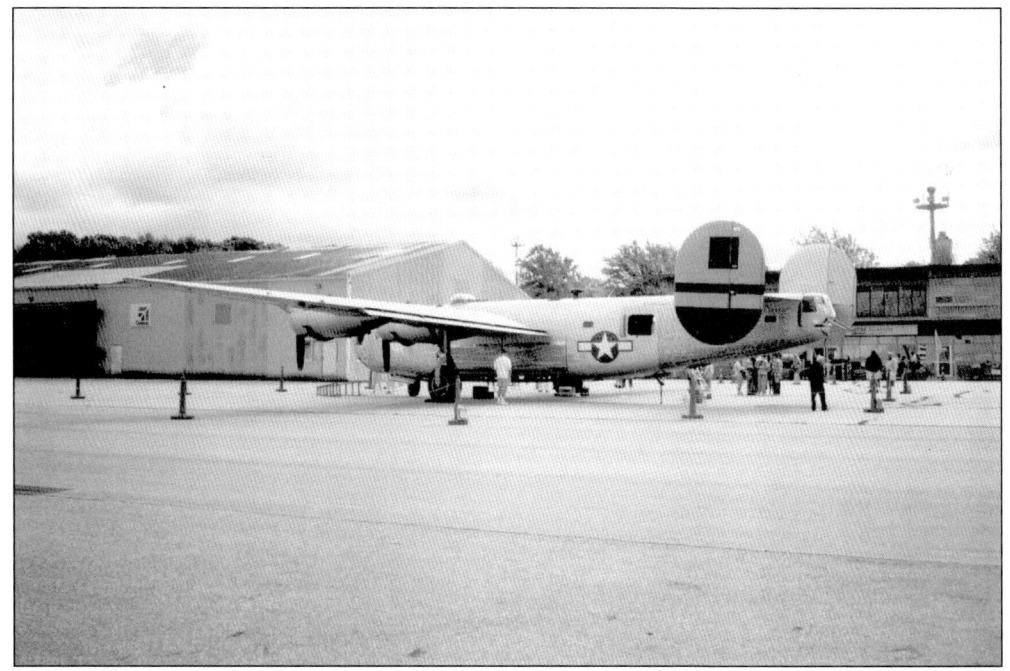
In September 2004, a restored World War II B-24 Liberator belonging to the Collings Foundation visited Smithfield. For a nominal fee, one could take a 30-minute ride in the vintage aircraft. (JI.)

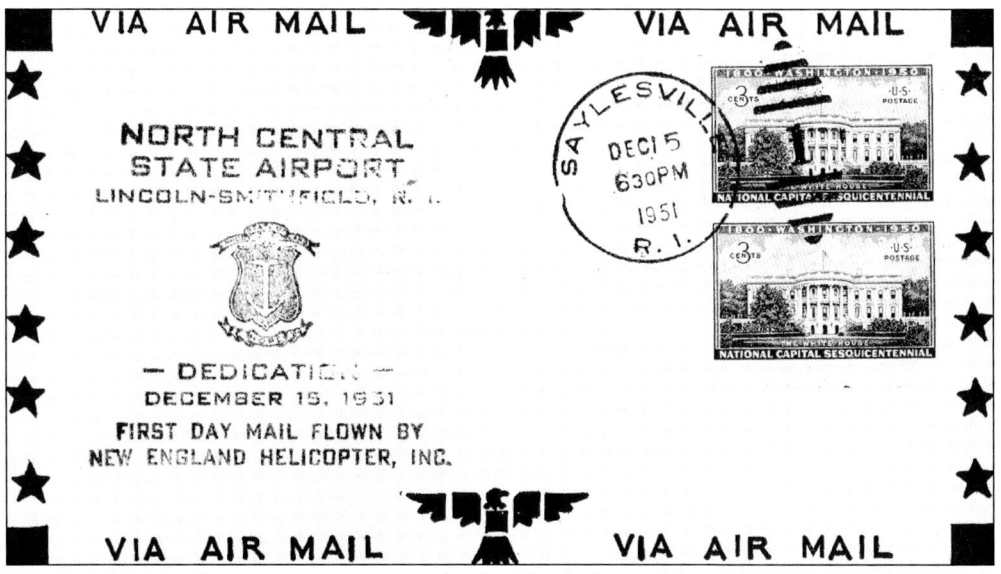
This first-day postal cover commemorates the day North Central State Airport officially opened, December 15, 1951. (TA.)

Eight
A Smithfield Photo Album

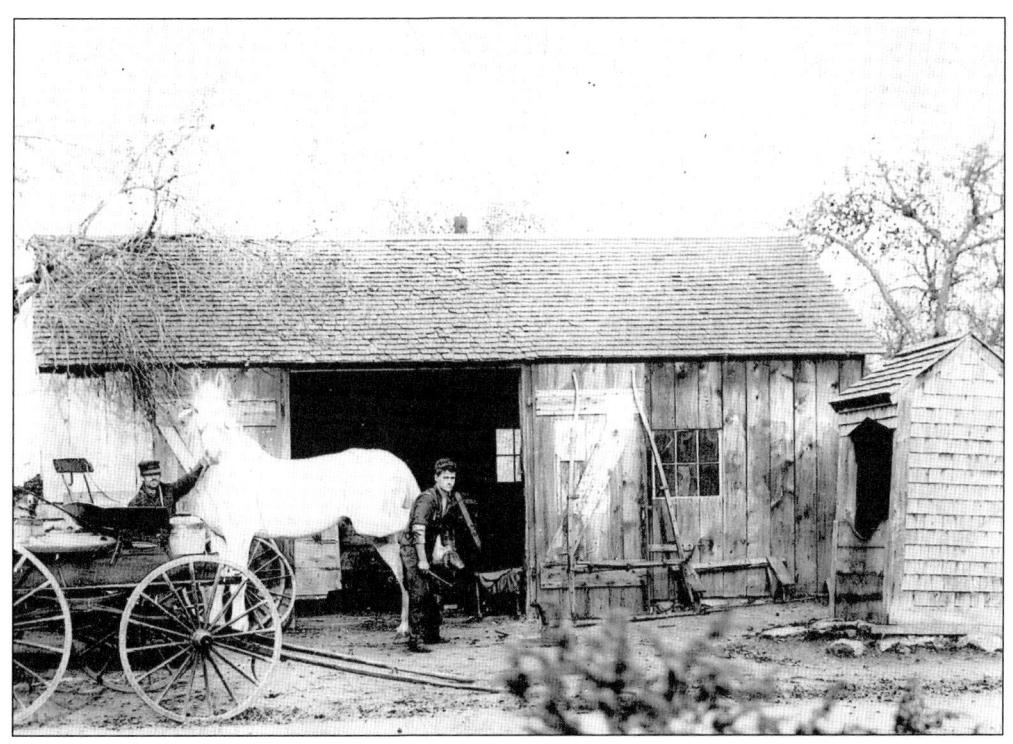

This photograph, taken about 1880, shows a blacksmith shop that once stood near the corner of Wolf Hill Road and Farnum Pike. (JE.)

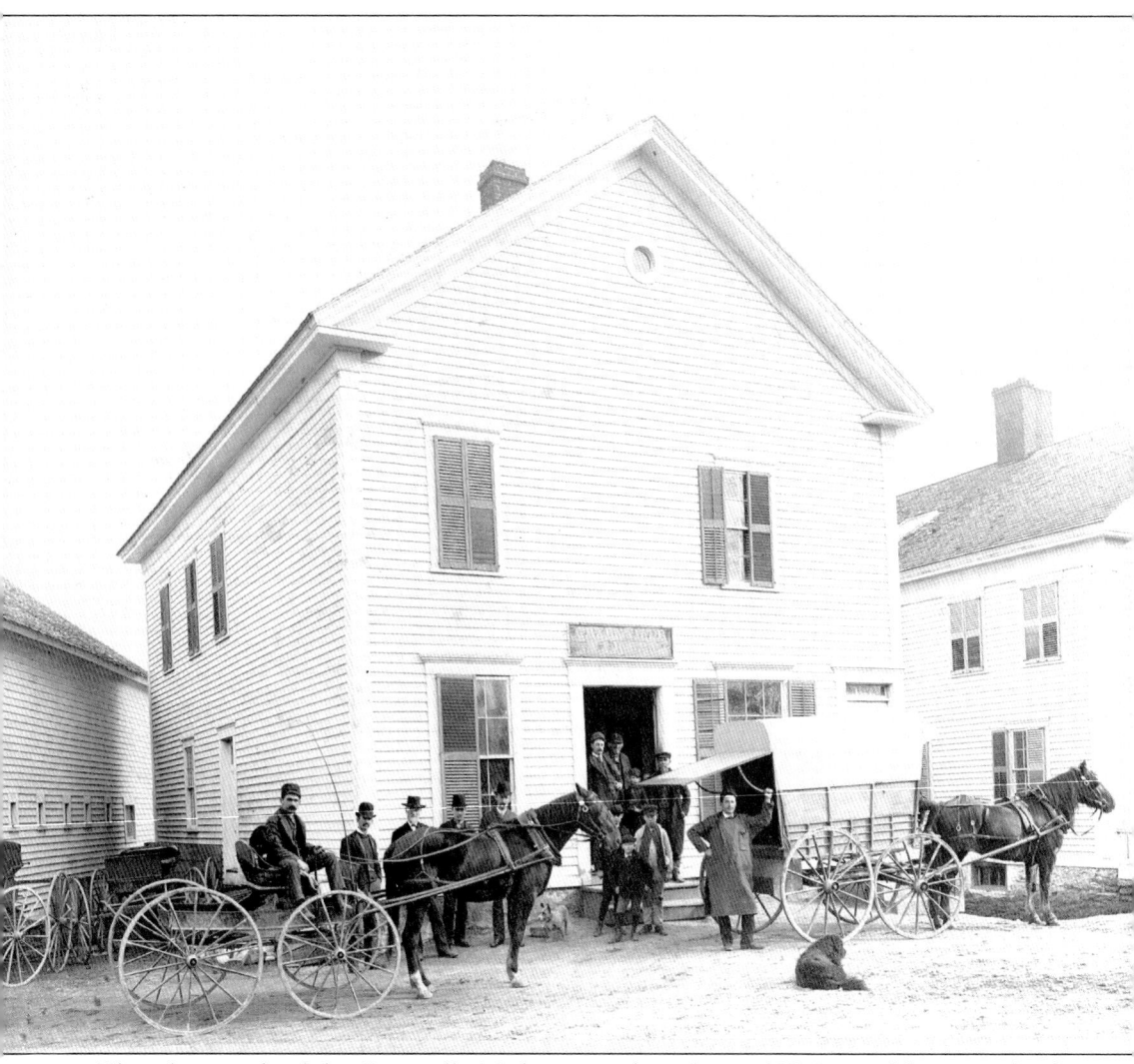

This photograph of the Greenville Market was taken about 1885. It stood between the first Masonic lodge (on the right) and a barn (on the left) on the corner of Austin Avenue and Putnam Pike. This building is still standing, but it has been substantially remodeled. (PH.)

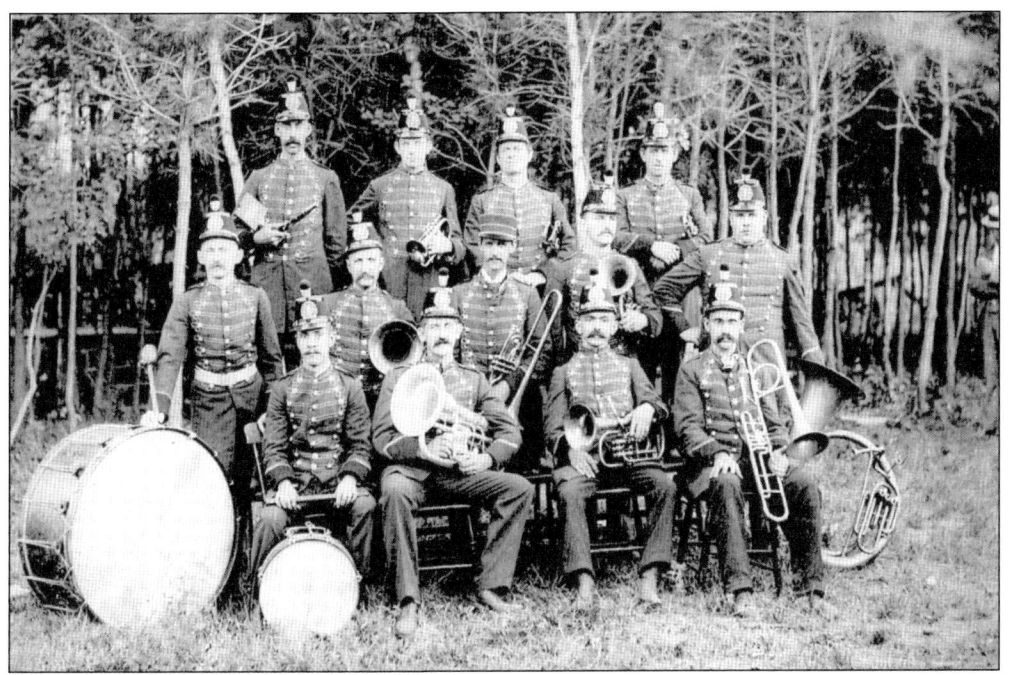

This is a photograph of the Greenville Cornet Band in 1890. (HSS.)

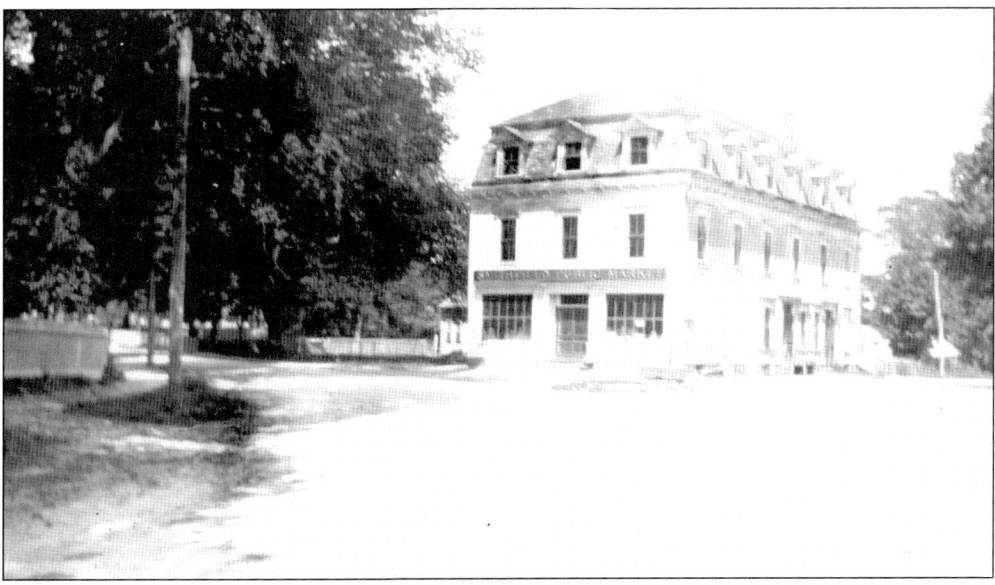

Wilkinson Hall once stood at Austin Avenue and Route 44. The first floor was a store, the second a Grange hall, and the third a dance hall. It was later replaced by a state garage in the 1920s. (PH.)

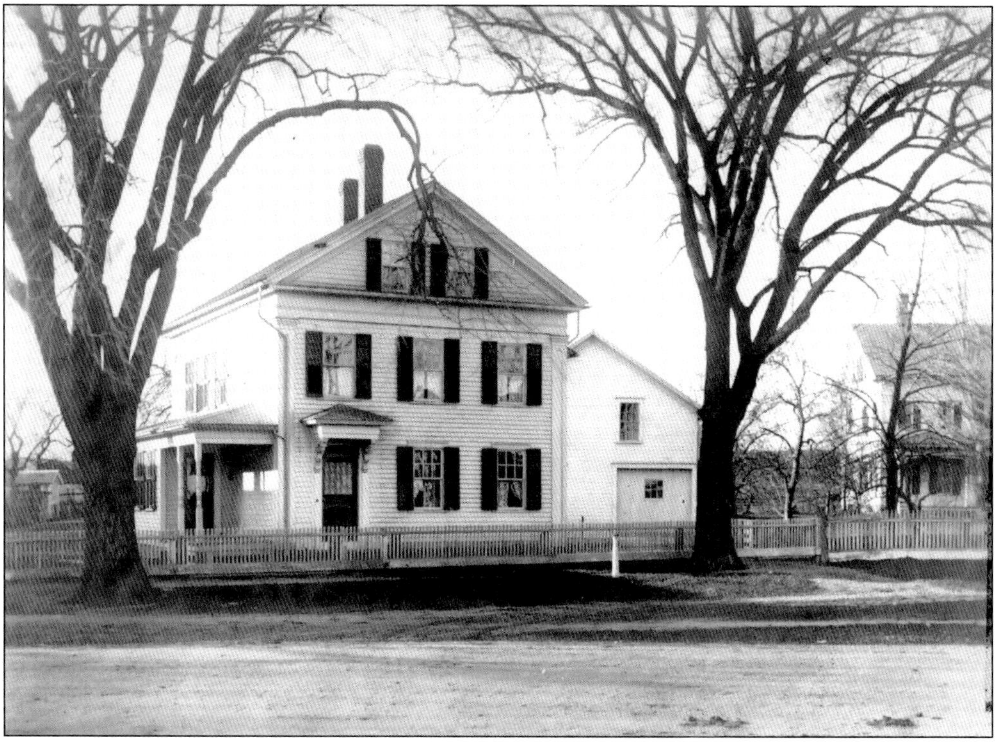

The Howard Hopkins House in Greenville stood between St. Thomas Church and the Winfield Funeral Home. Today a parking lot occupies this spot. (PH.)

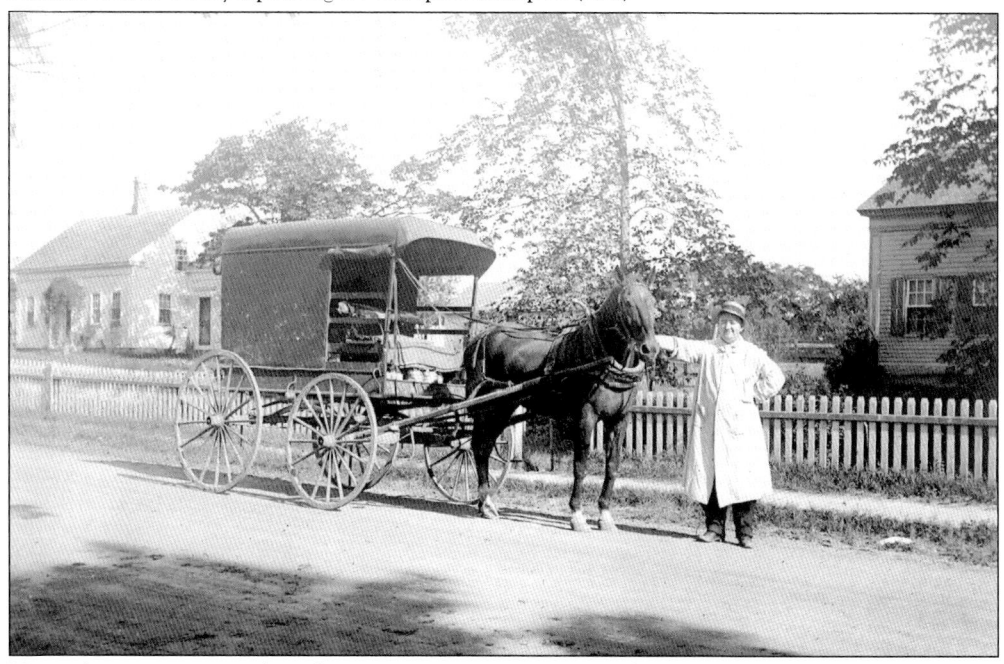

Horse-drawn wagons such as this one were once common sights around Smithfield. This picture was taken on Putnam Pike in Greenville just west of Austin Avenue. A shopping center now stands where the houses were. (PH.)

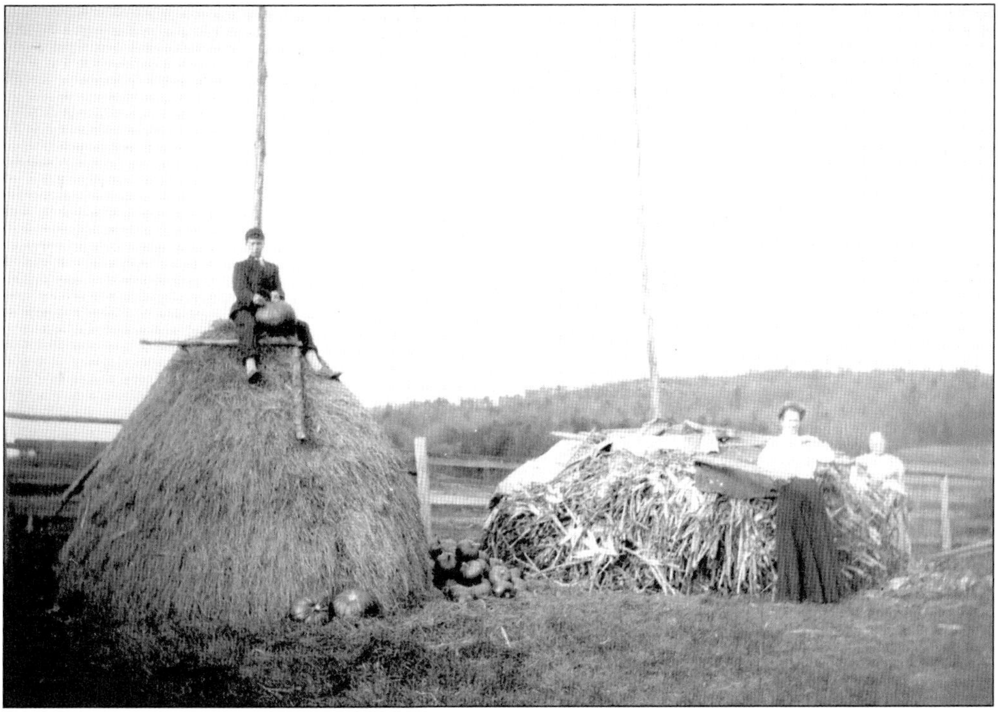

This interesting photograph was taken at harvest time at the Appleby Farm in Stillwater. (Note the pumpkins at the base of the haystack.) (HSS.)

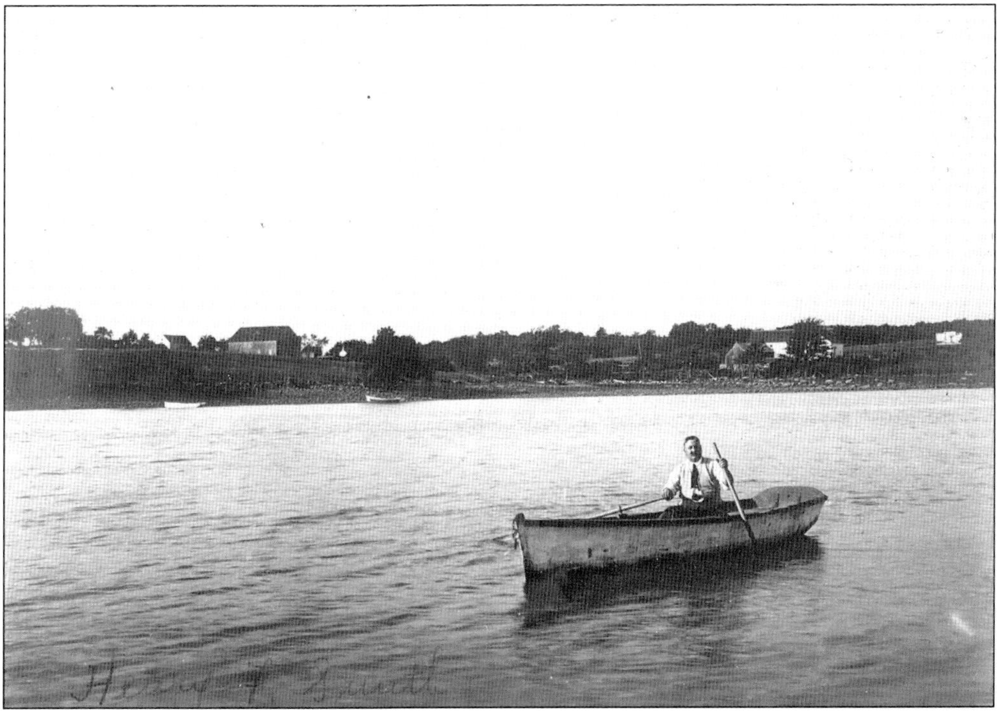

Before the days of outboard motors and jet skis, people enjoyed quiet boating on Waterman's Lake by using oars and sails. (PH.)

89

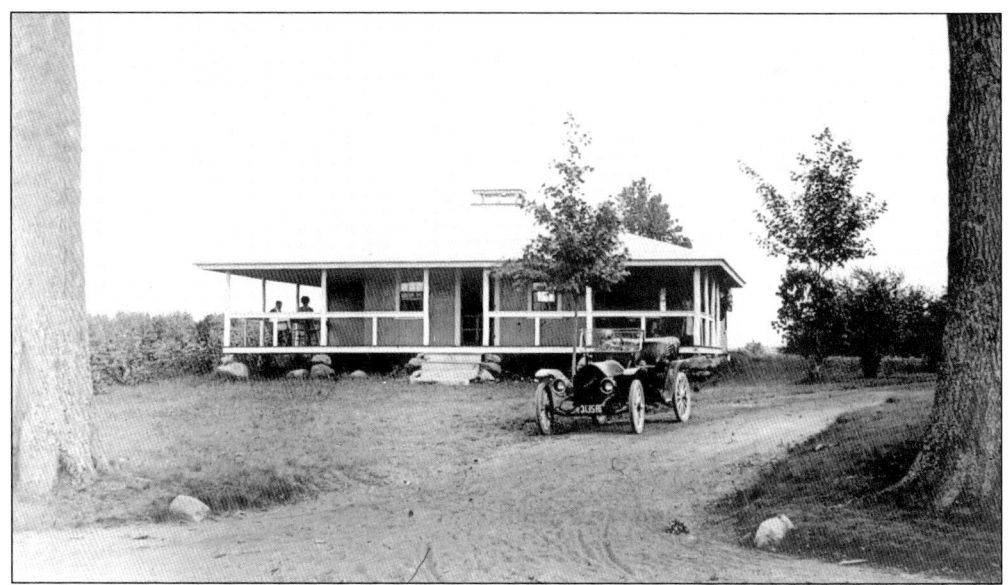

Frank Gavitt's Ice Cream Parlor was the first ice-cream shop in Greenville. At Christmas he sold ribbon candy. The shop stood on Putnam Pike across from West Prospect Street where a retail business is today. (PH.)

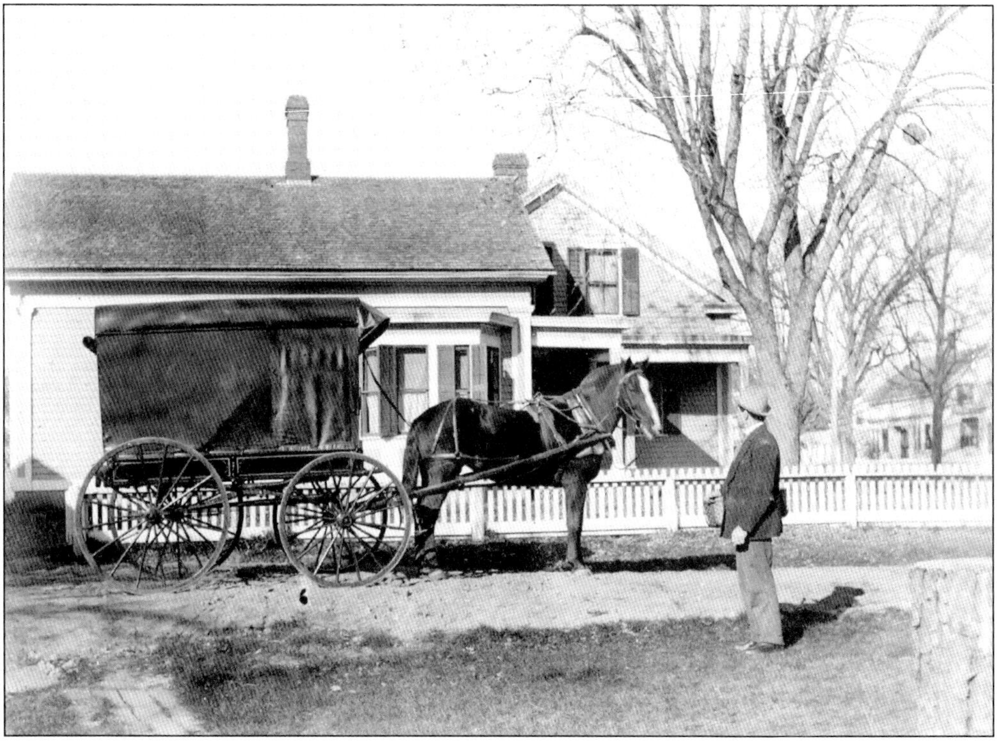

This was Oscar A. Tobey's delivery wagon parked next to the house at 594 Putnam Pike in Greenville. The house is still standing today. Tobey owned a general store in Greenville for many years. The man in the photograph is Harold Tobey Smith. Smith took some of the photographs seen in this book. (PH.)

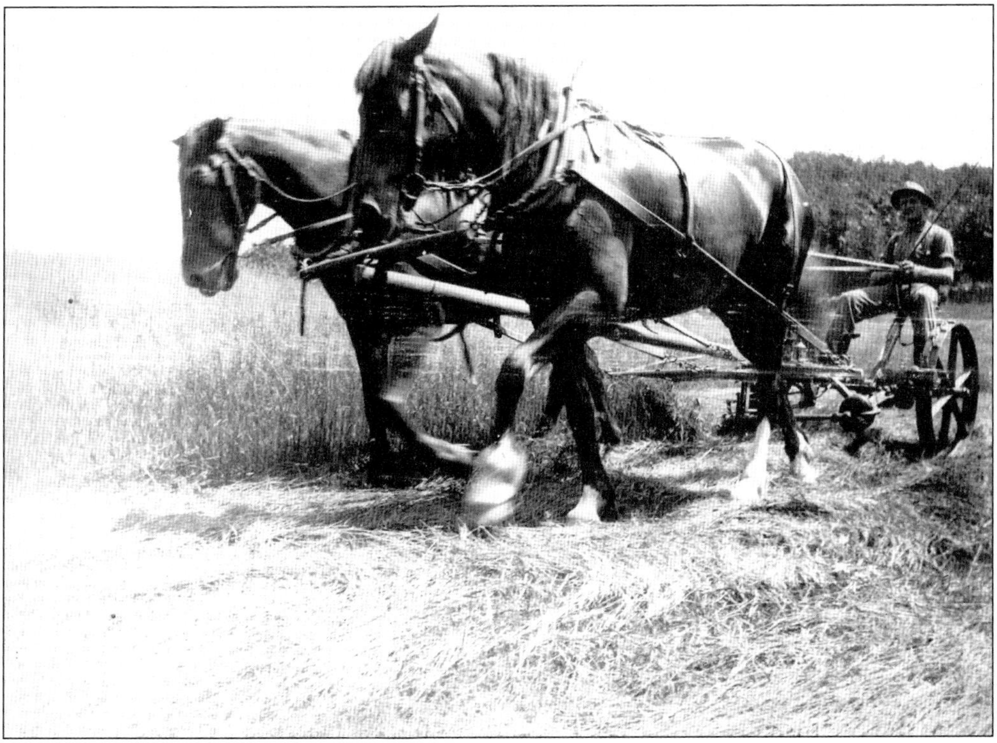

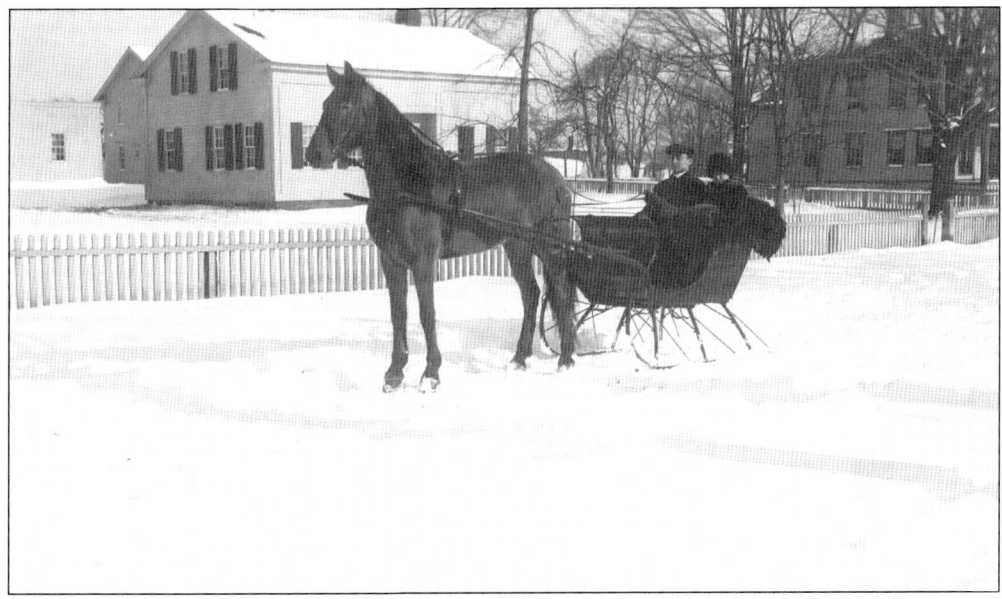

This photograph shows a farmer reaping hay in Stillwater around 1895. (HSS.)

Before snowplows and road salt cleared snowbound streets in the winter, the quickest mode of transportation was by sleigh. By spring, the melting snow turned the unpaved roads into a muddy morass. (PH.)

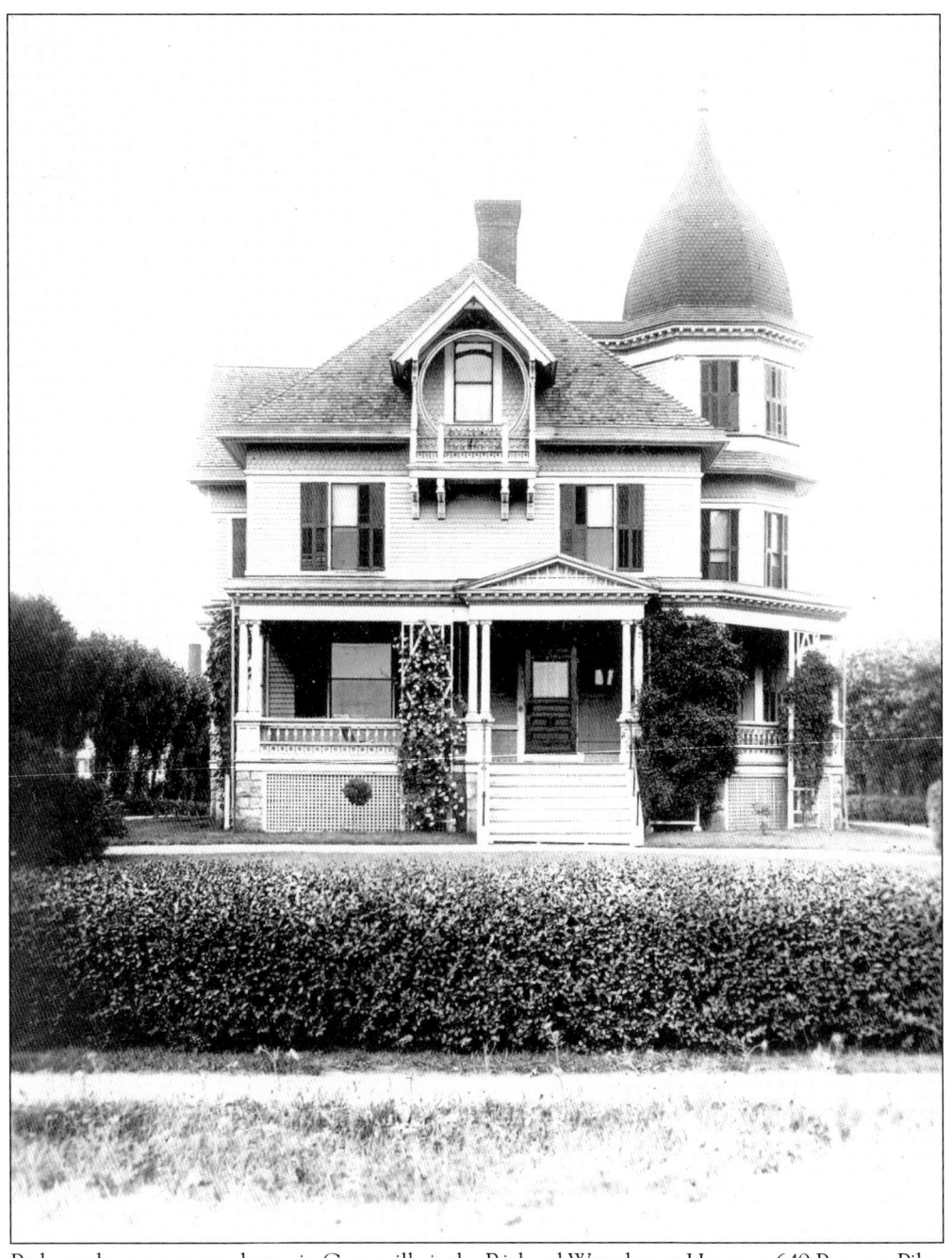
Perhaps the most ornate home in Greenville is the Richard Waterhouse House at 649 Putnam Pike. Today it is better known as the former Tucker-Quinn Funeral Home. The Queen Anne–styled house is considered one of Smithfield's architectural gems. (PH.)

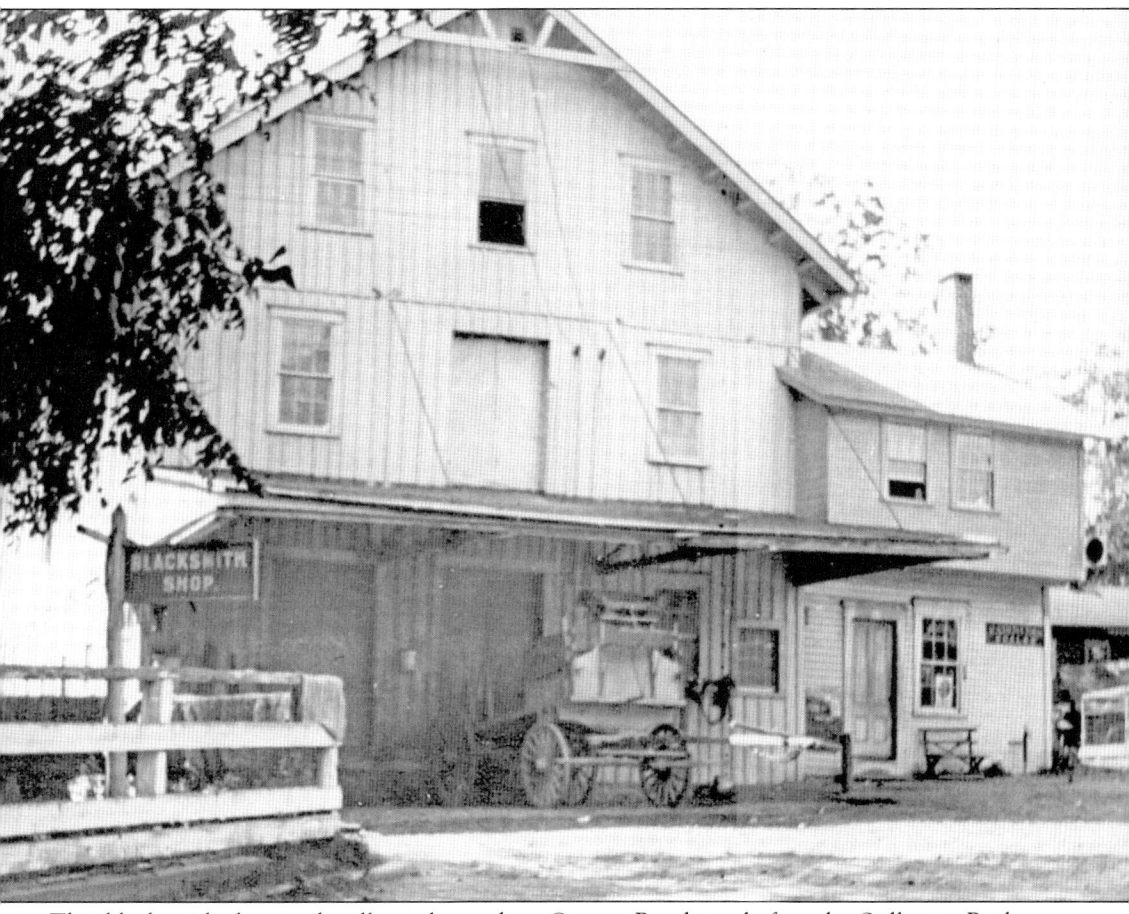

This blacksmith shop and mill was located on Capron Road just before the Stillwater Bridge. Even though the automobile began to slowly replace the horse and buggy, many local farmers still required the services of a blacksmith well into the 20th century. (JC.)

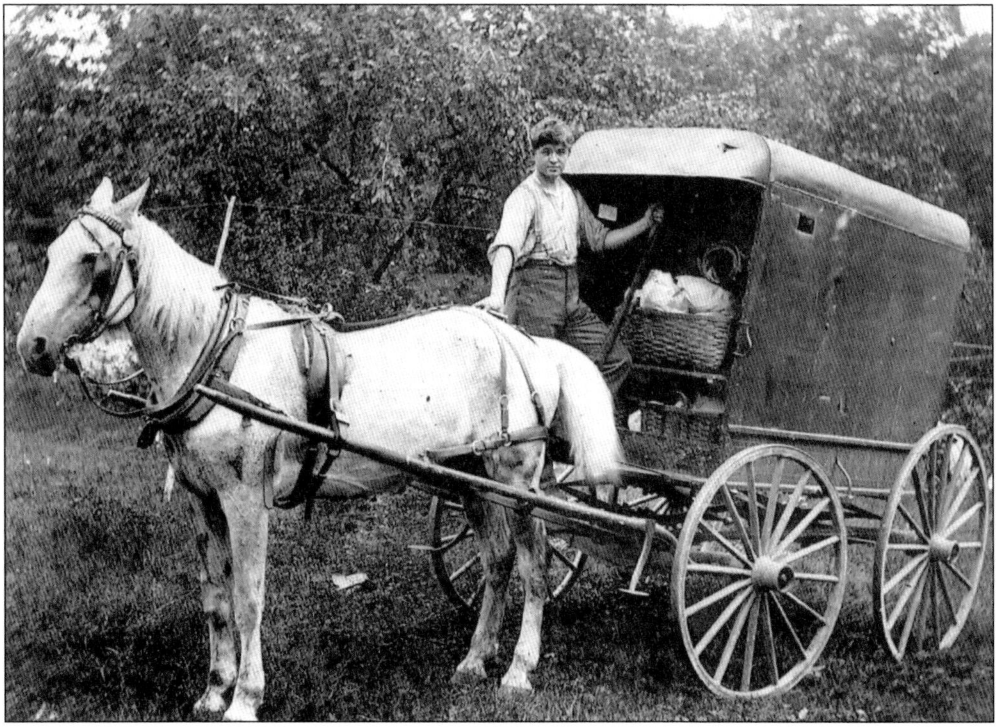

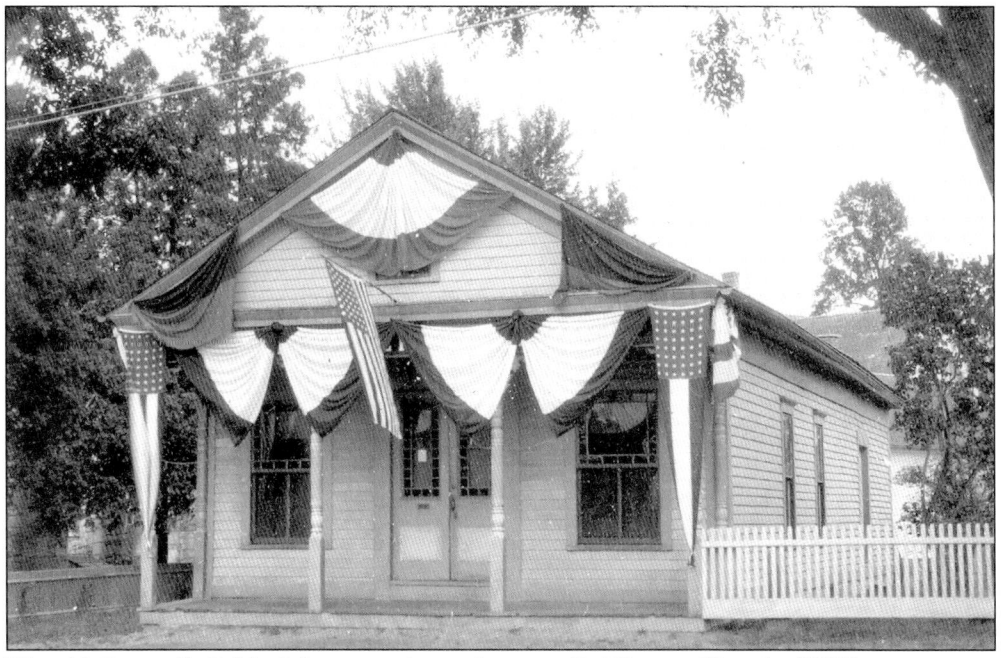

Leander Emin used this wagon to deliver groceries from the general store in Stillwater in 1900. Today the store is a day care center. (JE.)

The old Greenville Public Library was located next to St. Thomas Church. (WK.)

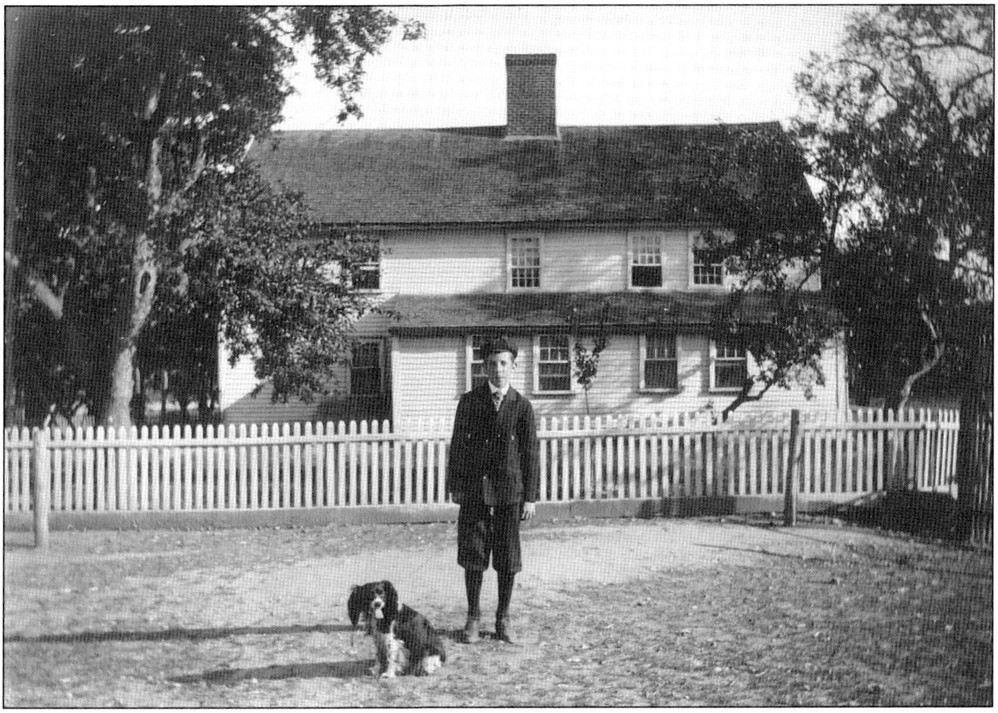

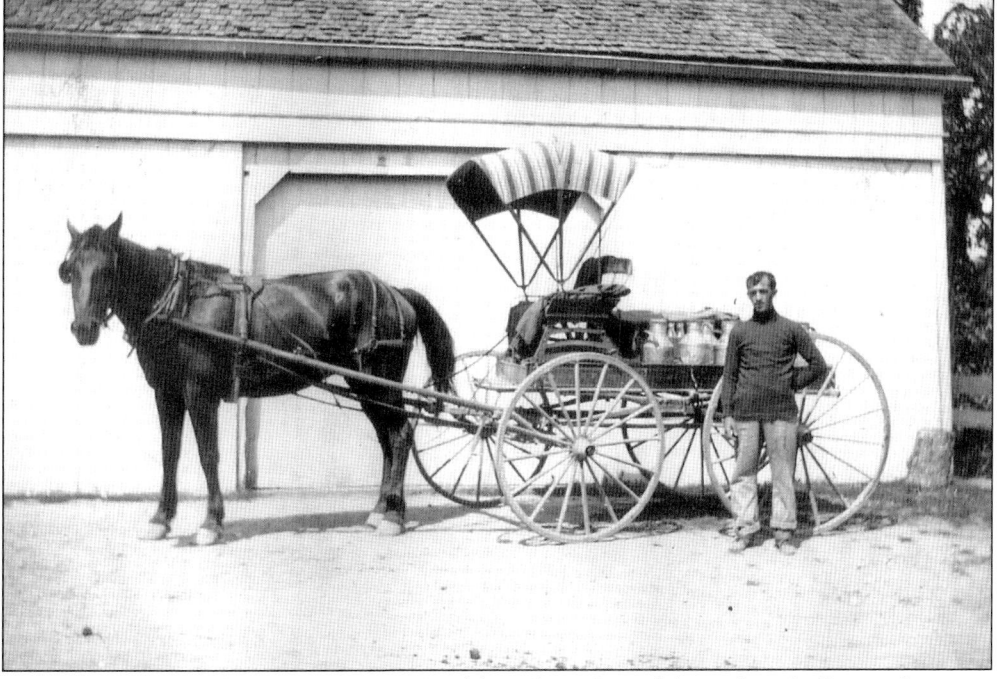

This photograph shows the Smith-Appleby House as it looked around 1905. The oldest part of the house dates from 1698. Today the house serves as the headquarters for the Historical Society of Smithfield and is Smithfield's only museum. (HSS.)

This milk wagon belonging to Maria Appleby's dairy farm delivered in Stillwater for many years. (HSS.)

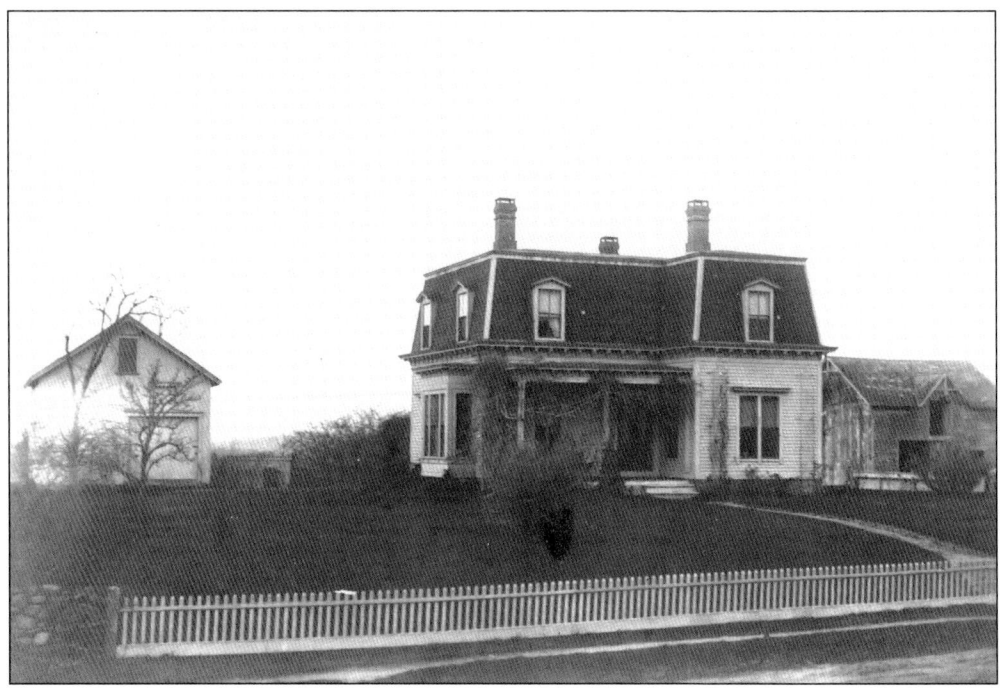
The Oscar A. Tobey House on Route 44 dates from about 1885. Tobey was the Smithfield town clerk from 1871 to 1917, a time span of 46 years. To date, he is Smithfield's longest-serving town clerk. (PH.)

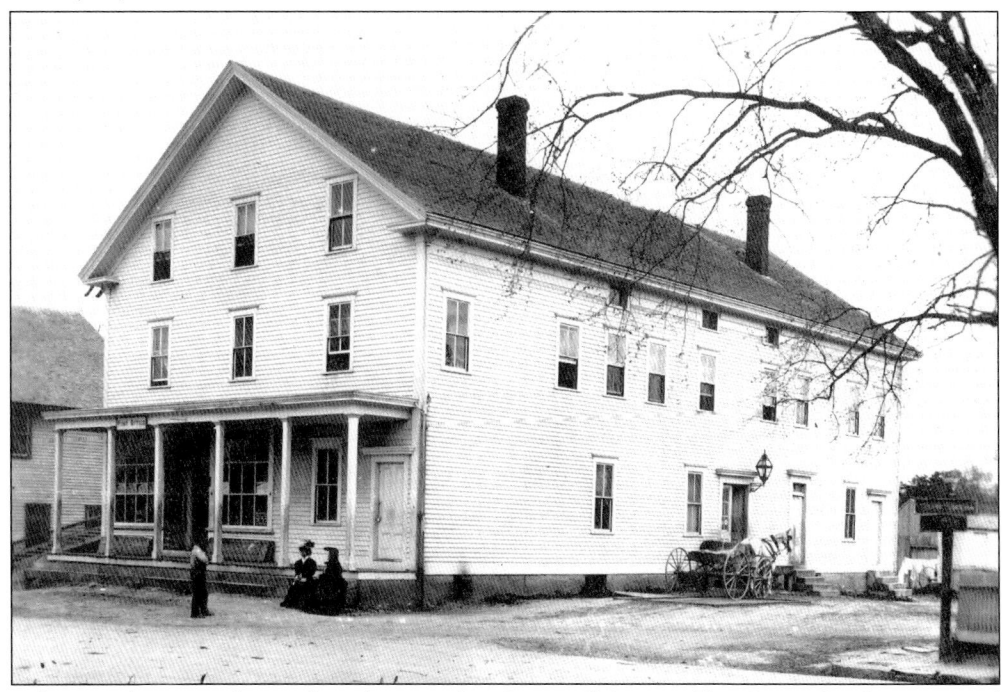
Tobey ran this general store that also served as Greenville's post office. It stood at Route 44 and Smith Avenue. While Tobey was the town clerk, town offices and records were located here. On February 2, 1924, it was destroyed by fire. (PH.)

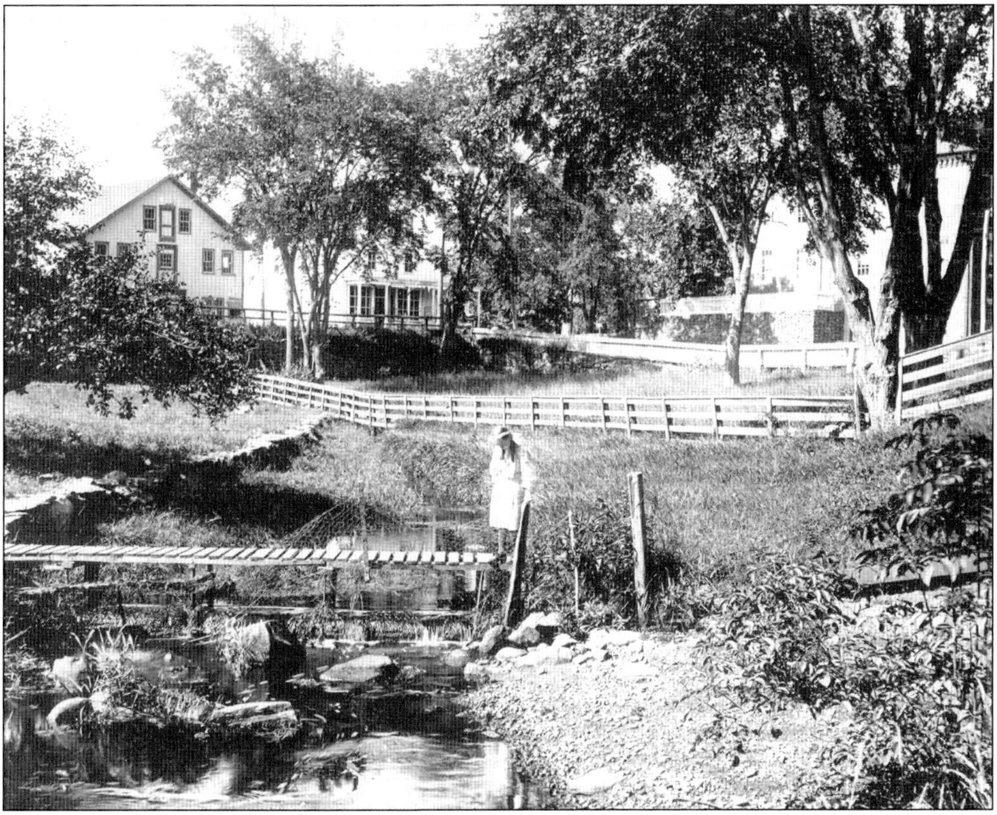

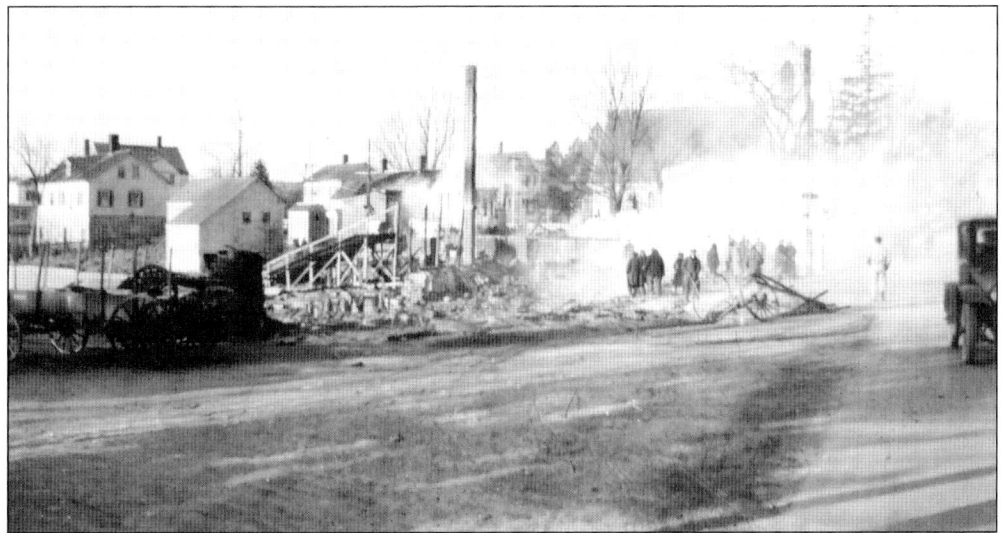

This summer landscape was photographed behind the old Smithfield Exchange Bank that is visible in the upper right of this photograph. The building in the upper left was the A. B. and W. A. Whipple Carriage Shop that burned in the early 1920s. The girl in the picture is J. Ethelyn Smith-Winsor. (PH.)

On February 2, 1924, the fire that destroyed Tobey's General Store also destroyed the old Whipple Carriage Shop in Greenville. (SFD.)

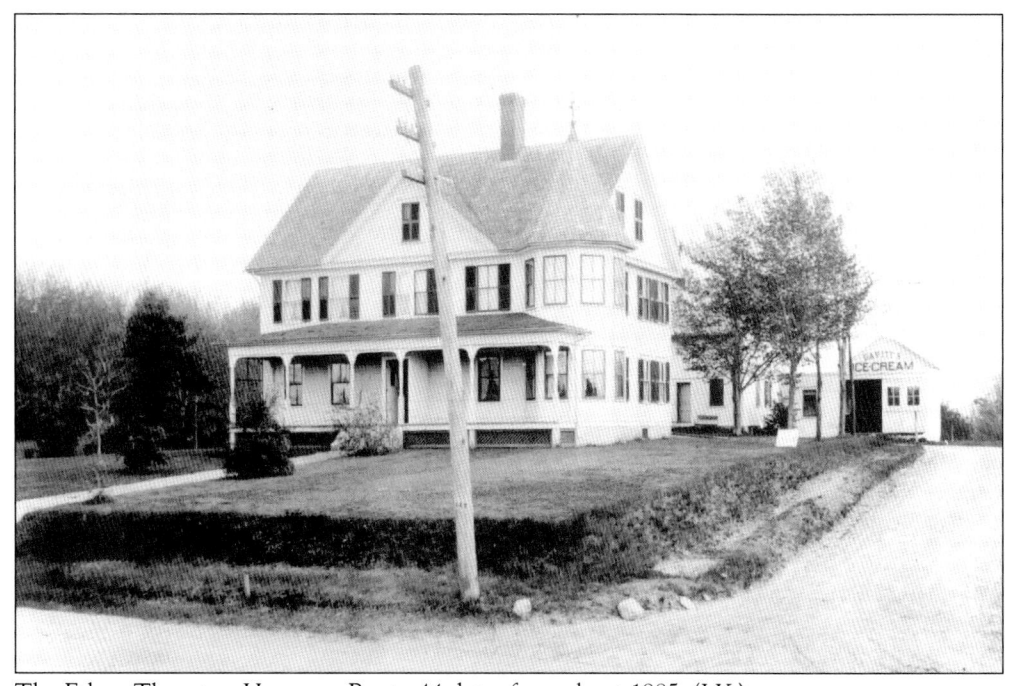

The Ethan Thornton House on Route 44 dates from about 1885. (LK.)

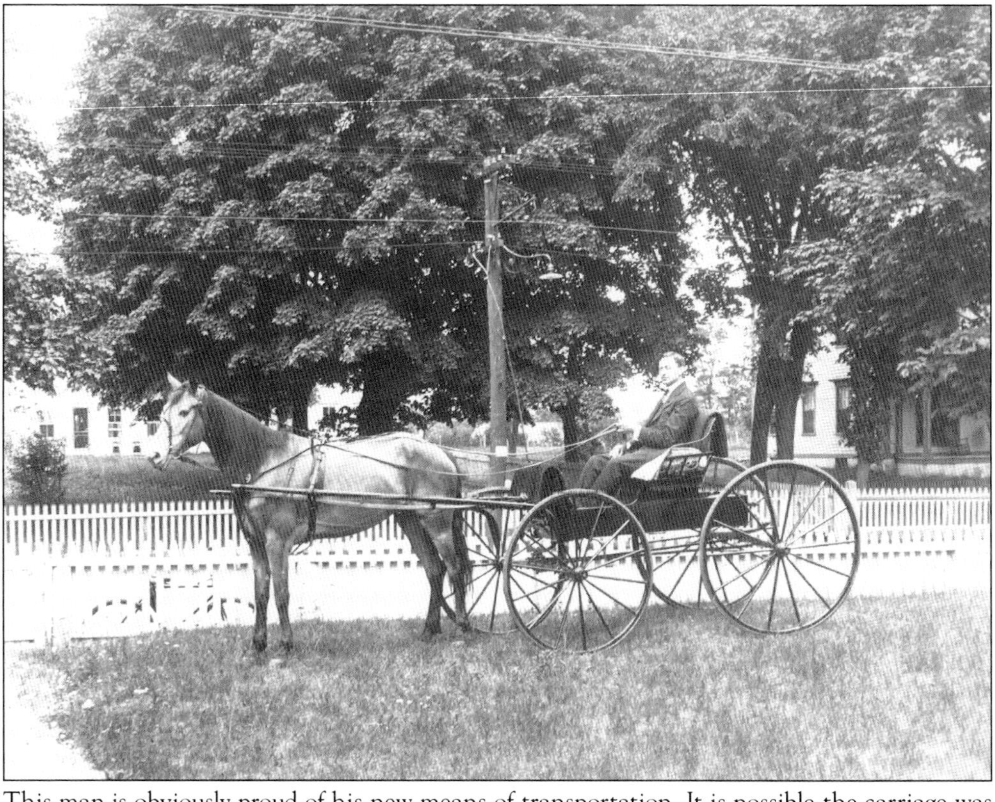

This man is obviously proud of his new means of transportation. It is possible the carriage was made in Greenville at A. B. and W. A. Whipple's shop. (PH.)

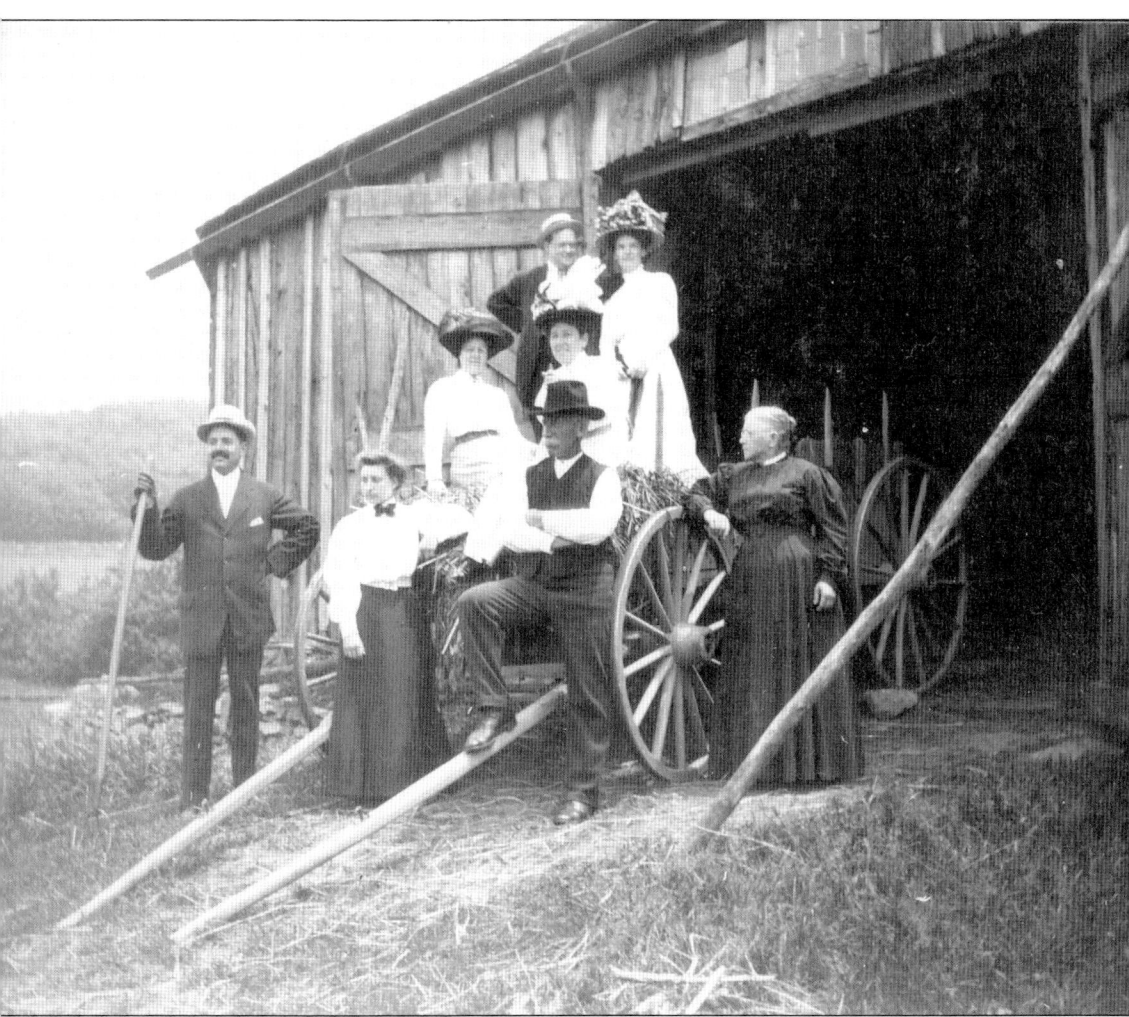

Maria Appleby, shown standing in front of the wagon, was a very industrious woman. She single-handedly built and operated Smithfield's only golf course in the 1920s. Known as the Stillwater Country Club, the golf course operated until the 1950s and was located where Route 295 crosses Stillwater Road today. (HSS.)

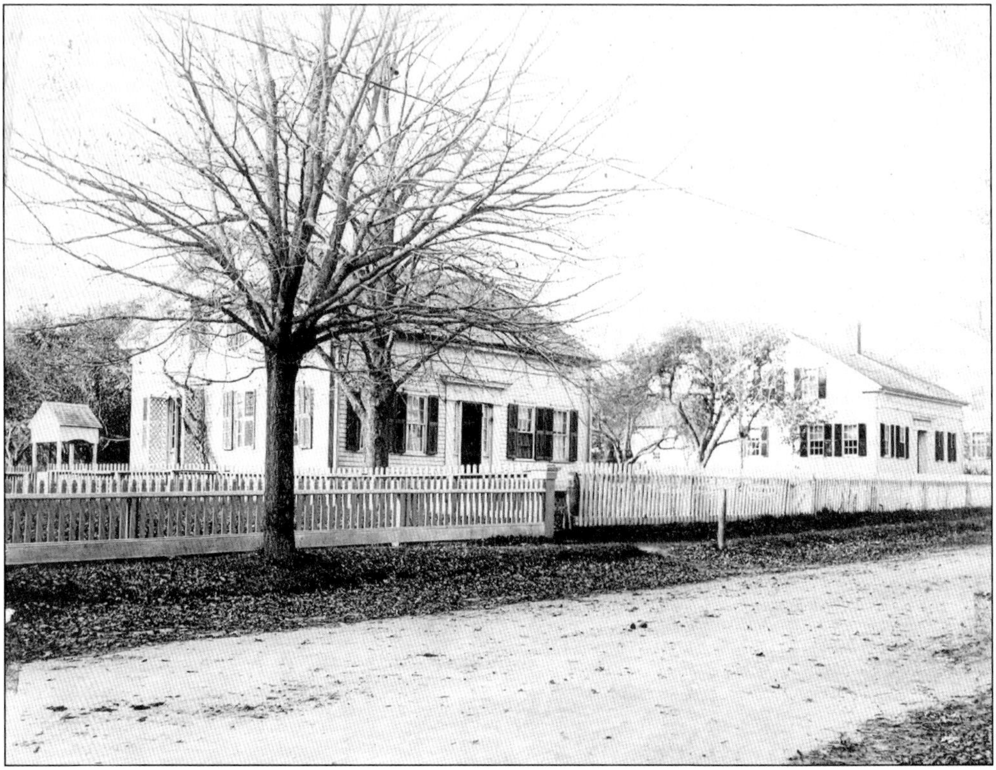

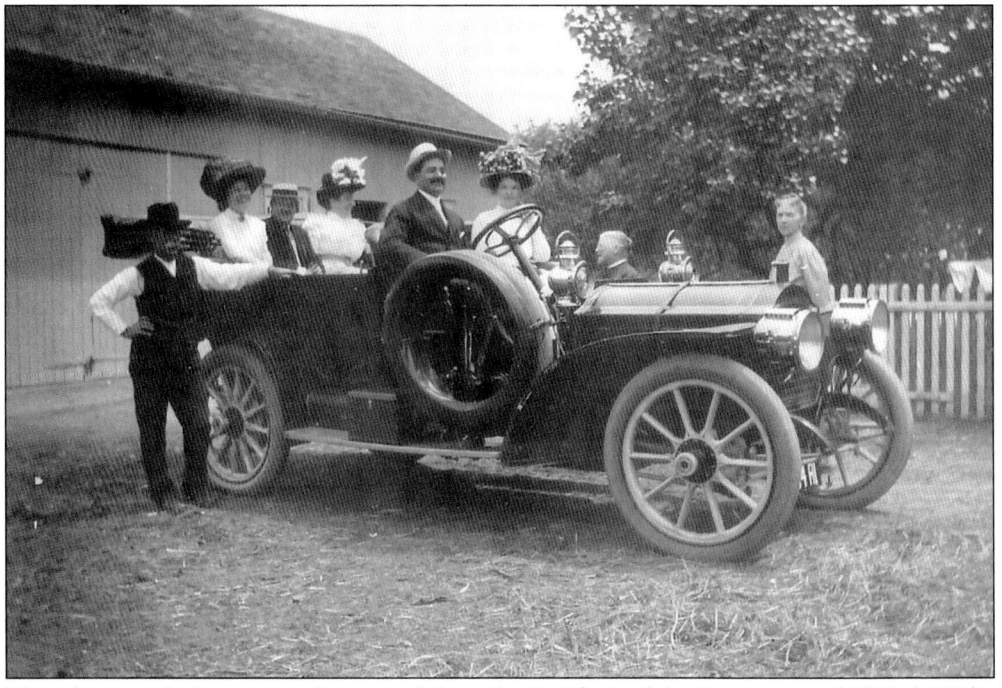

These houses on Route 44 in Greenville no longer exist. The last one was torn down in 2005. Today a commercial building occupies where they stood. (PH.)

This photograph shows an early automobile at the Smith-Appleby House around 1915. (HSS.)

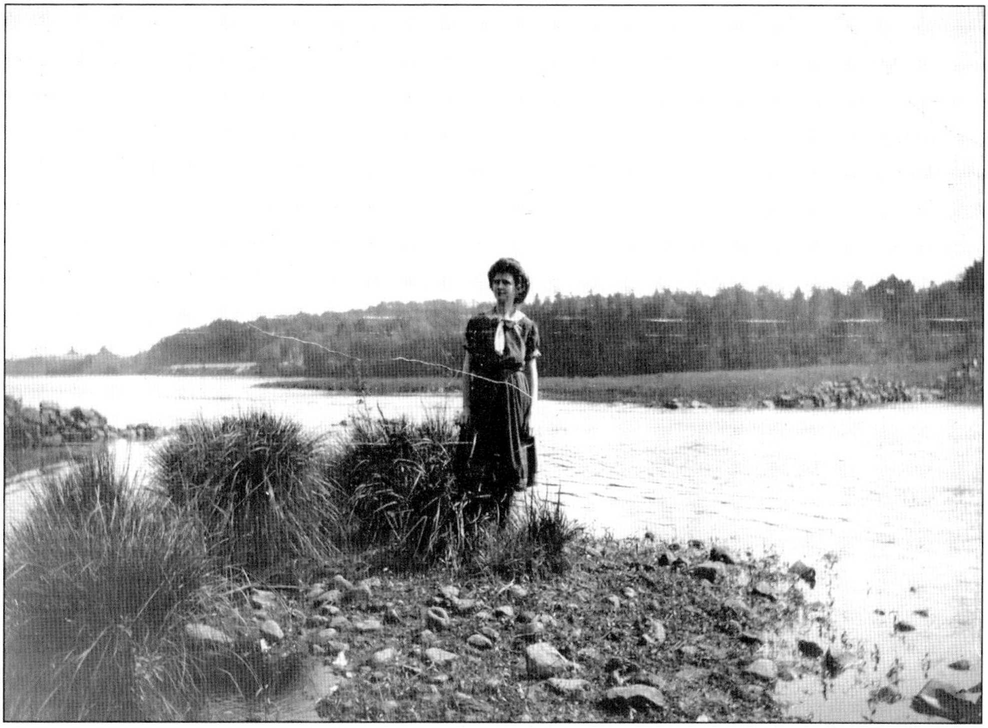

This photograph shows Stillwater resident Abbie E. Sargeant (1879–1963) standing on the shore of Georgiaville Pond around 1900 wearing a bating suit of the era. (HSS.)

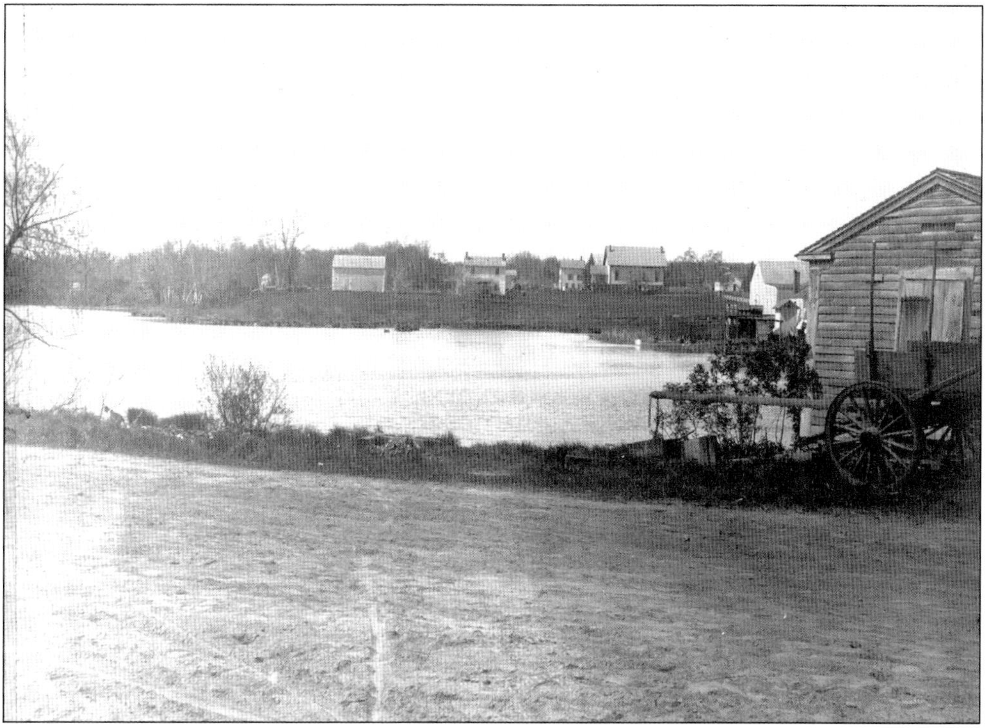

This is Hawkins Pond in Greenville as it looked from Greenville Avenue about 1905. (PH.)

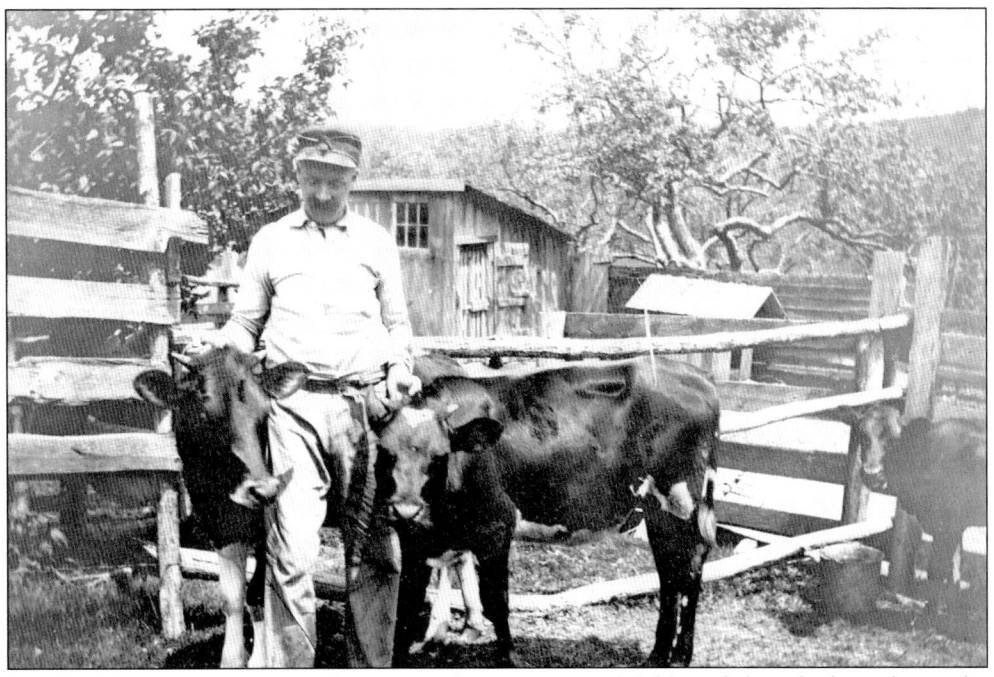

Dairy farming was once a thriving industry in Smithfield and lasted throughout the 20th century. The last dairy farm in Smithfield was Niles Dairy on Lime Rock Road. It closed in 1999. (HSS.)

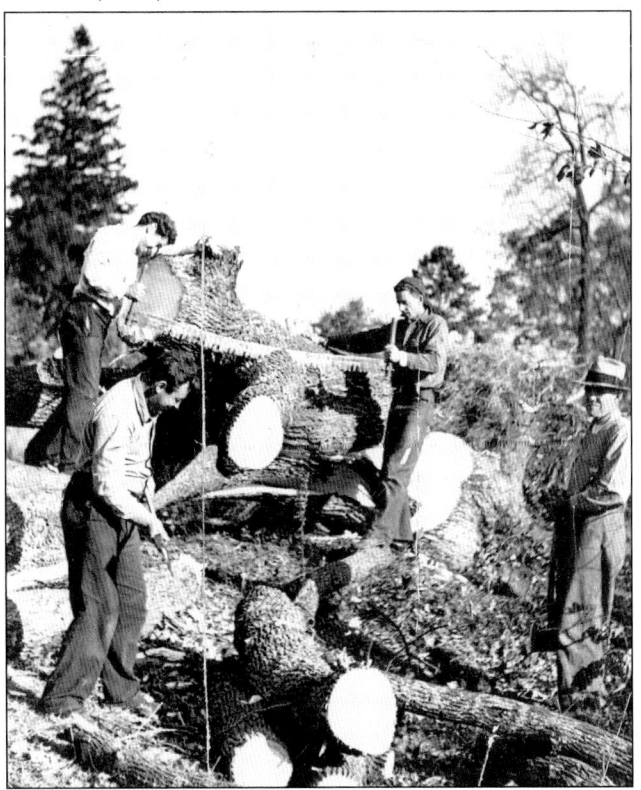

Woodcutting and logging was very important to Smithfield at a time when wood was used for virtually everything from building materials and wagons to cooking and heating. Even early automobiles had wood frames. Many residents owned wood lots, land used exclusively for logging. The work was hard and dangerous, but it was steady. (WK.)

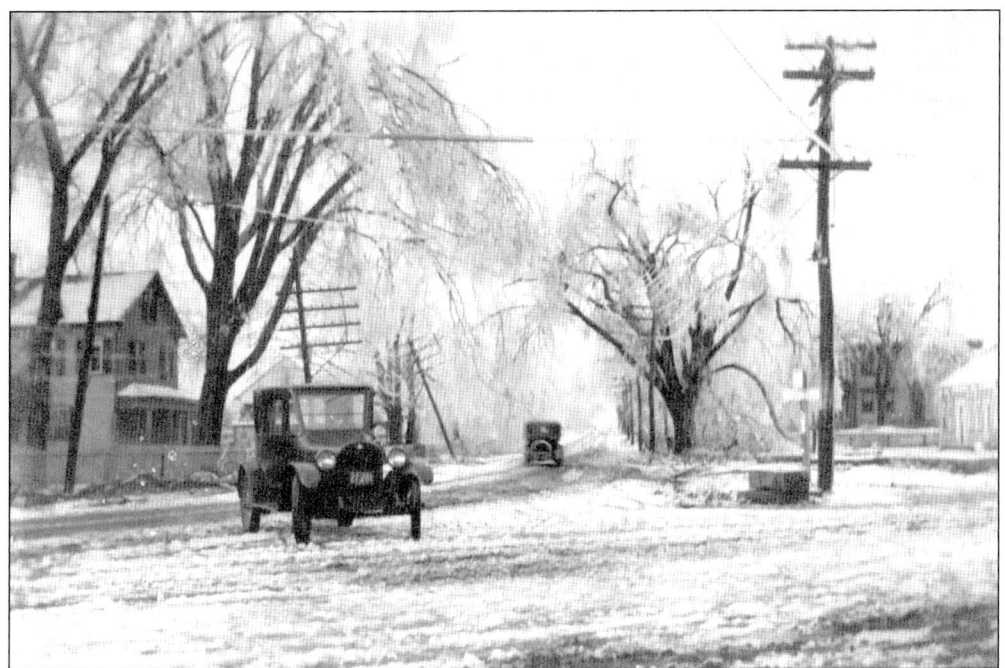

On December 6 and 7, 1921, a severe ice storm struck the area. This photograph was taken in Greenville Center looking west on Putnam Pike. (HSS.)

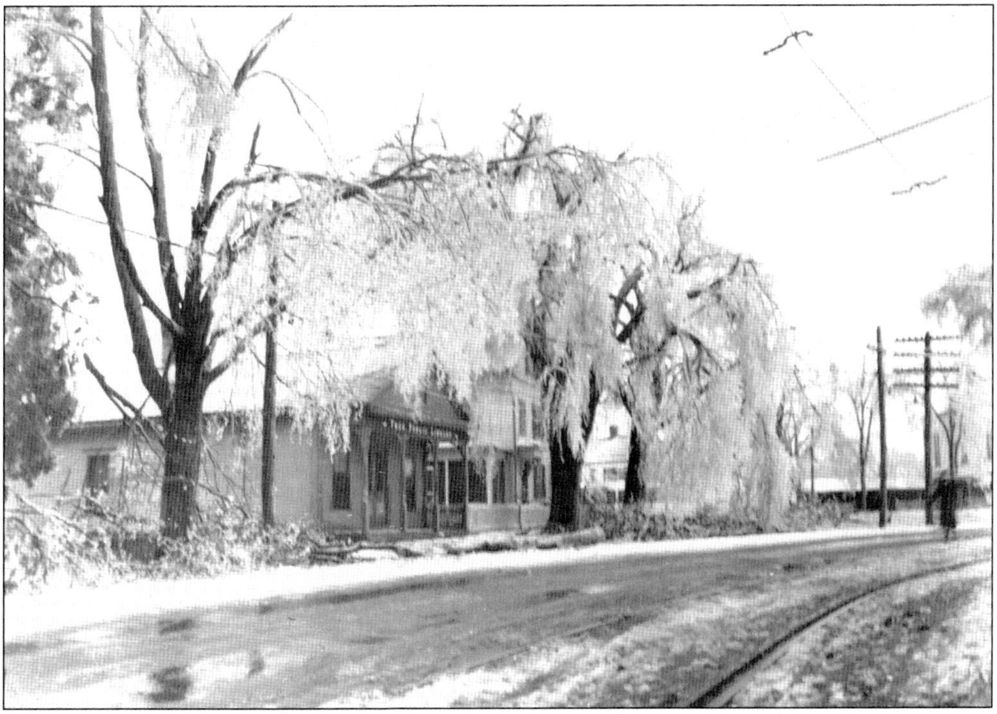

This view of Route 44 after the 1921 ice storm shows the Greenville Public Library and the Hopkins House on the left. (PH.)

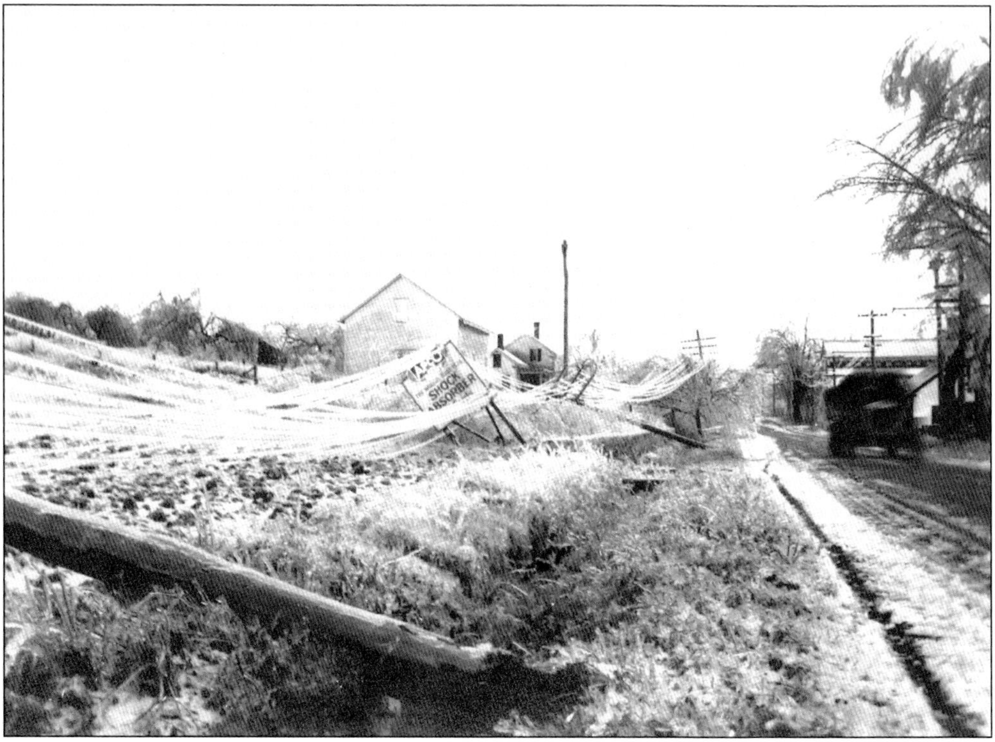

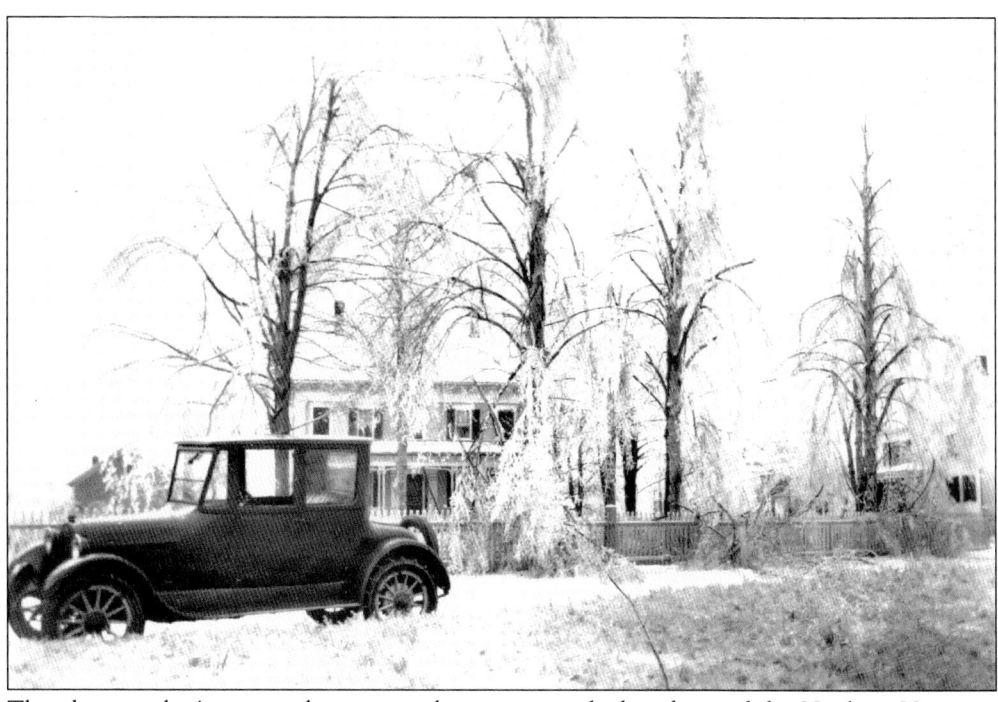

The ice pulled down power lines on Route 44 west of Greenville Center. (PH.)

The photographer's car can be seen in this picture parked in front of the Hopkins House in Greenville. (PH.)

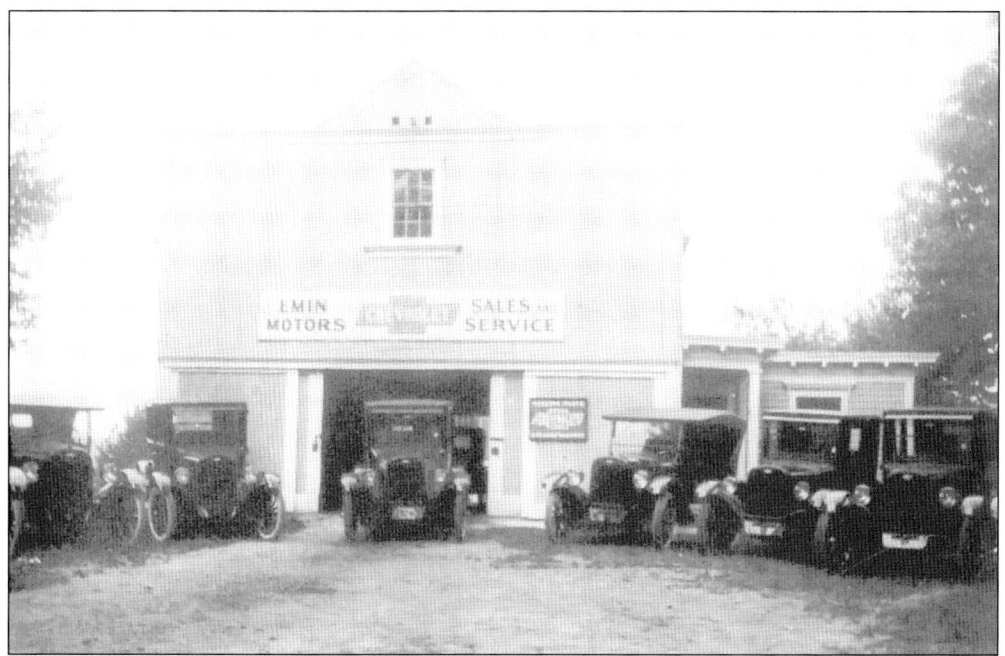

Emin Motors is said to have been the first Chevrolet dealership in Rhode Island. It was located on Farnum Pike near the town hall. (KD.)

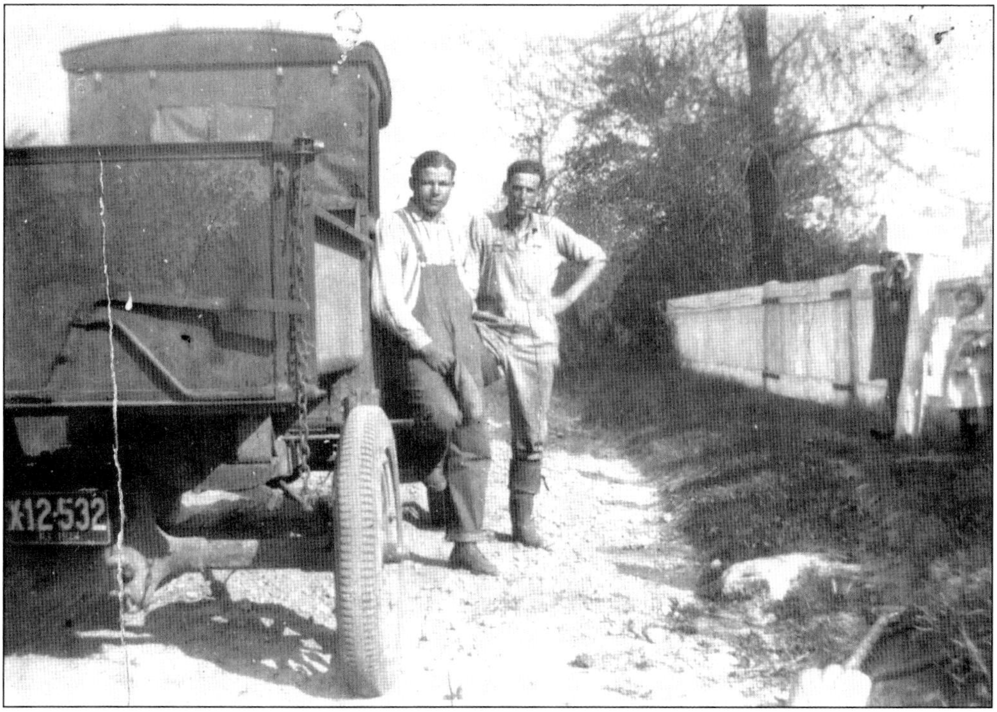

This photograph, taken on May 22, 1924, shows an early Department of Public Works truck. Many Smithfield roads of the era were still dirt or hard-packed gravel that needed constant attention. Rains caused washouts, and melting snow in the spring turned roads into impassible mud. (CS.)

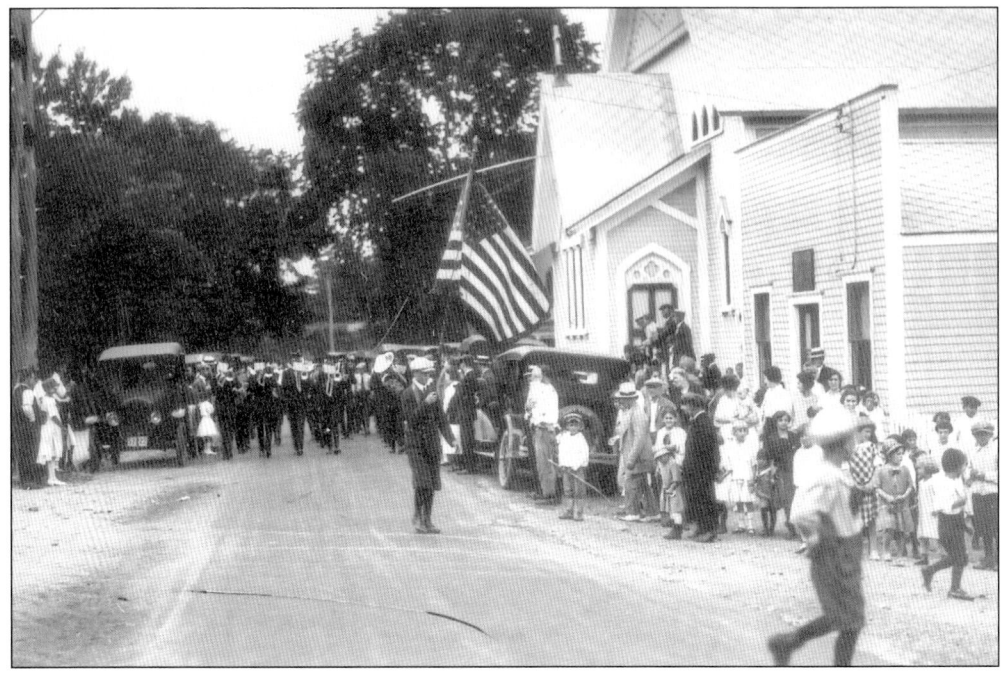

This view shows a street scene in front of the old St. Michael's Church on Homestead Avenue during the 1920s. (AS.)

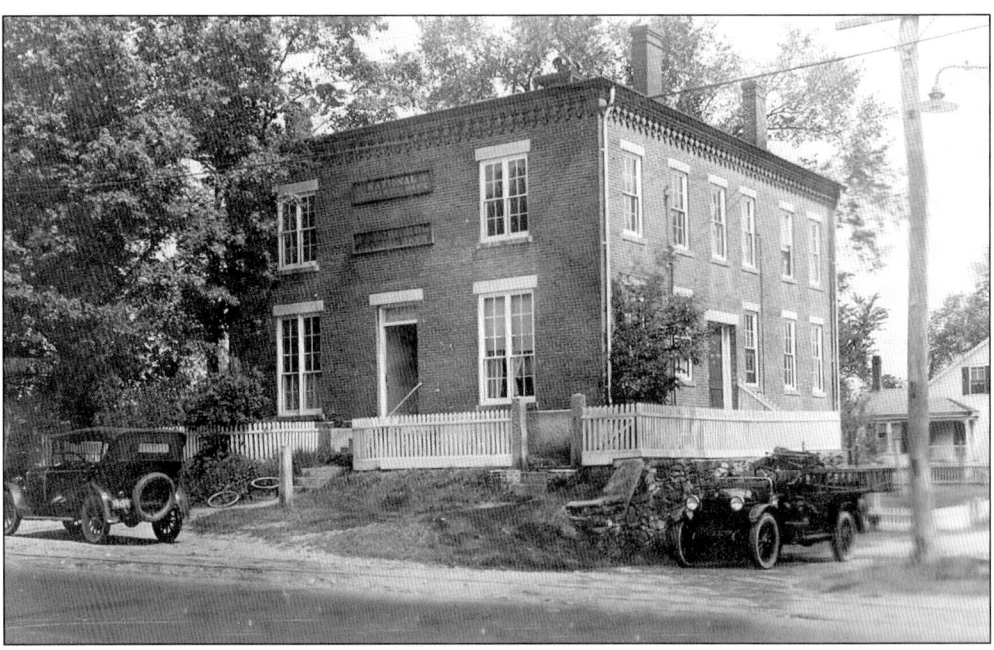

This photograph gives an early view of the old Smithfield Exchange Bank in Greenville built in 1856. Today it is a dental office. Note the fire engine in the driveway. (WK.)

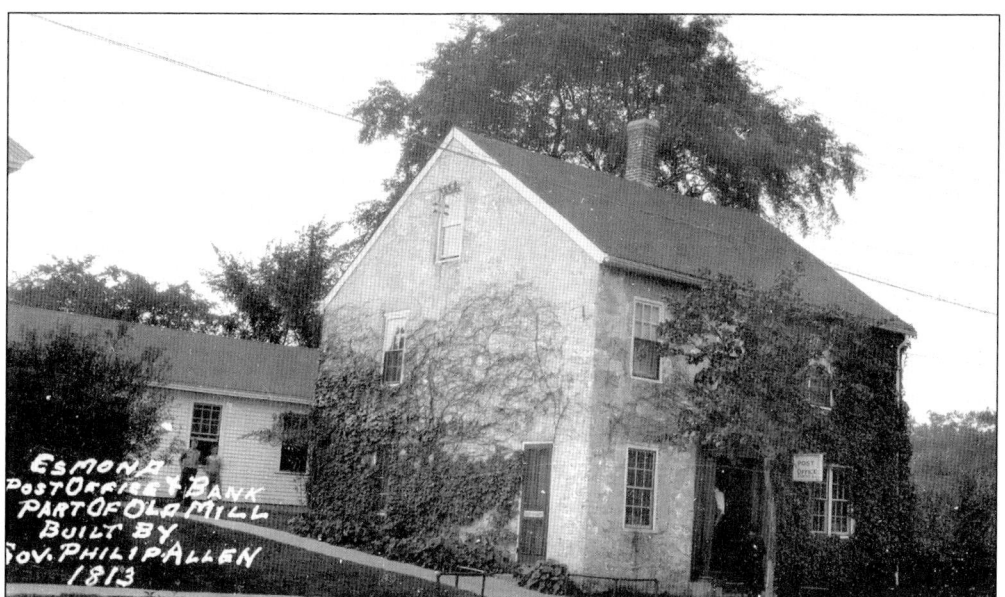

The Esmond Post Office and a bank were once housed in this building on Esmond Street that dates from the early 1800s. The back portion was once a bowling alley. (HSS.)

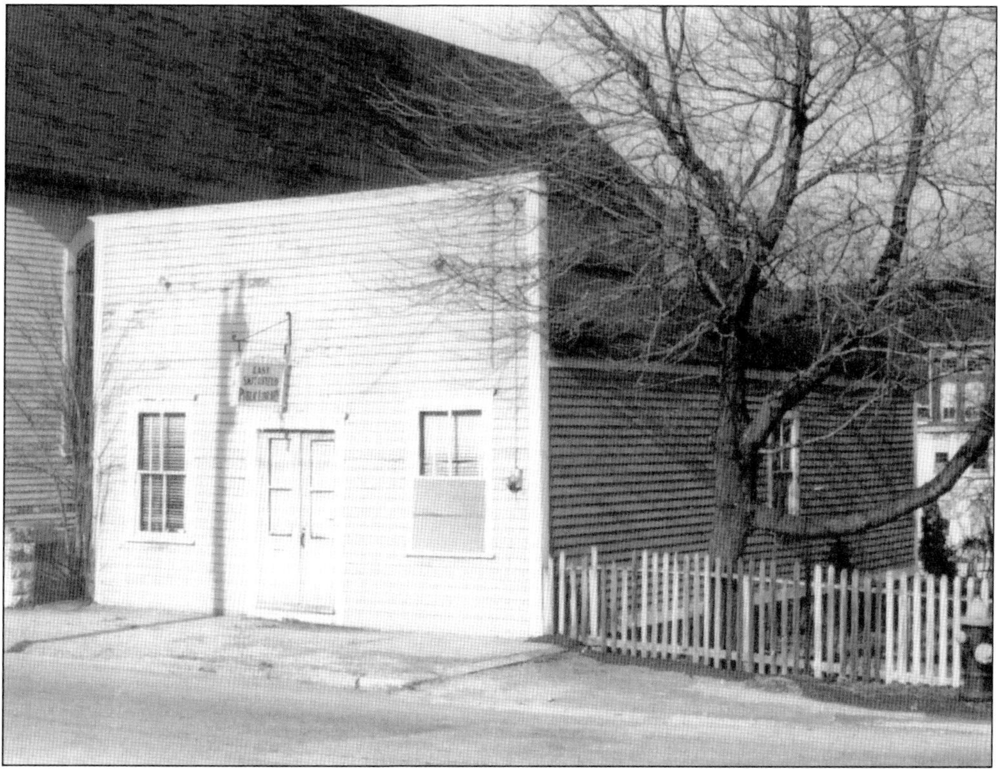

During the 1930s, the East Smithfield Public Library was located in this building on Homestead Avenue next to St. Michael's Church. (FF.)

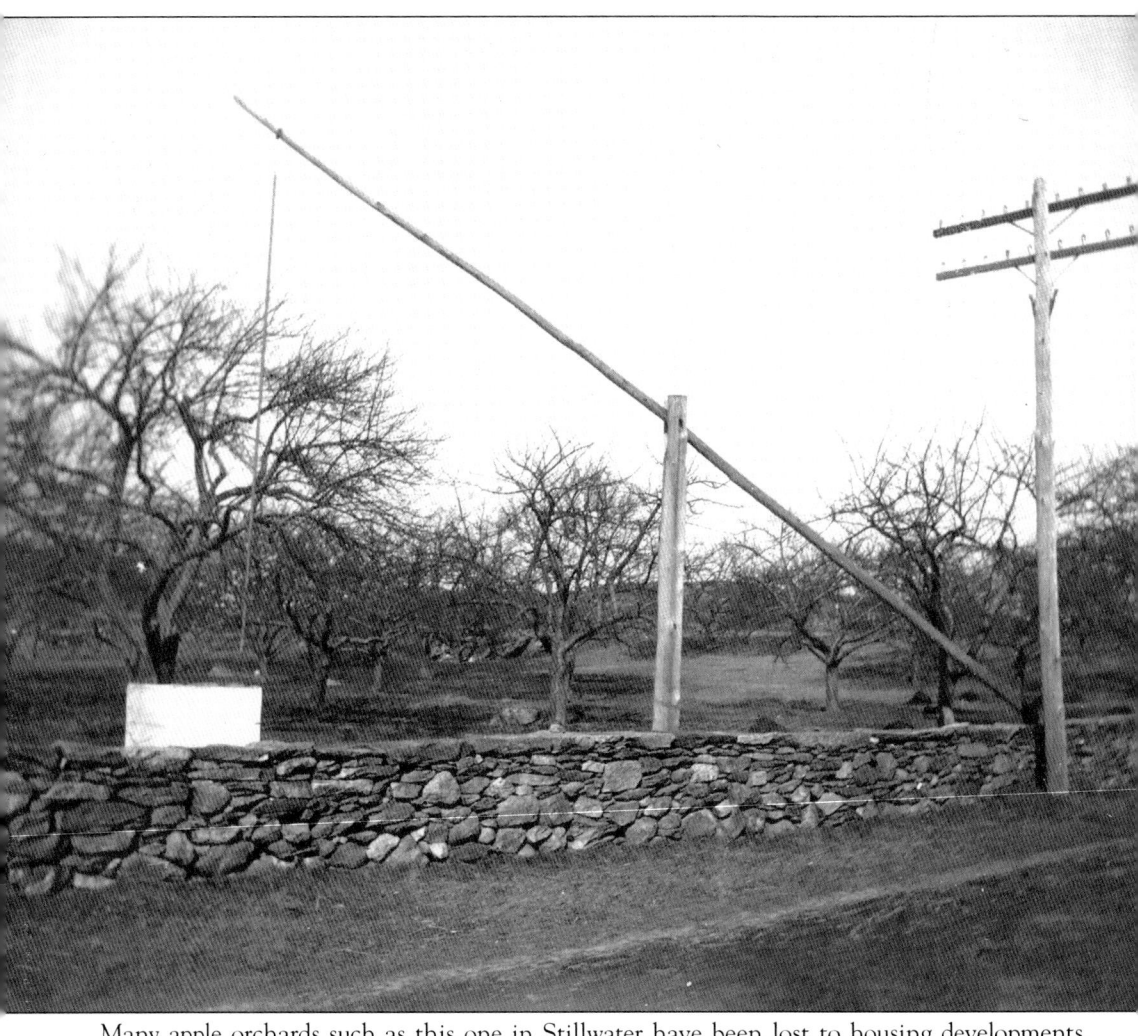
Many apple orchards such as this one in Stillwater have been lost to housing developments. What is interesting in this photograph is the lever-action well used to irrigate the trees. (HSS.)

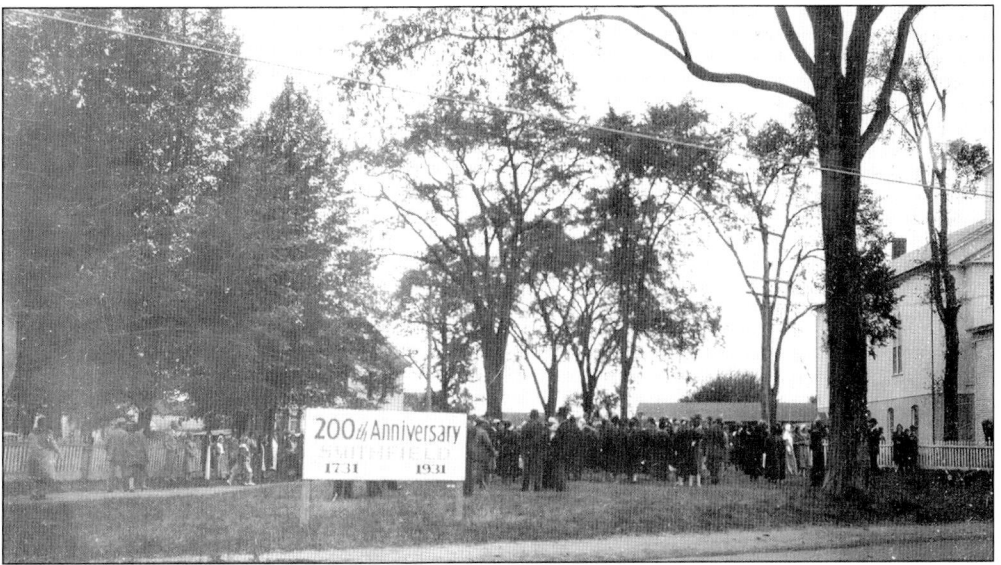

In 1931, Smithfield celebrated its bicentennial as a town with historical speeches and tours of local historic sites. This view shows the Greenville Common. (HSS.)

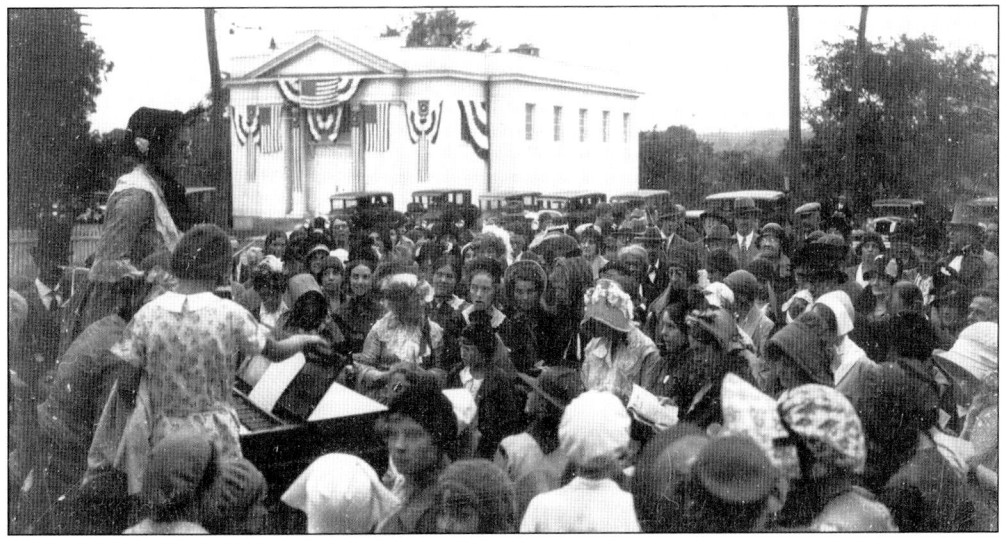

This photograph shows the old Masonic temple in Greenville decked out for the Smithfield bicentennial celebration. (HSS.)

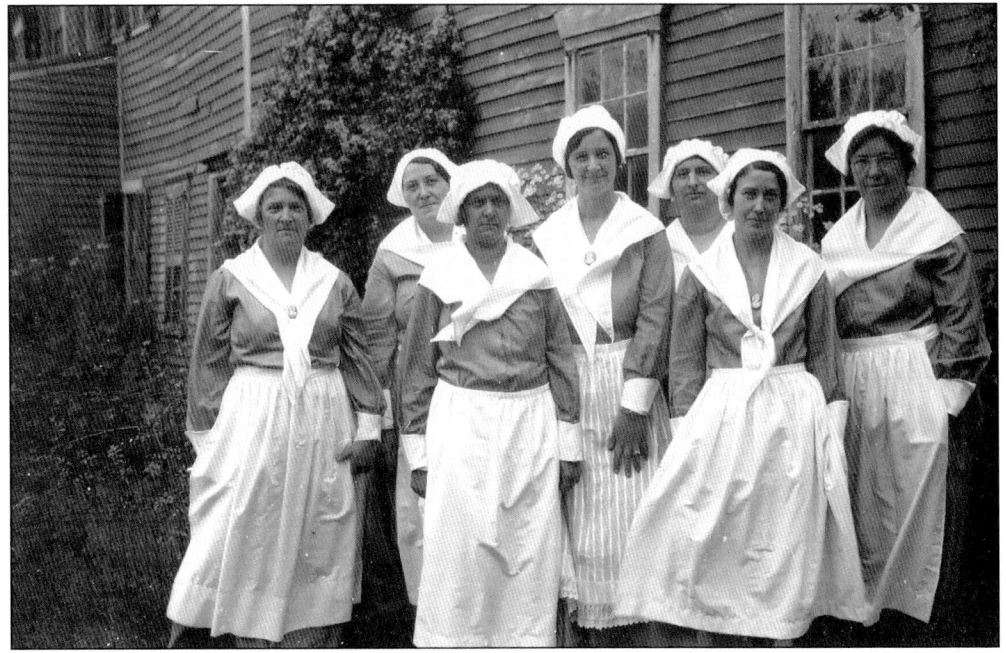
The photograph above shows the ladies of the Smithfield Bicentennial Committee. (HSS.)

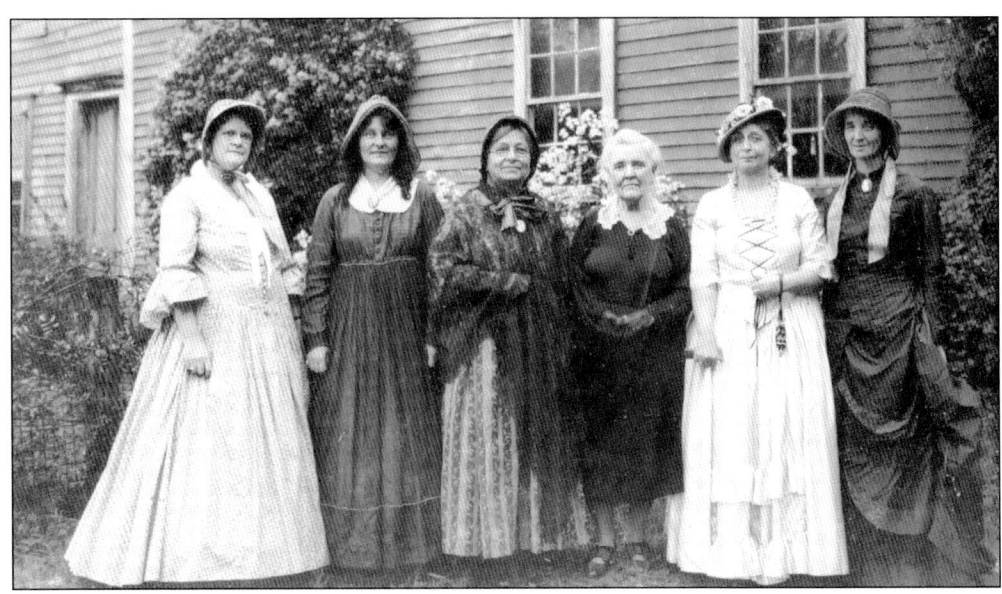
These ladies are dressed in period clothing for the bicentennial ceremonies. This photograph was taken next to the old Waterman Tavern in Greenville. (HSS.)

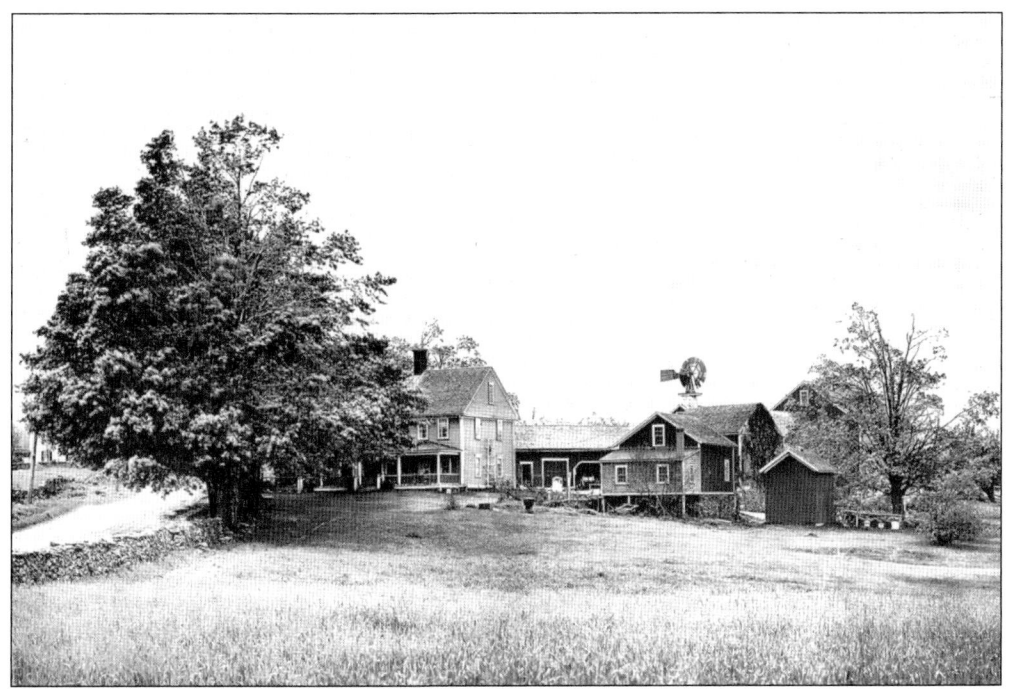
The Andrew Waterman Farm on Austin Avenue is seen as it looked in 1931. (GPL.)

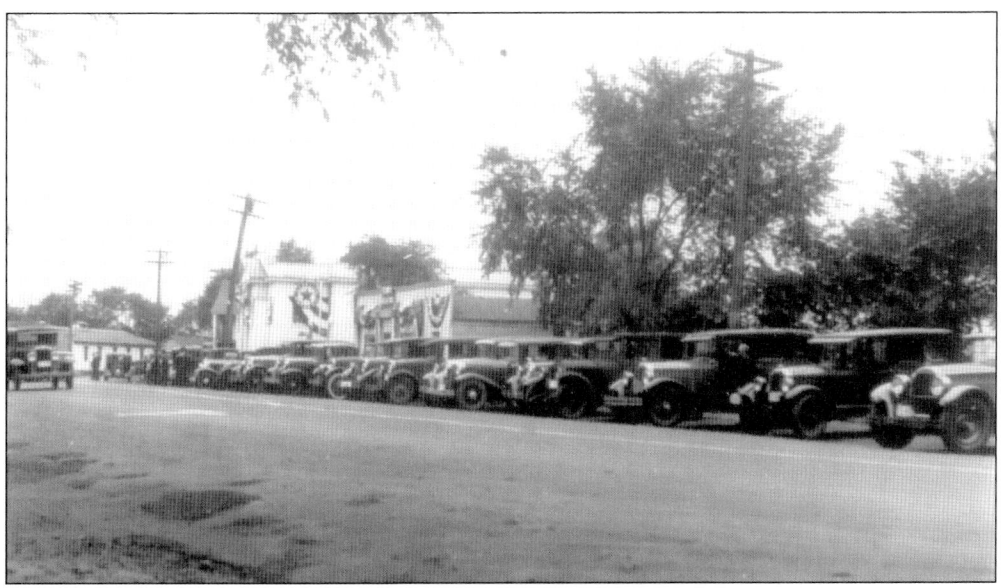
This street scene from the 1930s shows cars parked sideways in Greenville Center along Putnam Pike. (LK.)

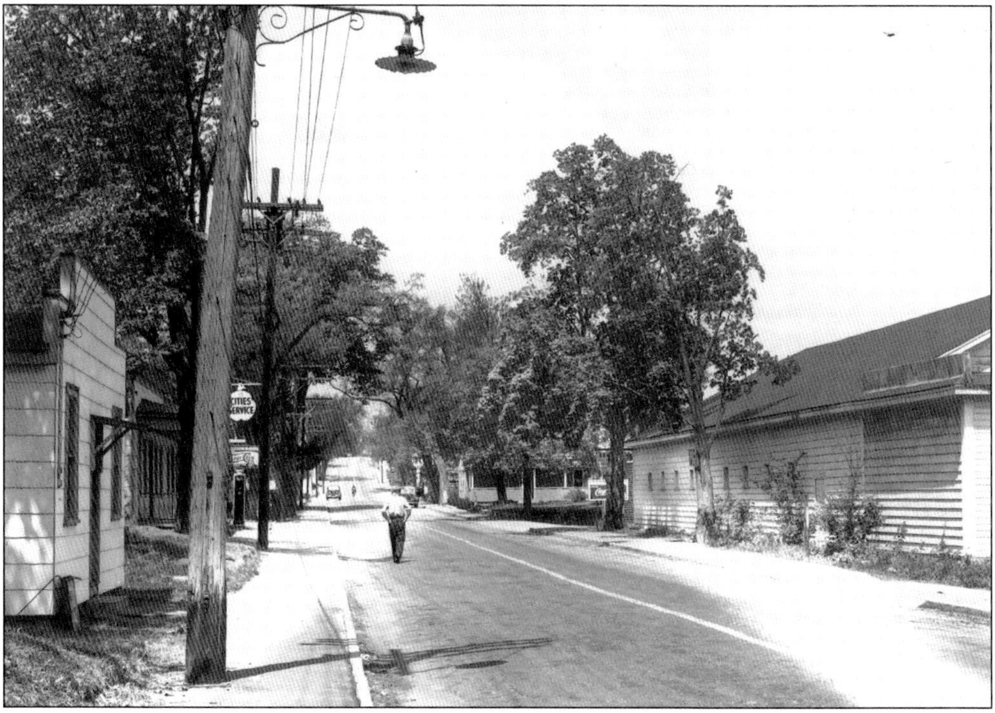

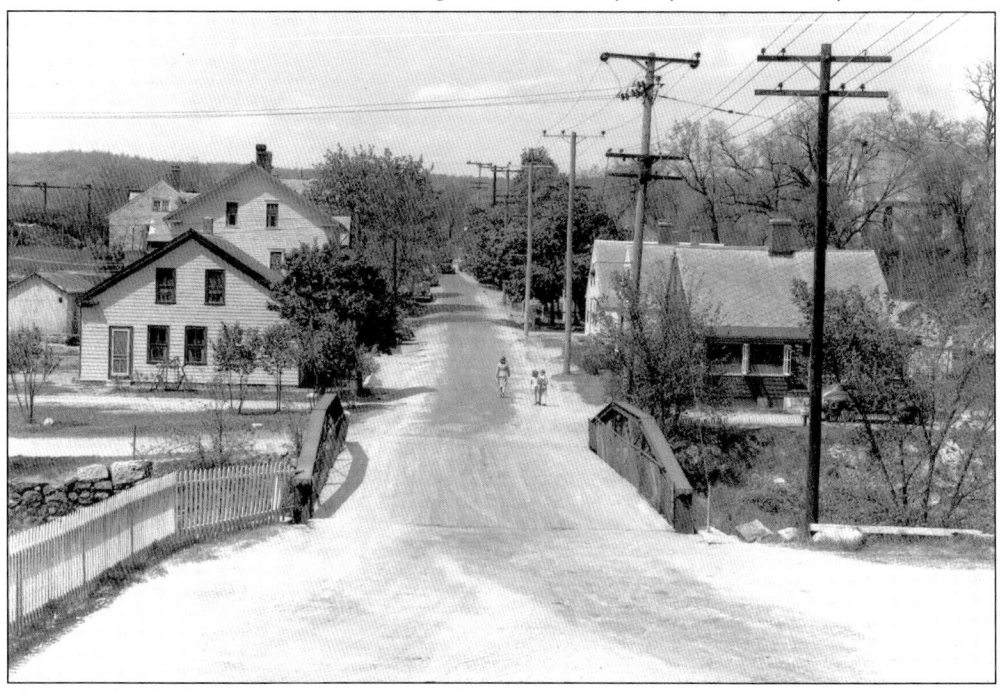

This street scene in Georgiaville from the 1920s shows Farnum Pike just south of the town hall. Walsh's Roller Rink can be seen on the right. It was destroyed by fire in February 1939. (CLL.)

Shea's Bridge, built in 1886, once connected Stillwater Road to Georgiaville. Today this portion of road is blocked off. When the bridge was dismantled in 1994, it was sold and reassembled in Cumberland, where it can be seen today. (CLL.)

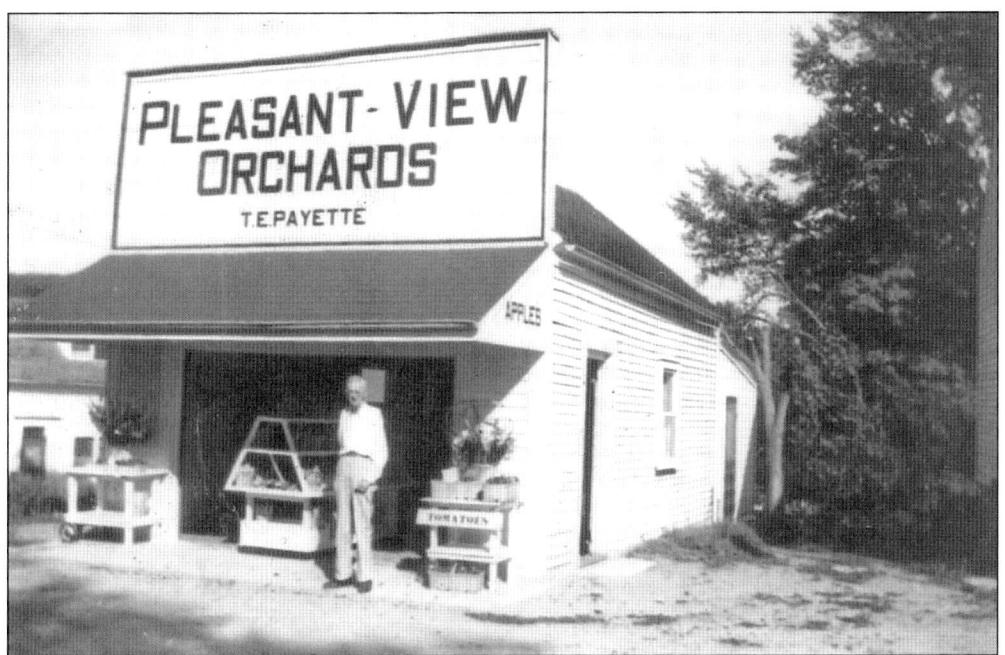

T. E. Payette's apple stand stood at the corner of Pleasant View Avenue and Mountaindale Road for many years before it was replaced by the current building bearing the same name. At one time, apple growing was a major agricultural industry in Smithfield and the area was widely recognized as "Apple Valley." Many local apple orchards have been lost to development over the last 25 years. (AP.)

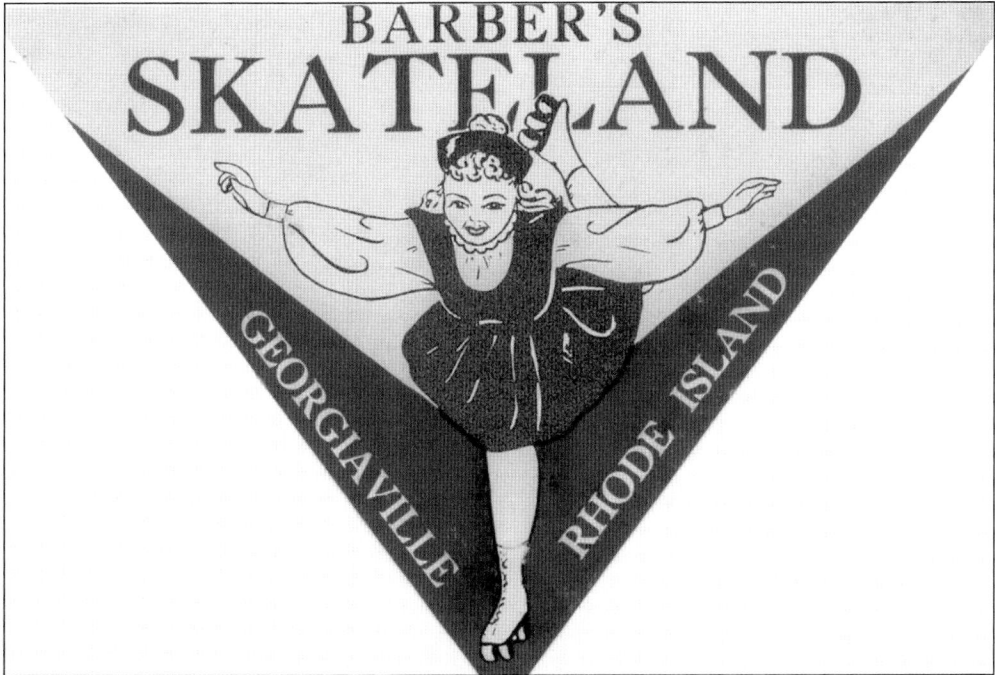

This label is from the boxes that once held roller skates at Barber's Skateland in Georgiaville. (TA.)

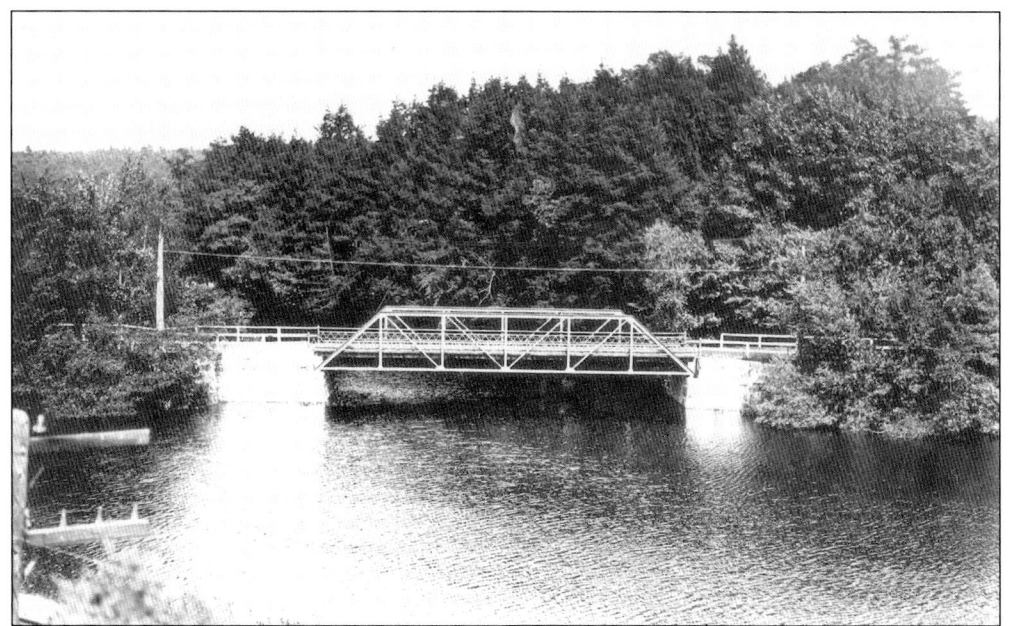

The "Suicide Bridge" once spanned the Woonasquatucket River between Georgiaville and Esmond. It was so named because between 1914 and 1933 twelve deaths occurred there. It was torn down in 1934. (AS.)

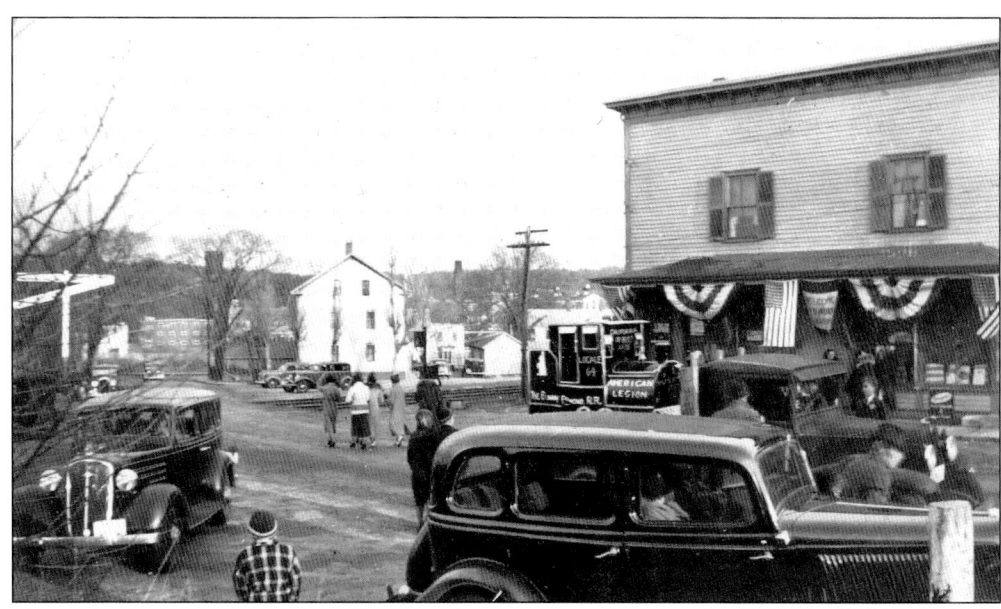

Cooney's Store was located on Rail Road Avenue in Georgiaville (now Stillwater Road at St. Michael's Way). This photograph was taken in November 1938. (AS.)

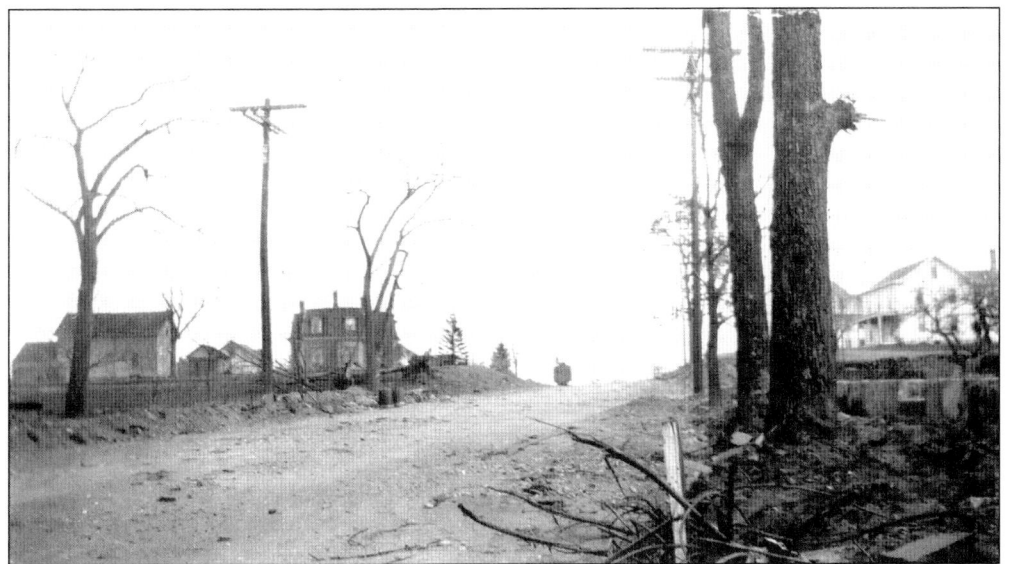

This is what Route 44 looked like after the Hurricane of 1938. The Oscar Tobey House can be seen on the left side of the road. (WK.)

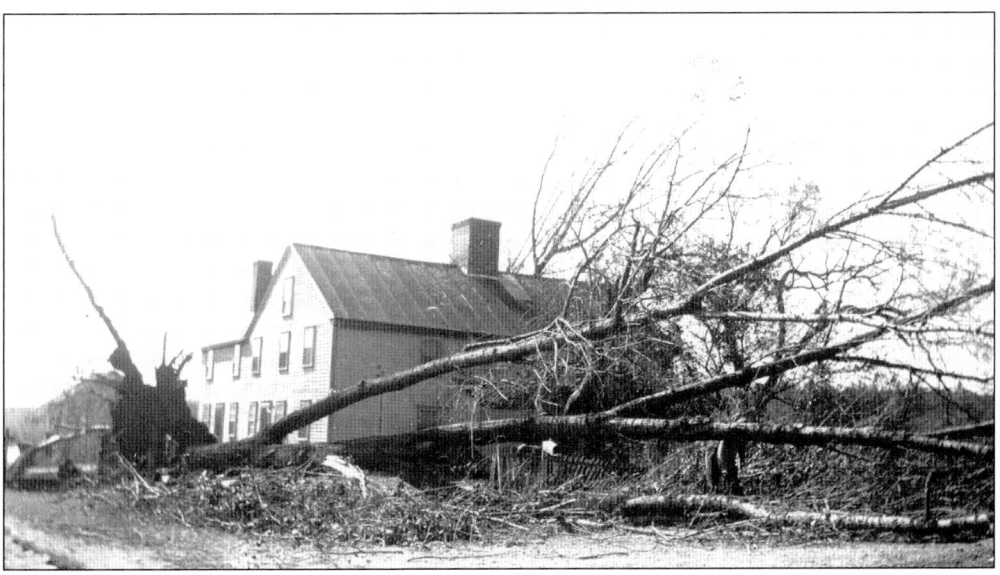

The Smith-Appleby House narrowly escaped being crushed by a massive maple tree that came crashing down during the Hurricane of 1938. (HSS.)

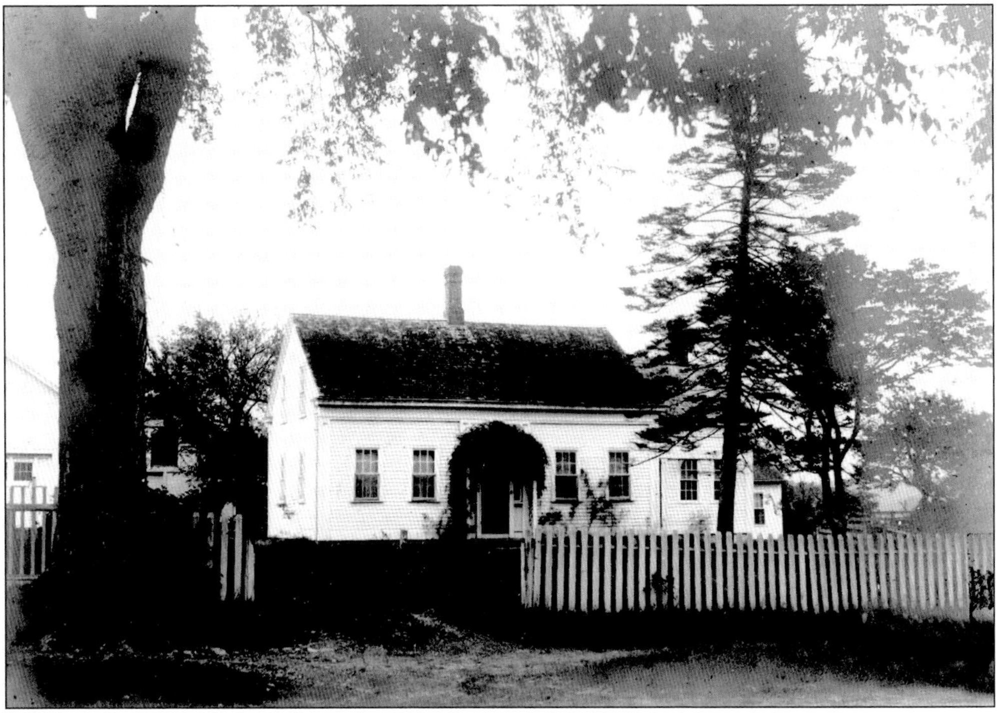

The E. S. Angell House once stood in Greenville just west of Austin Avenue where a shopping plaza is today. It was moved in 1956. (LK.)

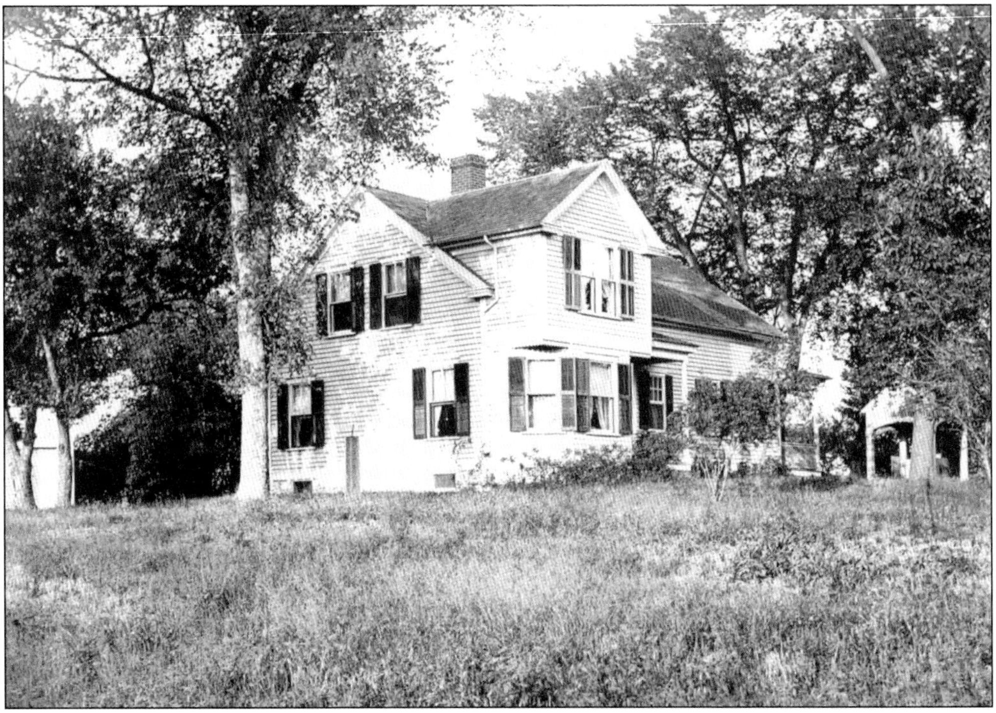

This house was known locally as "the Lilacs" and once stood where the Greenville Public Library is today. (LK.)

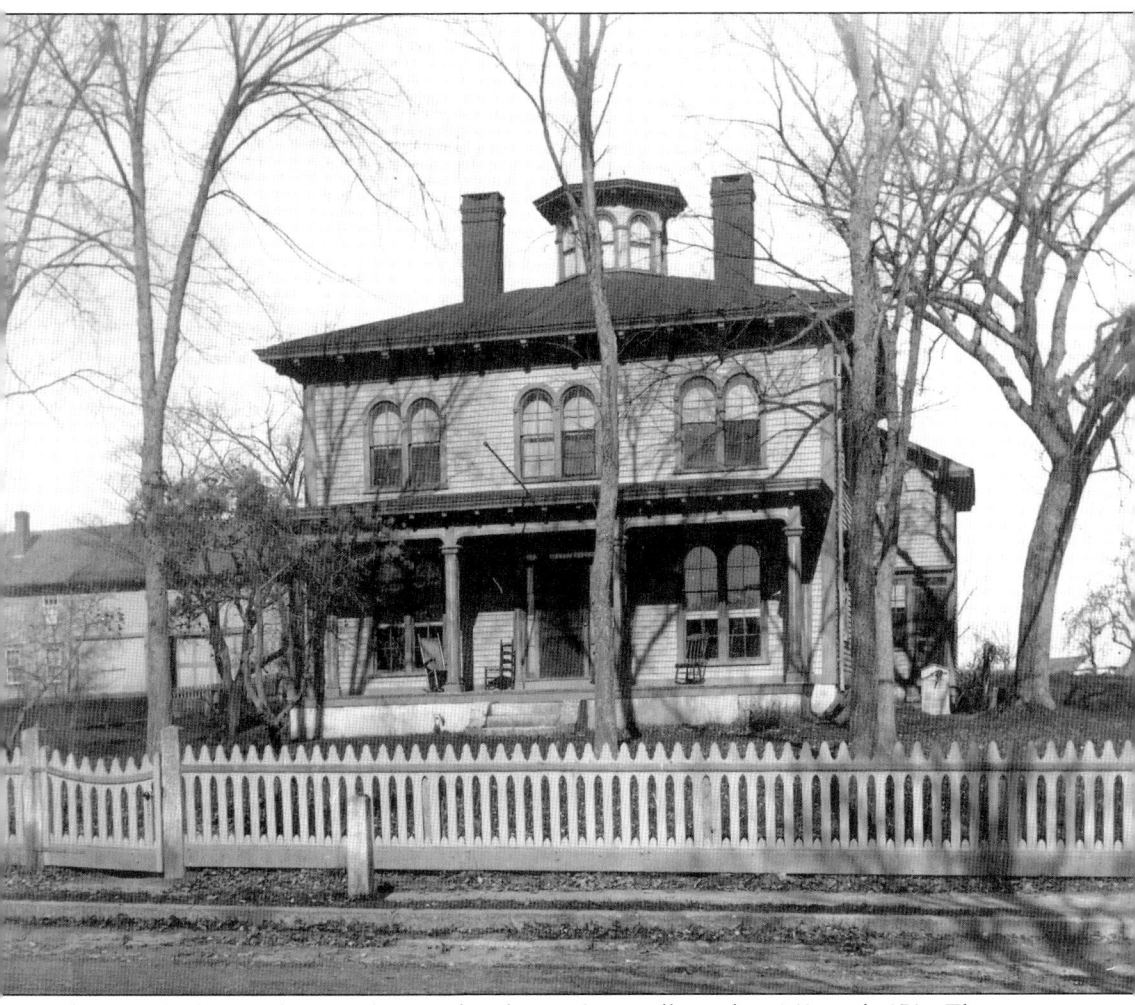

This was the home of P. Angel, an undertaker in Greenville in the 1860s and 1870s. The most interesting architectural feature is the widow's walk atop the roof, something normally found on old homes in shoreline communities. Legend has it that widow's walks were made for the wives of sea captains to watch for returning ships. The Angel House stood facing Route 44 just west of Austin Avenue. It was dismantled in the 1950s to make way for a shopping plaza. (PH/LK.)

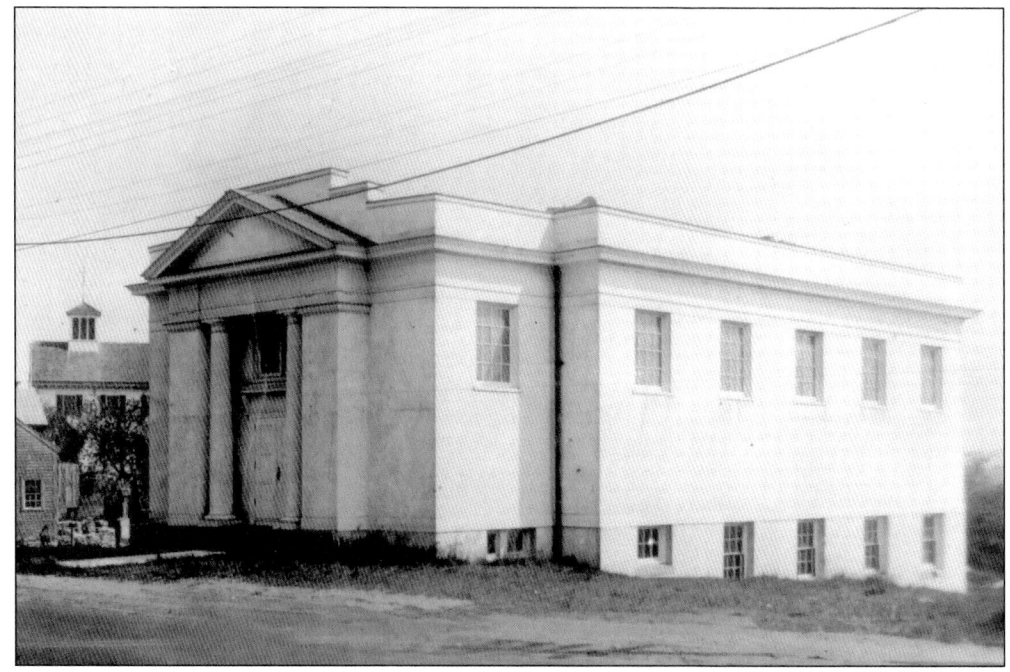
The Masonic temple in Greenville was at one time painted white, as evidenced by this picture. Today it is no longer a temple and its exterior is natural brick. (LK.)

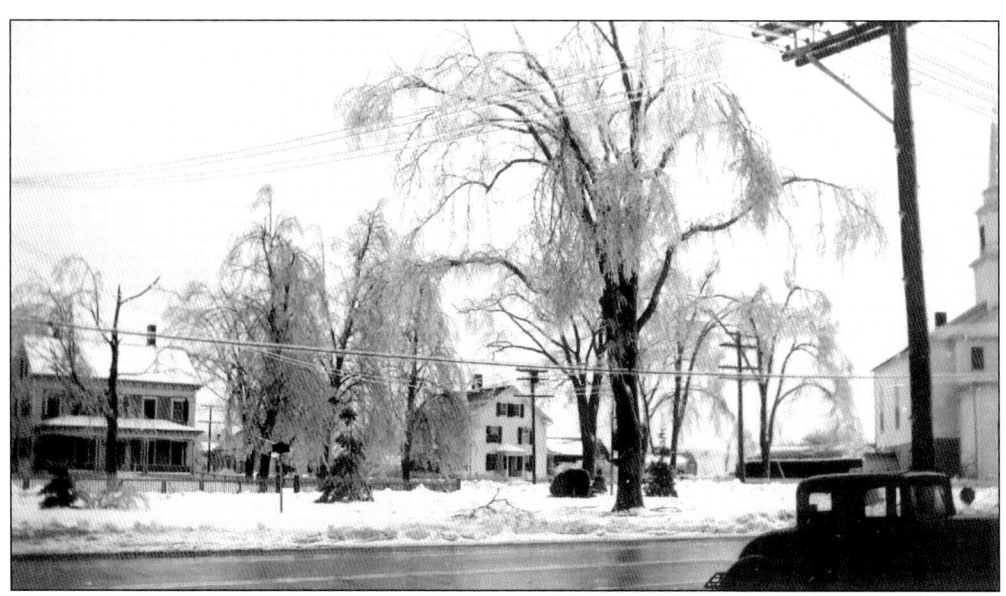
This view shows Greenville Center as it looked in March 1940. (WK.)

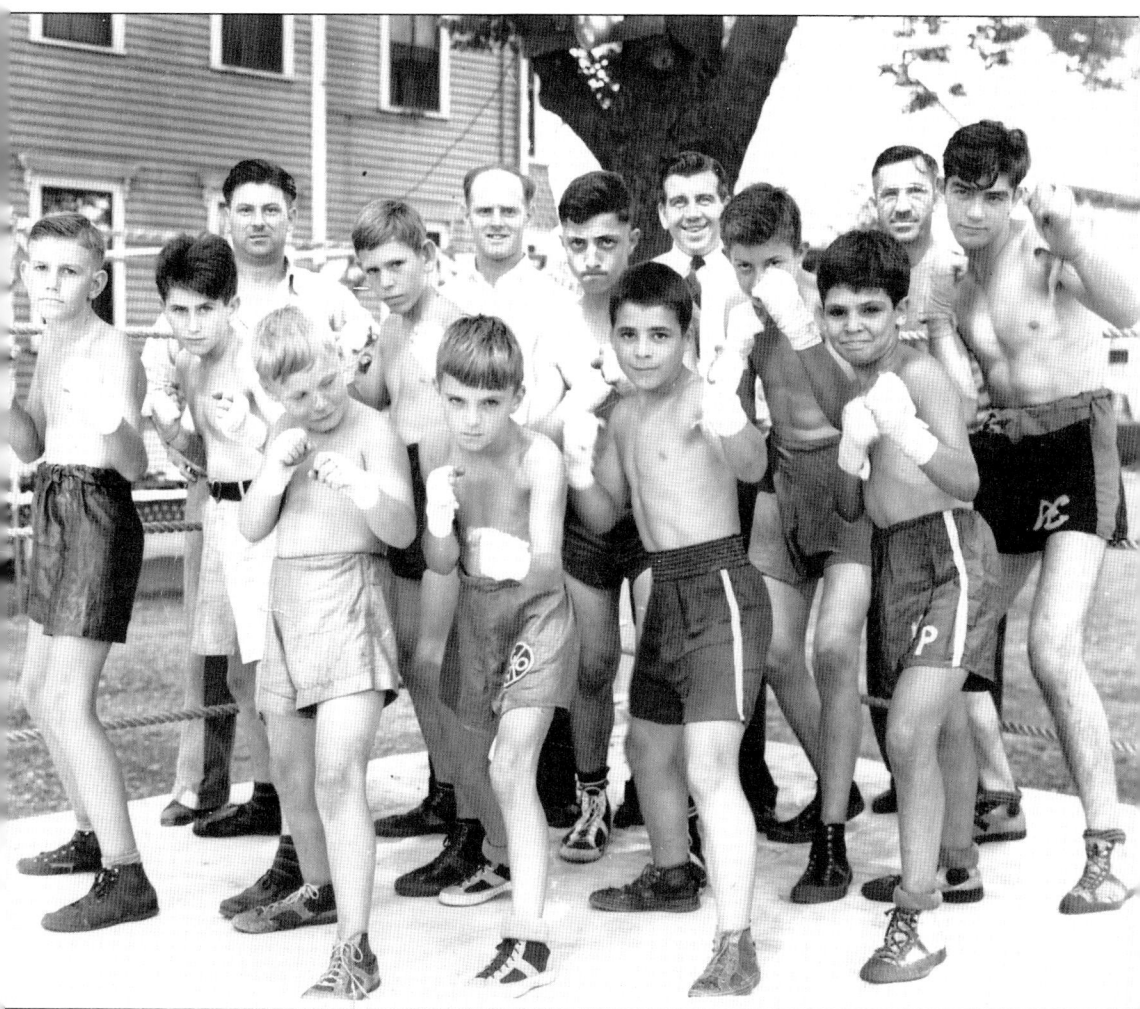

This photograph, taken around 1940, shows the St. Philip's Boxing Club. From left to right are (first row) J. Reynolds, L. Farley, B. Rathier, and R. Palmieri; (second row) H. Darby, J. Leach, L. Foster, S. Carbon, G. Jaswell, and G. Gaberiell; (third row) ? Farley (trainer), R. Kennedy (manager), S. Lauder (assistant manager), and ? Felix (assistant manager). (LK.)

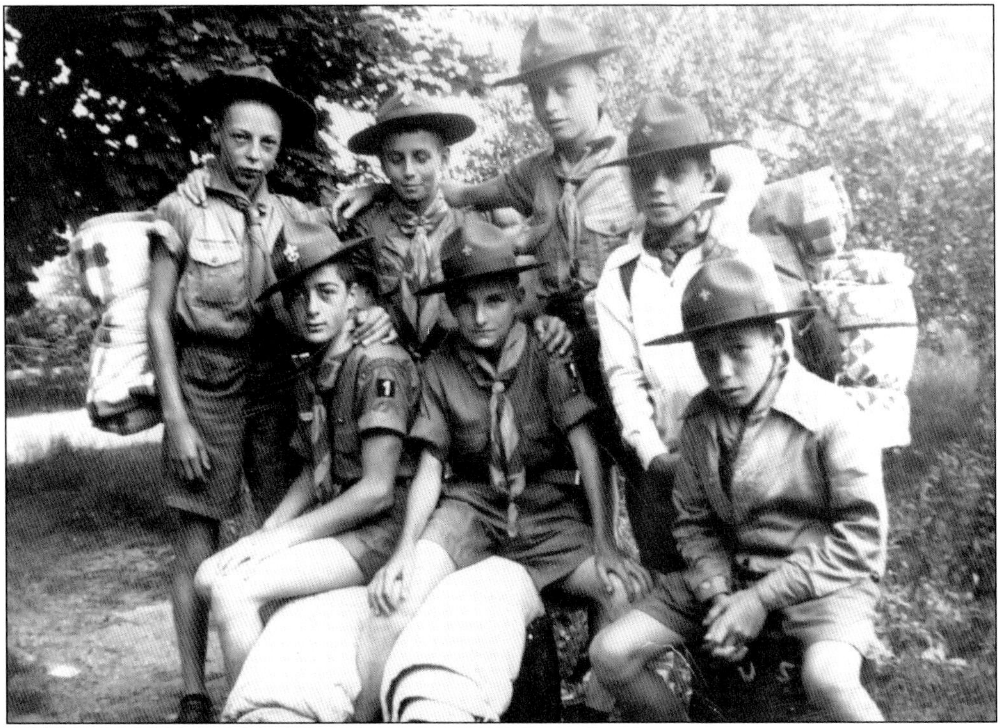

This image shows Georgiaville Boy Scout Troop 1 around 1942. From left to right are (first row) A. Schenck, R. Schenck, and L. Morvan; (second row) F. Arsenault, R. Lachapelle, C. Lachapelle, and D. Carrara. (AS.)

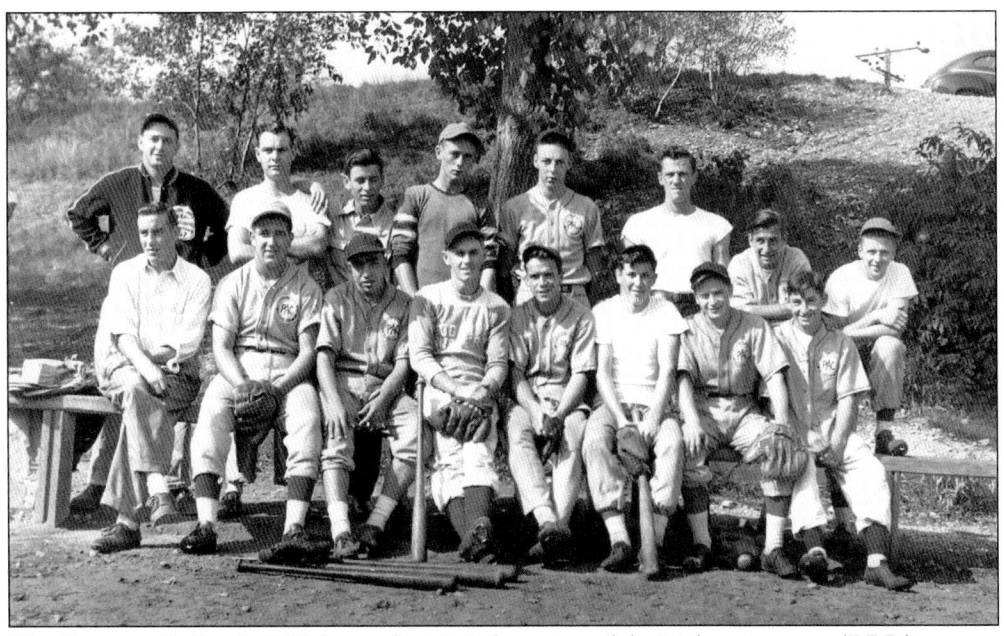

The Georgiaville Baseball Club was the 1948 champion of the Melrose League. (DDB.)

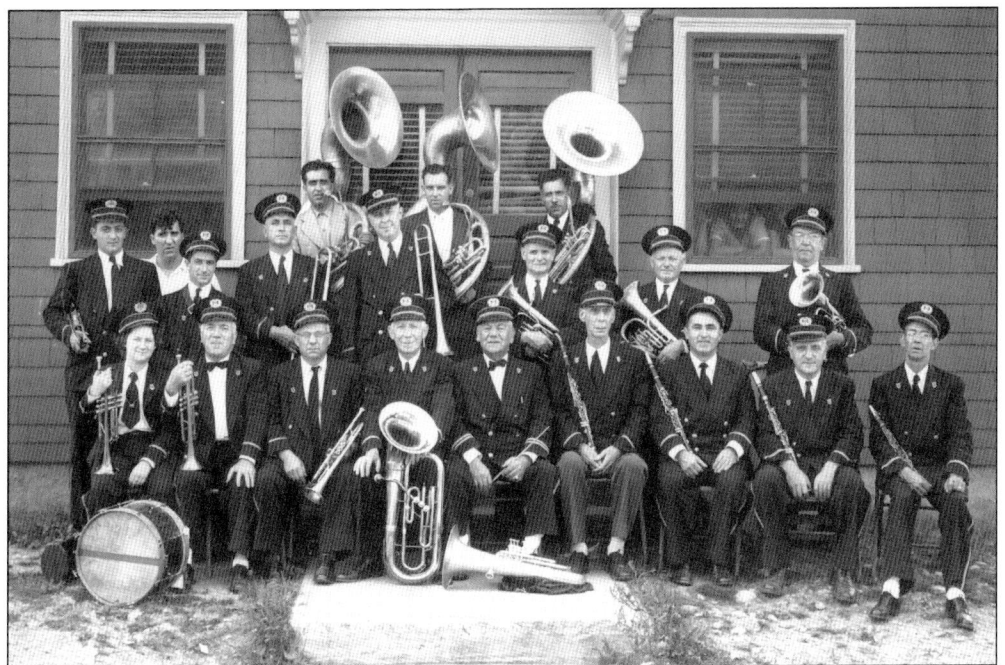

This photograph of the band at the Portuguese American Club was taken about 1945 and features some residents of Smithfield. Today the Portuguese American Club is located on Fenwood Avenue in Esmond. (TM.)

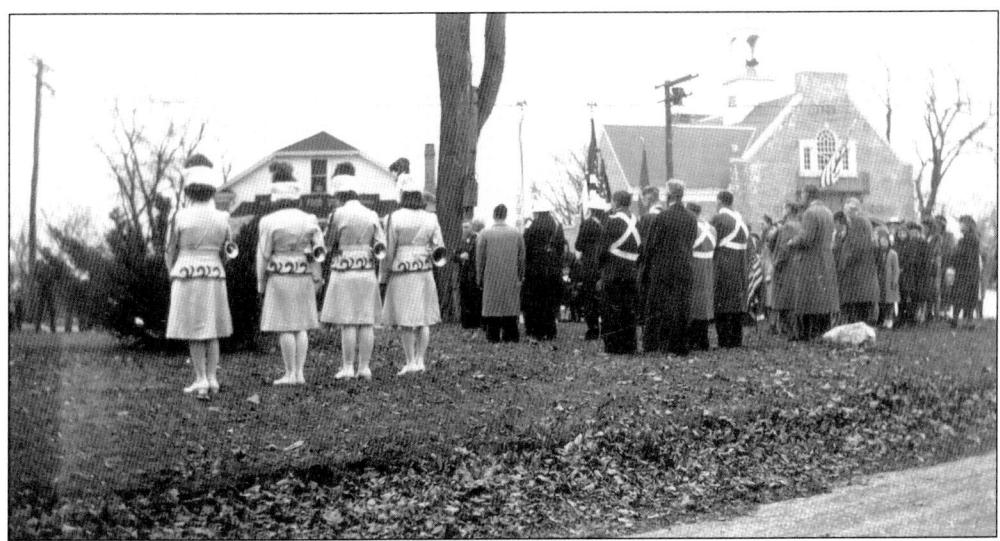

This photograph shows a Veteran's Day ceremony on the Greenville Common during World War II. The Greenville Fire Station is in the background. (WK.)

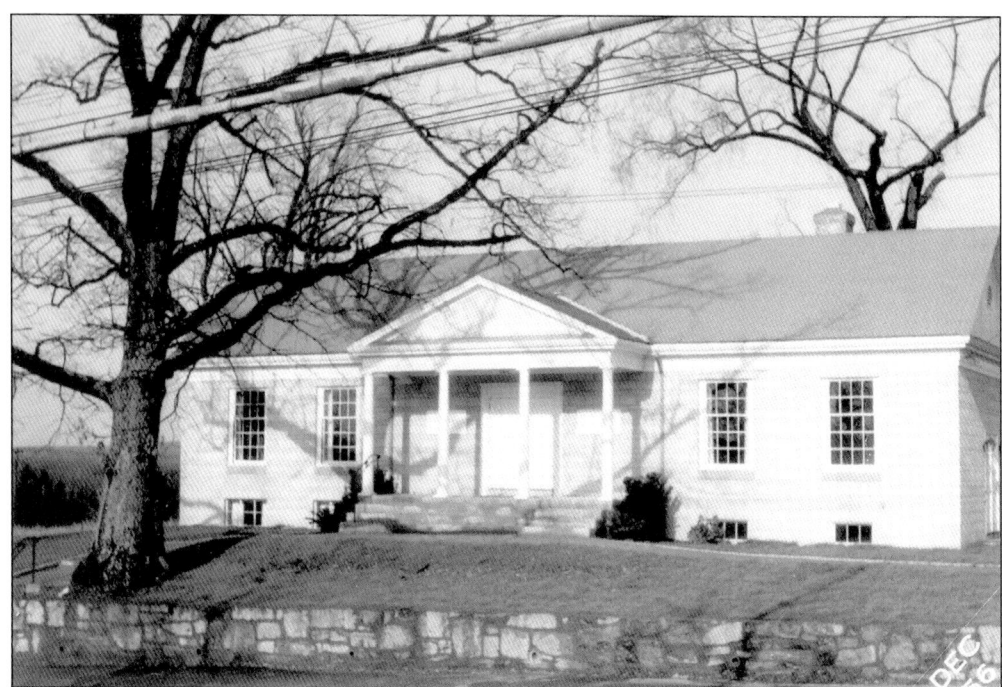

This photograph shows the "new" Greenville Public Library as it looked in December 1956. (WK.)

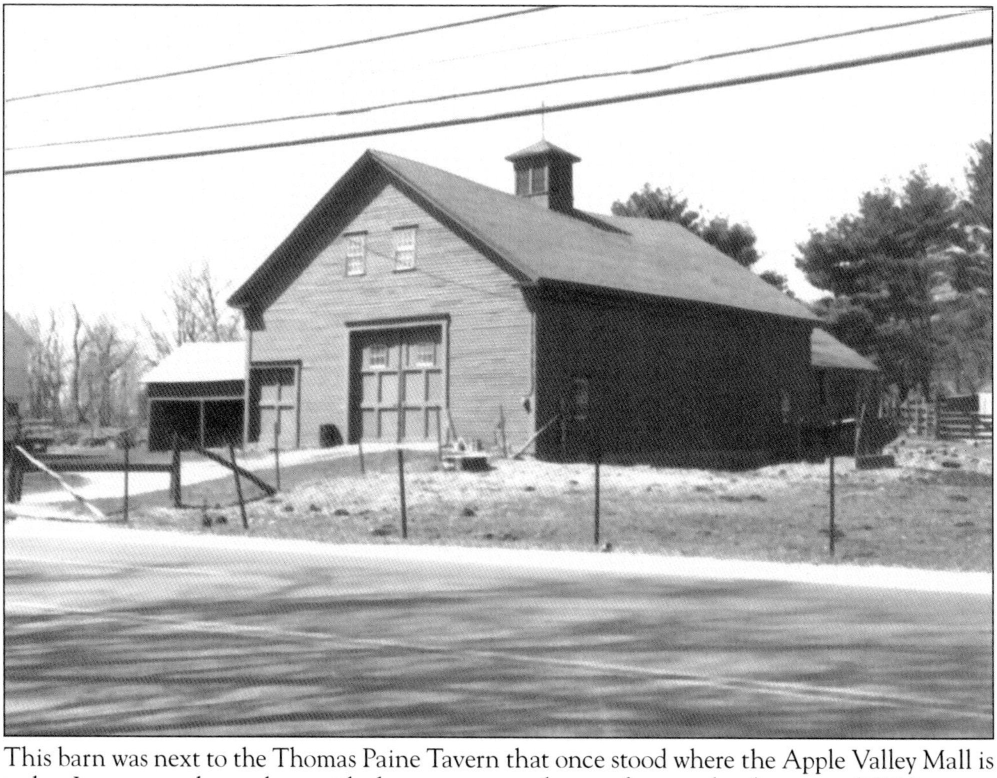

This barn was next to the Thomas Paine Tavern that once stood where the Apple Valley Mall is today. It was torn down along with the tavern to make way for new development. (WK.)

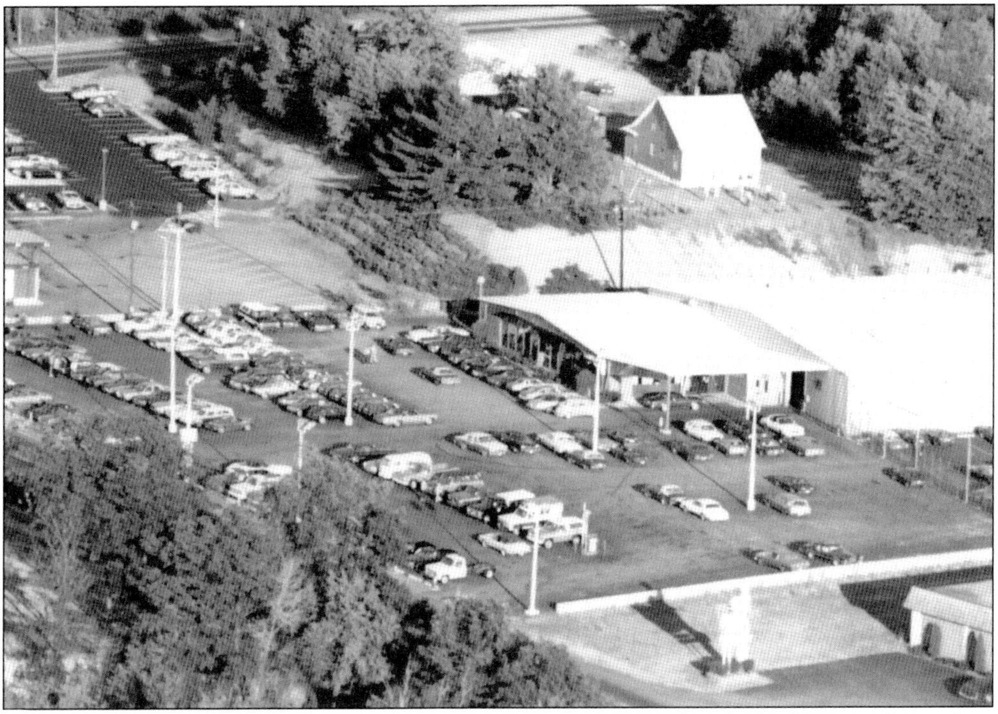

This aerial view of Scuncio Chevrolet was taken in 1977. The dealership was located at 446 Putnam Pike where a shopping plaza is today. (CLL.)

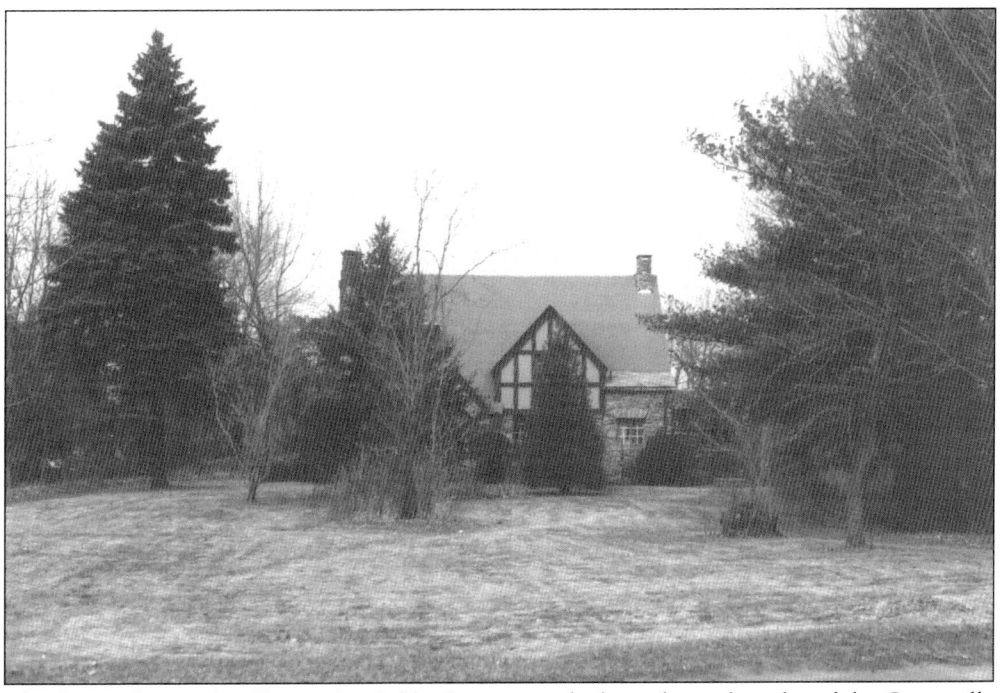

This house, known locally as "the Gables," once stood where the parking lot of the Greenville Public Library is today. (LK.)

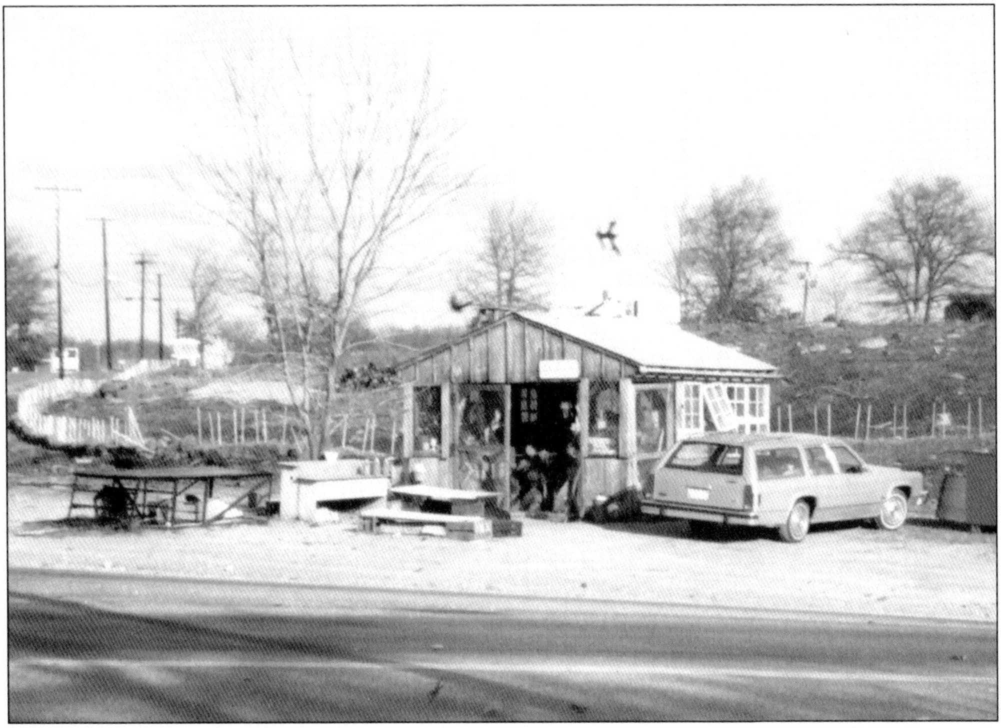

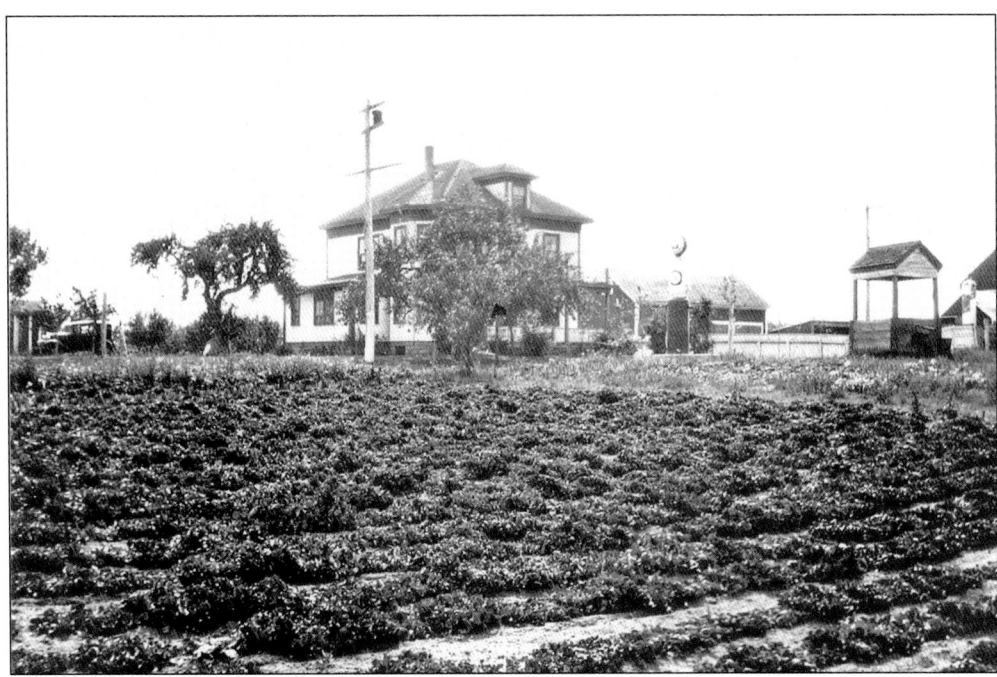

The Davis Farm Stand was located at Route 7 and Route 116 where the state salt barn stands today. It was torn down in 1989. (JI.)

This photograph of Jaswell's Farm on Swan Road dates from the 1950s. The farm was established in 1899 and has remained in the family ever since. (AJM.)

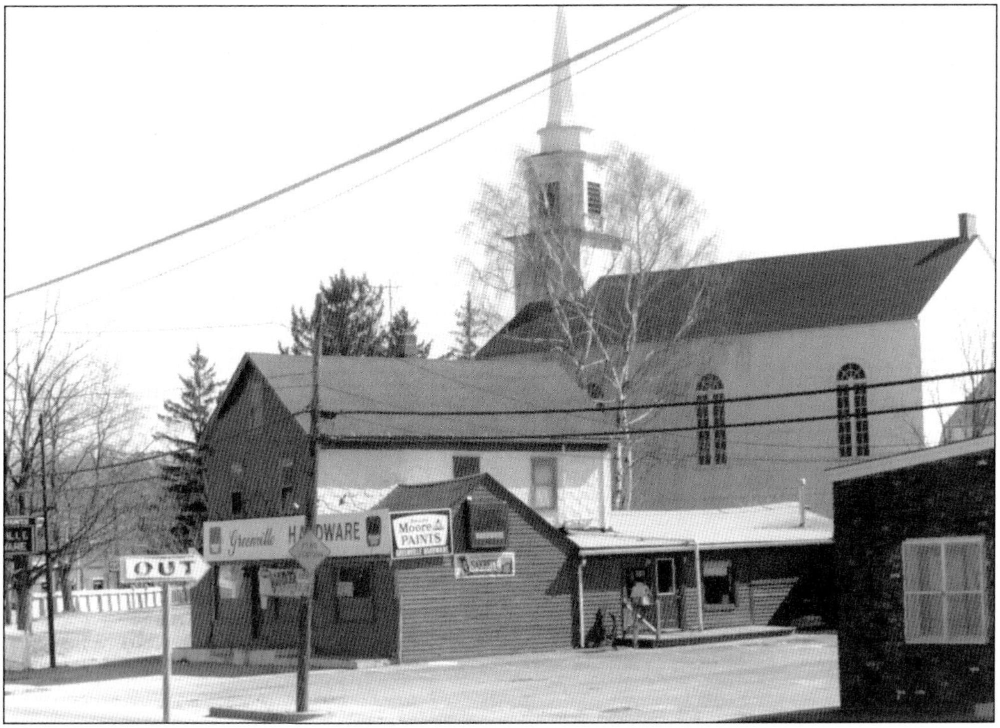

The old Greenville Hardware store used to be located next to the Greenville Baptist Church. This building was torn down, and now a bank occupies the site. (LK.)

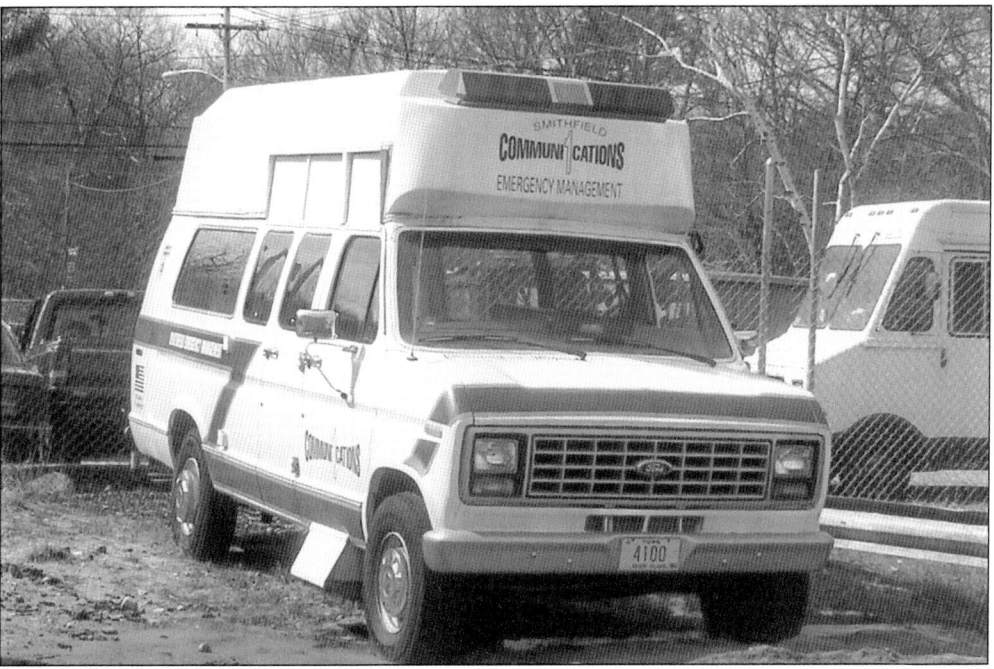

This photograph shows the old communications van used by the Smithfield Emergency Management Agency (EMA). The EMA assists other town agencies during weather-related emergencies. It began in the 1950s under Civil Defense. (JI.)

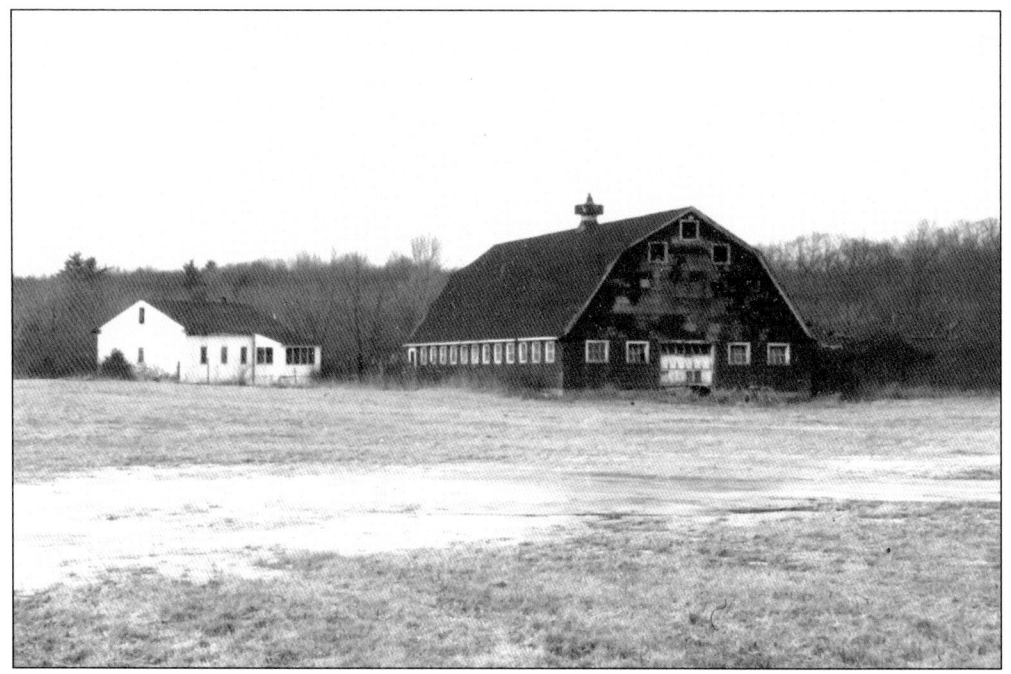

Between 1835 and 1871, the town operated the Smithfield Poor Farm and Town Asylum where the indigent and insane were housed. It was located on Douglas Pike just north of Lydia Ann Road where the entrance to an office park is today. The farm was closed in 1871 due to a scandal over the treatment of inmates and later became a private dairy farm. This photograph, taken in 1991, shows the buildings prior to demolition. (JI.)

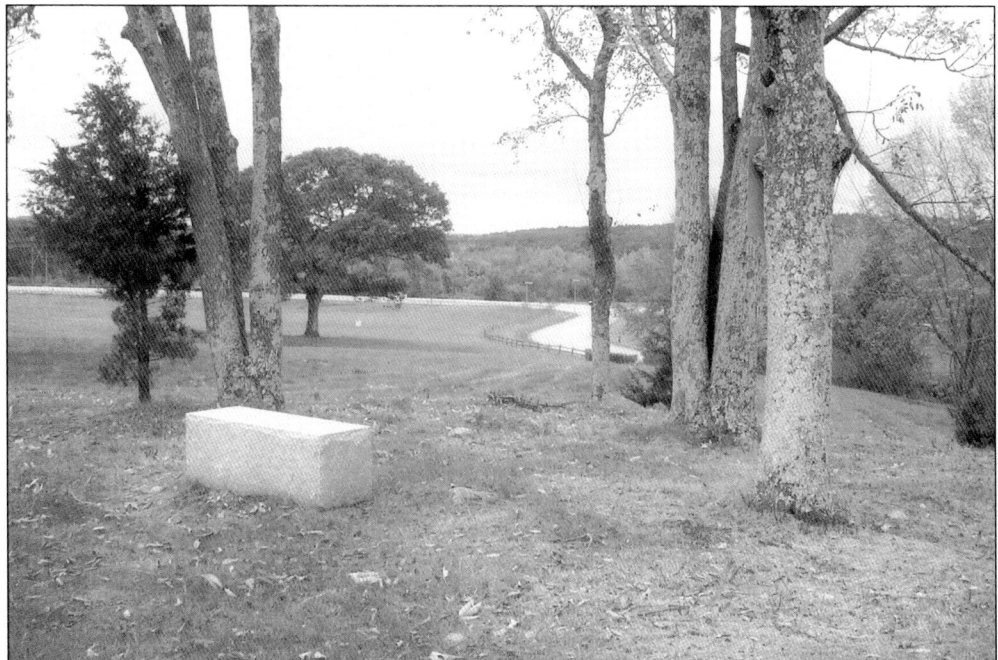

The Smithfield Poor Farm Cemetery sits atop a hill overlooking where the institution once stood. The graves are marked by simple field stones set in the ground. (JI.)

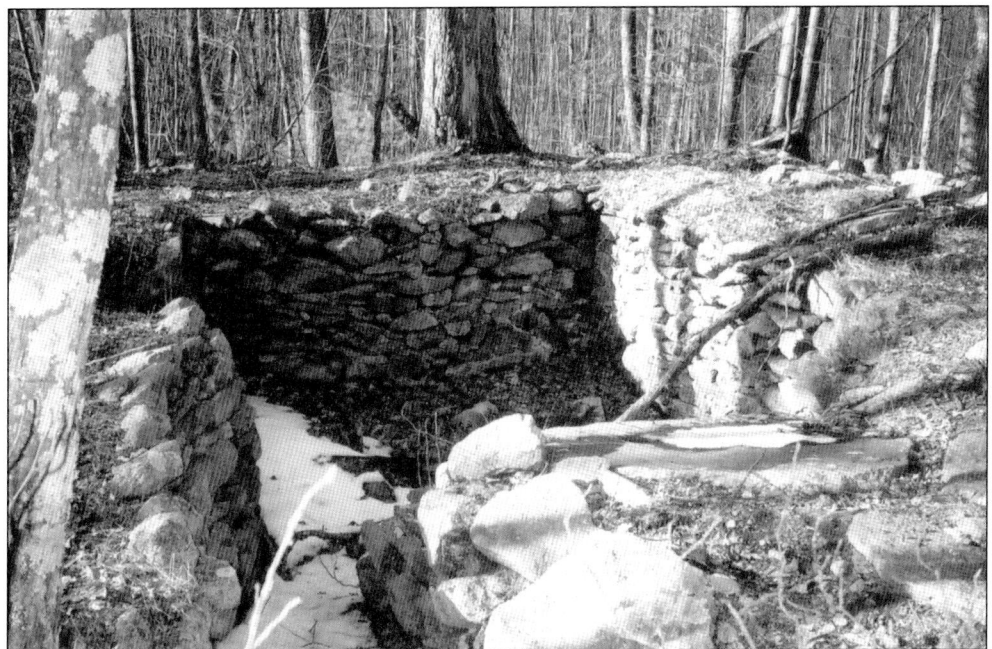

Buried in the woods in the northern part of town are the remains of a Colonial-era village known as Hanton City. The area has been the subject of folklore and speculation for generations as locals have theorized about the people who once lived there and what happened to them. Research indicates the settlement began in the late 1600s and thrived until the early 1800s when the inhabitants moved on out of economic necessity. Today only stone walls and cellar holes remain of the settlement. (JI.)

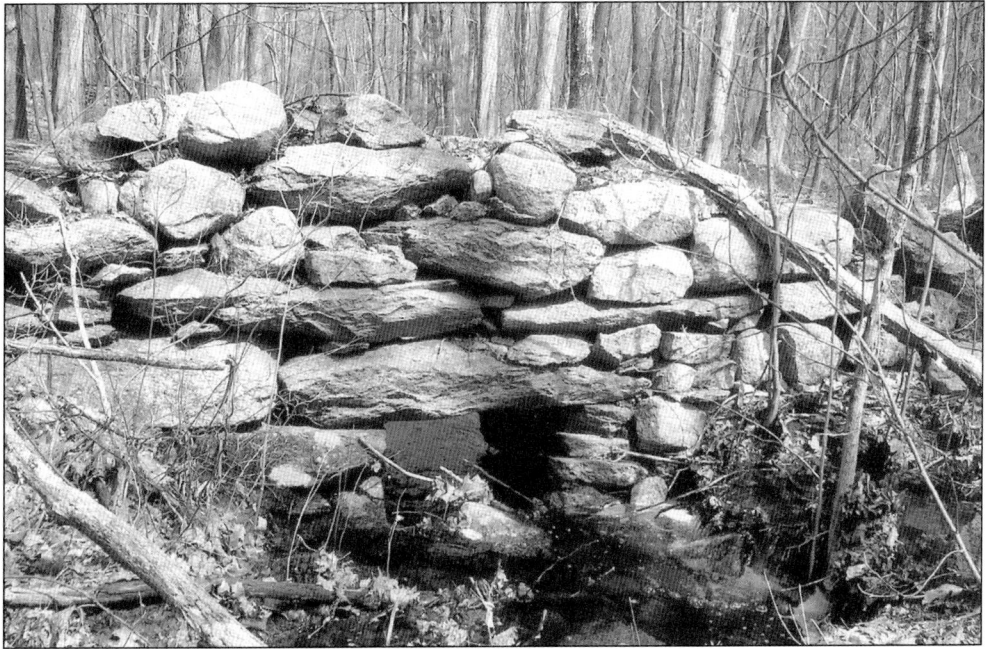

One interesting feature in Hanton City is this little known stone bridge that fords a small stream. The large rocks indicate it took quite a bit of effort to build. (JI.)

Discover Thousands of Local History Books
Featuring Millions of Vintage Images

Arcadia Publishing, the leading local history publisher in the United States, is committed to making history accessible and meaningful through publishing books that celebrate and preserve the heritage of America's people and places.

Find more books like this at
www.arcadiapublishing.com

Search for your hometown history, your old stomping grounds, and even your favorite sports team.

Consistent with our mission to preserve history on a local level, this book was printed in South Carolina on American-made paper and manufactured entirely in the United States. Products carrying the accredited Forest Stewardship Council (FSC) label are printed on 100 percent FSC-certified paper.

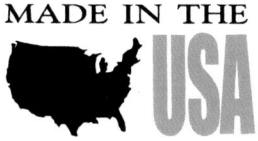